DUCATI
SINGLES

OSPREY
COLLECTOR'S
LIBRARY

DUCATI
SINGLES

All two- and four-stroke
single-cylinder motorcycles,
including Mototrans – 1945
onwards

Mick Walker

Published in 1985 by Osprey Publishing Limited
12–14 Long Acre, London WC2E 9LP
Member company of the George Philip Group

Reprinted early 1986

British Library Cataloguing in Publication Data
Walker, Mick
    Ducati singles: all two- and four-stroke
    single-cylinder motor cycles including
    Mototrans – 1945 onwards.—(Osprey
    collector's library)
    1. Ducati motorcycle—History
    I. Title
    629.2'275   TL488.D8
ISBN 0-85045-605-3

Editor Tim Parker
Associate Andrew Kemp

Filmset and printed in England by
BAS Printers Limited, Over Wallop, Hampshire

Contents

Foreword by Bruno Spaggiari

B. Spaggiari

Vencedor absoluto sobre DUCATI 285

XXIV HORAS DE MONTJUICH 1964

Bruno Spaggiari on the victorious record breaking 285
Ducati he shared with Giuseppe Mandolini; Barcelona 24
Hours, 1964. Many riders feel that an unfaired motorcycle
is essential for the tight Montjuich Park circuit

A telephone call from the publisher of *Ducati Singles* forced me to recall my motorcycling days in a way that I had not previously done – from the sole viewpoint of my involvement with Moto

Ducati. It gave me considerable pleasure mostly because it enabled me to greet my great friend Fabio Taglioni whom I still see, with a number of refreshed memories. Ingegnere Taglioni, of course, being the fountain of all that's great from Ducati. It also brought some heartache, but that I don't mind because I'm sure it makes one appreciate those good times more.

I first owned a motorcycle in 1955, it was a Ducati, at a time when I was a young mechanic. My memory fails me exactly what happened when but I found myself racing. In those days things were different for we didn't find ourselves on safe, enclosed tracks but on unsafe open roads which demanded both physical strength and stamina. Imagine racing from Milano in the north of Italy to Taranto in the south aboard a tiny Ducati non-stop – looking back, I wouldn't have done it if I'd known then what I know now.

For several years I raced the little Ducatis, then I had a spell with Count Agusta's MV team along-side World Champion Carlo Ubbiali, and a shorter spell with Benelli – it was exciting to ride the Benelli 250-four. I soon returned to Ducati because they invited me back, I knew it would work well and I was already under the Taglioni spell. I wanted to win, nothing else would do and I thought his Ducatis would do that for me.

Some of my fondest memories come from the period when I was seconded to the Mototrans factory in Barcelona where I worked as a *col-laudatore* or development rider, and a member of the race team. Using motorcycles which were built in Bologna but prepared and tuned in Spain we were very successful. My first win in the Barcelona 24 hours came in 1957, my last victory in 1964 when our little single was nothing short of a giant killer. After the finish of that race I made the sign of the cross on the track and said to myself, never again. During the rest of 1964 I raced an MV Agusta in Italy.

I didn't forget Ducati, though, for off and on I raced them until 1971 together with an MV and a Morini (two lovely machines, actually). 1972 saw me fail to go to Daytona with the brand new 750 V-twin because 'we couldn't afford to', instead playing second fiddle to Paul Smart at the Imola 200 for Ducati's classic one-two victory. I'm convinced Daytona that year was within my grasp. . . .

Time moved on and after spotting the young Franco Uncini at the Santa Monica circuit at Misano riding a Suzuki in 1973 I formed my own Scuderia Spaggiari. My *team* ran nine races in 1974 and won them all, honours being shared by Franco and Giulio Sabatini. For the one year only I used Ducati factory bikes race prepared by the team. Late that same year I realized that the time had come to stop – I had been racing for 18 years, most of them aboard a Ducati single cylinder road racer, and fate was being tempted. I moved quickly to selling Peugeot cars, switching to Fiat in 1980, and to a quiet family life. I haven't ridden a motorcycle since 1974 and I'm not about to let my two daughters ride them either. Today, I'm happier in a car.

But I have to admit that for those 18 years, life was adventurous, fun and fulfilling and it wouldn't have been the same without all my good friends around the world, Taglioni and Ducati. I'm proud to have been involved and happy to salute this book which should provide many an exciting moment for me and all fellow enthusiasts. Thank you.

Bruno Spaggiari
ex-Ducati factory rider with perhaps
more victories than any other; 1955–74
Reggio Emilia, Italy
February 1985

Acknowledgements

The author (left) with a youthful Barry Sheene about to cut the tape to a new Mick Walker Motorcycles showroom, June 1973

The story of the Ducati singles would seem an obvious choice for my first book, given that this unique lineage has dominated my own motor-cycling over the last quarter of a century.

Strangely, although the subject was a natural choice, the task was anything but easy and, in fact, I found compiling my second book (*Ducati Twins* – Osprey Publishing) much simpler! This was not just because by then I knew what to expect, but that there is a much more readily available bank of information on the twins.

With the singles much vital information was never documented, so even though I was for-tunate to have my own records, extra material often needed a level of investigation which I'm sure would have given Sherlock Holmes more grey hairs. However, I did find that my love for the tough little singles from Bologna drove me on when sometimes the more sensible thing would have been to have taken up a new interest altogether!

All this would never have come about except for a chain of events which were to follow my ride from Wisbech to Manchester on my 350 Mark 3 in May 1982 to attend the AGM of the British Ducati Owners' Club! It was at this meet-ing that I met an owner of a 750 Sport who as a journalist for *Motorcycle Enthusiast* asked me if I would provide him with information for a series on the Ducati marque, which he intended writing for the magazine. To cut a long story short, he left *MCE* before he started.

I then received a phone call from the editor,

Howard Lindley; would I write it? Having done most things in the motorcycle world, I agreed. A few months on and I had become editor of *MCE* and then came an offer from Tim Parker of Osprey Publishing, to write a book for the Collector's Library series.

I would also like to acknowledge the debt I owe my many close friends, both in the motorcycle trade and fellow enthusiasts without whose help and encouragement. . . . It is at times like these that the real proof of just how important something is comes out. If only Ducati Meccanica could harness that adoration their products are held in. In Britain so many helped; it is impossible to list but a few, yet I thank everyone even though their name might not be listed. The few who represent many – Brian Henley, Tony Scothern, Nick Menditta, Garith Jones, Barry Davis and Doug Curran.

Two people in America provided much valuable information including photographs, Ron Tittener and Syd Tunstall to whom I am particularly grateful. My old friend, Franco Valentini of Ducati Meccanica helped in several ways, as did Bernard Adey who brought back an experimental engine from Italy which I was able to study and photograph. I also received a wealth of information from several riders who had raced all types of Ducati singles from the mid-1950s up to the classic racing events of today.

Photographs came from many sources – Don Upshaw and Doug Jackson in particular, but also and in no special order, Alan Cathcart, Tim Parker, the EMAP archives (ex *Motor Cycle, Motor Cycling* and *Motor Cycle Weekly*), John Day, Mike Clay, Tom March, J. Stoddard, C. J. Mayhew, Len Thorpe, Kenneth Simmons, Terreni, Alden, Mark Berlin, Publifoto, Jan Heese, E. Puigdengolas, G. Berghini, Nick Nicholls, G. V. Kneale, Colin Chisholm, R. Baldock, Hollingworth & Martin, Cecil Bailey, Alan Kirk and Stewart Kendall. Thank you all.

Bruno Spaggiari was my first choice for the foreword – I was so pleased he accepted this task. He is surely one of the heroes for all involved with the singles.

A special thank you goes to my wife Susan who both accepts and supports my love of motorcycles. To my brother Richard who has ably supported my efforts both on and off the track – his technical ability is second to none.

Finally I want to thank Osprey Publishing and Andrew Kemp for it is their combined efforts which have converted my knowledge of Ducati singles into what I hope will be hours of good reading.

Mick Walker
Wisbech, Cambridgeshire
February 1985

Early days in Bologna

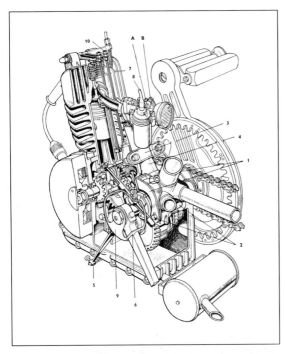

The Cucciolo 'micromotor' engine which carries the distinction of putting the name Ducati on wheels

Few of the world's great motorcycle marques have their origins in the myth-making machines that weave legends around their maker's name. On the contrary most were launched from humble beginnings in the manufacture of cheap transport for the masses. Even today, it is often the bread-and-butter machines that provide the life blood of many factories better known for their exotic creations and their track exploits.

Ducati was no exception. Like so many others, both in the classic British period, and in Japan and Italy postwar, its fortunes as a motorcycle producer grew from the bottom up. The story begins in a war-torn Italy hungry for cheap transport – and not even with a true motorcycle or moped. Ducati's first motorcycle product was a clip-on micromotor – an auxiliary power unit to pep up a bicycle and save the rider's leg muscles.

But humble is not necessarily pedestrian. Even in this first foray on two wheels there was a hint of the sparkle of inventive genius that was to characterize the company's production of single-cylinder machines for the next 30 years until 'rationalizations' forced Ducati to concentrate production in a newer range of twins. In between, the Ducati story touches on almost every facet of motorcycling from commuter bikes to World Championship winners. They built scooters, mopeds, superbikes, road racers – even trials, motocross and grasstrack machines.

The Ducati company dates back well before the war, when they were a major producer of

The 48 cc Cucciolo engine offered a reliable, economical means of transport with less leg work

The 1950 Ducati 60, the Bologna factory's first 'real' motorcycle

radio components. With the coming of war, production diversified into military hardware, and the workforce grew.

At the end of the war, they were in trouble – like so many others in a shattered Italy. But as part of a national reconstruction plan, the government stepped in and looked for an outlet for the Ducati company's vast production facilities. They found it in a diminutive petrol engine.

Transport was desperately short, but even in the early 1940s, some had foreseen this and laid plans. One such was Aldo Farinelli, whose highly innovative little engine, or 'micromotor', was ideal for the nation's needs. Ducati were now commissioned by their new owners to make it.

The story of Ducati motorcycles starts in the late 1940s in Borgo Panigale, a suburb of northern Bologna, Italy. The factory gates open to let out a man on a pedal cycle, much like any other, but in the centre of the bicycle frame is an engine. Looking just like a miniature motorcycle power unit, it is a 50 cc four-stroke, with finned crankcase and overhead valves using pull rods instead of the conventional pushrods.

It will fit to any existing pedal cycle frame and offers all the performance of the bicycle without the effort – save for a little euphemistic 'light pedal assistance' on steep hills. Amazingly, it is capable of almost 300 miles on one gallon of low-grade petrol. It is called the 'Cucciolo' or 'little pup'. In the words of the owner's handbook of the period: 'The "Cucciolo" is an Auxiliary Unit designed to fit ordinary pedal cycles for the purpose of substituting motor power for human effort, every other advantage connected with cycling being fully retained. There are well over 250,000 "Cucciolo" units in everyday use on the Continent, and many more in other parts of the world. It is a precision-built four-stroke overhead valve engine, of advanced design which incorporates every desirable feature of the bigger class motorcycle engine, at a record minimum of running expenses.'

Extravagant claims maybe, but all of them justified. The Cucciolo was an innovative machine that achieved a well-deserved success – and to it, more than any other, goes the credit for spawning the moped boom. It also carries the greater distinction of putting the name Ducati on wheels.

There's a world of difference between making proprietary engines, however good they are, and producing a complete motorcycle. Originally Ducati's aim had been only to build and market engine assemblies; however the idea of building complete machines had come from several companies who manufactured complete bikes using Cucciolo power units. Of these firms perhaps the most successful was one called Motoclipper. Their first complete machine featured an open frame, with leading-link forks and torsion bar rear suspension.

Soon Ducati were to consider offering complete machines themselves. Their first effort appeared at the 1948 Milan Show; this, however, was not a two-wheeler, but a three-wheel truck which was powered by a Cucciolo engine bored out to 60 cc and labelled the T3. Although this project was a failure, the factory's management were convinced. During 1949, with production and demand for Cucciolo engines accelerating, the factory made a firm decision to market a complete motorcycle themselves. Initially the task was more difficult than it might have seemed to the casual observer, for although the factory had produced around 200,000 engines in a relatively short space of time, it possessed absolutely no experience whatsoever in cycle part design and construction. It was therefore decided that this called for a joint venture with another company. Contact was made with Aero Caproni, part of the Caproni Group based in Trento, a town situated in north-east Italy, near

The 1952 175 Cruiser scooter, its advanced technical specification failed to win it many customers

the Austrian border. Caproni, like Ducati, had been heavily dependent on the manufacture of war materials, but in their case this had consisted almost exclusively of aviation products. (Since Italy's participation in World War I, Caproni had been one of Italy's most important aircraft manufacturers with, at their peak in the mid-thirties, factories throughout the country, including Taledo, Milan; Ponte San Pietro, Bergamo; Vizzola Ticino, Varese; with smaller plants at Reggio Emilia and Rome.) This contact was curious – Caproni had no motorcycle experience either.

The result was a small, lightweight motorcycle powered by a 60 cc Cucciolo engine, producing 2·25 bhp at 5000 rpm. Although a limited number of machines were built, the marriage did not last and after a few months, in May 1950, Caproni broke up the partnership to concentrate on producing their own machines. Theirs used Caproni-designed engines – not Ducati – and were to lead to a range of motorcycles sold over the years as the Capriolo.

Ducati, meanwhile, had found that demand for engine units was slowing, as by now other manufacturers were also offering bolt-on power units, albeit two-strokes. The most successful of these was to be the Mosquito produced by Garelli, which by 1956 had sold over two million units! Not only this, but the scooter craze was just starting with the arrival of several new designs, including the first Lambretta and Vespa models.

Progressively the Cucciolo engine was updated and improved, its ultimate development being the 55E, which was introduced in late 1954. Ducati made the logical progression from clip-on motor to a true moped. Their moped had what was for the time a very modern styling with a chassis that featured full suspension from front leading-link forks and a rear swinging-arm with proper motorcycle-type suspension units. Its power output was now slightly up at 1·35 bhp as against the earlier Cucciolo's 1·25. The engine

A Ducati advertisement from the 1954 Giro d'Italia programme showing 65 and 98 cc pushrod models

used a full motorcycle-pattern silencer and exhaust system to replace the Cucciolo's expansion box type. Another improvement was the fully enclosed valve gear, which had been partially exposed on the original engine.

As an indication of what grass roots motorcycling cost in those days, some sample spares prices from the British 55E parts list make interesting reading: piston 15s., big end £5 2s. 2d., conrod £1 3d., silencer 18s., petrol tank £2 9s.

The 55E sadly never approached sales figures to equal those of the early days of the Cucciolo and by 1956 was being phased out of production. The first 'real' Ducati was conceived back in

Ducati Singles

British journalist John Thorpe trying the 65T for size at the factory in December 1954

1950 following the collapse of the Caproni venture. This was simply called the Ducati 60, and was something of a cross between a motorcycle and a moped. The 60 was powered by a suitably enlarged Cucciolo engine, in fact the same unit as was used to power the abortive *Duca proni*. This had a bore and stroke of 42 × 43 mm, with a three-speed footchange gearbox, which was in unit with the engine. Maximum speed hovered around 40 mph. A kick-starter was fitted to the offside of the engine, as was the heel-and-toe gear pedal. With a dry weight of 104 lb, cantilever frame, leading axle telescopic front forks and friction damped swinging-arm, together with 18 in. wheels, roadholding and cornering abilities were exceptional for its day.

To test market reaction one of these machines was imported into Britain during the summer of 1951, by Britax Ltd. This was tested by John

Thorpe of *Motor Cycling*. Just prior to this Britax had become the British importer for the Cucciolo engine, and, in fact, produced several complete machines of their own design with the Ducati engine as a base. Amongst their first efforts in this field was in 1953, with a frame and cycle parts from the Enfield Cycle Co. Ltd (Royal Enfield). This was a very basic design featuring a conventional pedal cycle frame in a heavier gauge tubing; it had a motorcycle-type steering head, together with pressed steel fork blades and a 3-band rubber suspension, similar to that used at the time on the Royal Enfield range of lightweights. The brakes, again Royal Enfield products, had 4 in. diameter hubs. Equipped with the Ducati Elettronica flywheel magneto and Lucas cycle-type lighting, its specifications was augmented with the bare essentials; a bulb horn, cycle tyre inflator and a luggage carrier.

However, Britax's two most unusual offerings were both launched at the 1954 Earls Court Show – the Scooterette and Hurricane.

The Scooterette was just as its name implies, but an uglier device would be hard to imagine. The actual 1955 production models differed from the prototype shown at Earls Court by virtue of the use of the 55E-type engine with its 1·35 bhp at 5130 rpm, 6·7 to 1 compression ratio, fully enclosed valve gear and improved primary drive – which meant a much quieter engine than the earlier Cucciolo had been. Other details included a Weber carburettor, 20 in. wheels, 1¼-gallon fuel capacity and link-type Royal Enfield front forks. The whole machine was encased in panels beaten in 19-gauge sheet steel and finished in maroon paint. With all the various panelling sections in place the only parts of the machine visible were the bottom half of both wheels, the finned crankcase sump and the chrome silencer, which was incidentally dangerously mounted underneath the sump very near the road surface! List price in August 1955 was £99 18s.

Typical of the type of wording amongst the

press road tests of the period was the *Motor Cycling* tester's optimistic comments: 'The Britax Scooterette – an under £100 weather-protected single-seat runabout – was without doubt one of the major attractions at last year's Earls Court Show. Since then production has gone ahead with few snags, and a number of these attractively styled little machines are now appearing in the dealers' showrooms.' Yes, the Scooterette was awful! The customers must have agreed with me because records show very, very few were ever sold and it is doubtful if even one survives today.

The Britax Hurricane was a 50 cc over-the-counter racer, again Cucciolo powered. Its only claim to fame was the polished-alloy streamlining which gave it the honour of being the first British bike so equipped as standard. Sadly, though, its performance did not match its name and works rider Arnold Jones achieved very little in the way of results. After 1955 Britax's efforts faded and with the exception of odd machines brought in for evaluation, only engines were ever imported.

Ducati themselves had meanwhile been pressing ahead at a purposeful rate, and had found it necessary to diversify into other designs, rather than just go on updating the Cucciolo-based machines. Therefore, as far back as the Milan Show of 1952 two completely new models had been introduced. The first of this duo was a pushrod ohv with a capacity of 98 cc, initially produced only in touring form. It featured a bore and stroke of 48 × 52 mm, producing 5·8 bhp at 7500 rpm, with an 8:1 compression ratio in its original form. This was to prove the forerunner of one of Ducati's most successful early designs, culminating with the later sporting 98S and a couple of 125s.

Sharing the same stand was a complete departure for the Bologna factory – a scooter. Called the 'Cruiser', this had been developed to counter the successful two-stroke designs then coming off other production lines and being

The 1953 98 cc TL pushrod, four-speed gearbox, swinging arm suspension and conical brake hubs

snapped up all over Italy. Ducati reasoned – wrongly – that by producing a four-stroke, more technically advanced scooter, it could steal sales away from its rivals. In practice Ducati's Cruiser was too advanced for its own good, with a specification more akin to that of a sports motorcycle than a humble form of commuter scooter. Because of its four-stroke engine, the Cruiser was also much heavier than its competitors, but in theory it did have one design advantage – power. Unfortunately, even this was to be denied, as production versions had to be detuned to meet government regulations. All this, together with the production costs of a four-stroke and a complexity which was not appreciated by the average scooter owner, quickly led to an early demise.

With the exception of the unwanted Cruiser, the motorcycle side of Ducati's production was now picking up with the new 98, together with an updated version of the 60, now called the 65, which together with the various versions of the Cucciolo engine represented Ducati's two-wheel production efforts during 1953 and into 1954. But it was in the latter year that the company, rather surprisingly partly owned by the Vatican, made the move which has shaped the history of virtually every Ducati model made since. They decided to take on a new designer.

The man selected for the job was Ing. Fabio Taglioni. Ing. stands for Ingegnere, the Italian for engineer. In a country with as proud an engineering heritage as Italy, it's a title which commands respect − almost reverence − and it's men like Taglioni who made it so. Taglioni is a visionary and was soon to become a legend, and to a large extent any history of Ducati is a biography of Taglioni.

Taglioni was and is an innovator of genius, who brought with him designs and theories which others have only tried to follow. Without him Ducati would not have been the same company, and I do not believe that the world would have seen machines of the calibre of the famous ohc singles and the V-twins which followed. It

is also unlikely that we would have seen the desmodromic valve system used so successfully or on such a wide scale. And, above all, we would be poorer for the lack of such unique sportsters as the Formula IIIs, Mach 1s, 750s and SSs. It was machines such as these that became, for many riders, the real Ducatis that created the legend and inspired such loyalty and dedication in all who rode them. Amen to Fabio Taglioni. Before his arrival Ducati had only produced two-wheeled machines; now they were to produce real motorcycles.

Taglioni's greatest love and enthusiasm was road racing. This is why the best Ducatis have been real road racers or genuine sporting roadsters with their hearts on the track. The factory has never produced a really successful touring

98 Sport, pictured at the 1953 Milan Show offered a lively performance

bike, certainly not one which sold well compared to the sportier models in the range. I am also certain that without Taglioni it is doubtful if Ducati would ever have achieved any real success in racing. This goes not just for the factory-sponsored efforts. The design flair and enthusiasm that characterized the new breed of Ducatis has inspired hosts of privateers the world over, and the machinery which they have converted for the track has done its part to swell the list of Ducati honours.

As early as late 1954, the factory may have shown some of Taglioni's influence on their pushrod-engined models when they catalogued their first sports models, the 65 and 98S. With an overhead valve four-stroke engine, the smaller engine had a capacity of 65 cc with a bore and stroke of 44 × 43 mm, and it was good for 44 mph – impressive for the time. Its frame carried a rear swinging-arm and telescopic forks. From these modest beginnings, the two machines gave the first hint of the famous sportsters that were to come in the future.

These were followed in 1956 by improved versions, now with flyscreens and more racy lines to produce some of the most sporting-looking bikes of the period. In the 1950s Italy was the world's premier motorcycling nation. It was a country which favoured the small-capacity motorcycle, with few legal restrictions and low costs. Above all, the young men who made up the bulk of the market valued style and performance – even if they did have one eye to economy, the bikes didn't have to look as though they did. The 56 mph top speed and good looks of the 98S made it a firm favourite for *la passeggiata* – the Italian version of street cruising. Predictably it sold in large numbers.

Also available was a touring version, known as the Cavalline. The engine of both models had a bore and stroke of 48 × 52 mm and was fitted for the first time with a four-ring piston. On this type of piston the two compression rings were fitted above the gudgeon pin, while a pair of oil

The 98 Sport by 1956 looked like this. Flyscreen, dropped bars and bulbous tank all added to its sporting aura

scraper rings were fitted below. It was to become a common Ducati feature, being used on most models from then up to the mid-sixties. The last to use it was the 1968 250 Monza (never sold in Britain and not to be confused with the 1966 model of the same name which sold in Britain in 1968–70; more of these later).

The Cavalline was listed as the model 98T in its original form in 1952. Touring features included a single-pivot sprung saddle (known as the TL with optional dual seat), built-in rear carrier and touring handlebars with fixed lever positions. A screw-type petrol filler cap replaced the quick-action, race-style version used by the sports model – and the wheel rims were chrome, not alloy as on the 98S. Maximum speed was down to 50 mph, although the fuel economy was improved from the sportster's 120 mpg to 138 mpg. Perhaps because of this, the Cavalline fuel tank was smaller, holding $2\frac{1}{2}$ gallons as opposed to the $3\frac{1}{4}$ of the 98S.

Ducati's complete model line-up for 1955 consisted of the following machines: M55, 55R, 55E, 65T, 65TL, 98N, 98T, 98TL and, the top of the range, the sporting 98S. The suffixes incidentally stood for: T – Touring, S – Sport, TL – Touring

The 1954 48 Britax, a Ducati Cucciolo engine in cycle parts supplied by the (Royal) Enfield Cycle Co

Lusso; and M, R and E were moped designs.

In late 1956, Ducati followed the success of the 98 series by introducing a 125 cc version. The engine unit of the 125TV was clearly an enlarged 98, but the majority of the cycle parts were completely different. Its frame, forks, petrol tank and headlamp were all new, although British riders of the period commented on the origins of the headlamp design, which looked for all the world just like an Italian copy of the famous Triumph nacelle! A slightly less expensive version, the 125T, was also produced. Both were offered for a short period in late 1957/early 1958 in Britain by a company S. D. Sullam Ltd of London; the 125TV sold at £187 2s. 6d., while the 125T was £181 13s. 10d.

This time the frame was a neatly crafted double cradle, while the forks and brakes were more robust than those seen on earlier Ducatis, and the alloy hubs were now full width. The petrol tank had the same $3\frac{1}{4}$-gallon capacity as the 98S, but its contours were changed. Despite the extra cubic capacity, the 125 had the same top speed as the 98S – 56 mph.

With the exception of a budget priced range of models of 85, 98 and 125 cc, all titled under the Bronco label, the pushrods were made instantly obsolete when the new range of overhead-cam Ducatis appeared. These final variants of the original pushrod design lingered on into the sixties and were expressly intended for the US market, although a few did reach other shores. The 85 Bronco was a sleeved-down 98, with a bore of 45·5 mm, but retaining the latter's 55 mm stroke. It produced 6·5 bhp at 7500 rpm, and like the other Broncos featured four speeds. The last Bronco (the 125) was still listed by the Berliner Motor Corporation as late as 1968.

The story of Ducati's overhead-cam engine goes back to 1955, which saw the factory's first serious attempts at racing; up to Taglioni's arrival, the works had converted standard machines to take part in local events, which, for the most part, meant either trials or long distance road races.

The road races of the time were *real* road races, held on the open public highways, which were not closed for the event. They included several outstanding events, some of which were on an annual basis. Amongst these were the classic Giro d'Italia, and the Milano-Taranto. As the name implies, the latter was derived from the historic city-to-city races, which dated back to the earliest days of motor sport.

Ducati machines were always extremely reliable in competitive events but stood no real chance of success. While Ducati were running stripped-down roadsters, other factories were racing pukka works machines – out-and-out racers fitted with the bare minimum of road equipment needed to qualify for the event.

Ducati set out to reverse this inequality and aimed first for the popular and well-contested 100 cc class. The machine that carried their hopes and was soon to shock their rivals was Taglioni's first racing design for Ducati. This was the 98 cc single overhead-cam engine, and proudly cast into its cam cover were the words

'Ducati 100 cc Gran Sport'. Very soon it was being produced in quantity, and helped to launch the racing careers of such acclaimed riders as Bruno Spaggiari, Alberto Pagani, Francesco Villa, Alberto Gandossi, Franco Farne and Giuseppe Mandolini. The tale of these men and other famous Ducati riders is told later.

While it featured such items as a kick-start and other road-going equipment, the 100 cc Gran Sport was a genuine production racer. The engine unit was a pure racing design, but except for the cylinder head it looked, externally, just like the single overhead-cam sportsters which followed it. The original versions of the Gran Sport had exposed hairpin valve springs and external oil pipes. Its light alloy barrel with cast-iron liner had nearly square dimensions with a bore of 49.4 mm and stroke of 52 mm, and carried a forged 3-ring piston. The crankcases smacked of being from a small production run, since they were sand cast, as were the side covers. Its kick-start arrangement was different from that adopted for the roadsters, and transmission was through a close-ratio four-speed box with straight-cut primary drive gears. Power on the first models was 9 bhp at 9000 rpm on an 8·5:1 compression ratio. This was later increased to 12 bhp at 10,500 rpm, which took the maximum speed up from 80 mph to 87 mph. The rev counter drive was taken off the front of the cylinder head, unlike the later roadsters, where it came off the triangular cam cover.

Fuel consumption was outstanding, giving around 100 mpg at racing speeds, breathing through a 20 mm SS1 Dell'Orto carburettor with remote float. This carburettor was very steeply inclined and had an insulating rubber between it and the head. Ignition was by Bosch TJ6 oil-filled coil with a 6-volt SAFA battery.

The racer ran on 17 in. WM1 wheel rims. It was fitted with a lightweight alloy petrol tank which had a special large side cutaway to clear the carburettor bellmouth. Colours of the machine were dark red with white transfers on the fuel

The 55E, an early attempt to produce a modern moped (again with a Cucciolo engine), was offered for sale 1955/57

tank, which was also painted, despite being alloy. Later the 125 and 175 versions (all featuring exposed valve gear) also appeared.

The Gran Sport project had not been conceived just so that Ducati could win races, there was also a serious commercial production purpose behind it. The ultimate aim of the factory was to launch a new range of overhead camshaft models on to both the home and the world's export markets. Working broadly with the proven Gran Sport design, the intention was to come up with brand new 100, 125 and 175 cc power units. However, to achieve the level of worldwide sales that would make such an exercise profitable, Ducati had to become known outside its native land.

Racing was and is a quick way to fame – but only if you are supremely confident of the ability of your products to deliver the results. Ducati was, and so launched an intensive racing programme. This was to include both Grand Prix events and endurance racing – for Ducati was concerned to emphasize their machines' reliability as well as their speed.

Early days in Bologna

19

Ducati's first 125, the 1956 TV, still pushrod, but with duplex frame and full width hubs. Note Triumph-type headlamp nacelle

In November 1956, a Gran Sport engine of the original 100 cc capacity was fitted with a special, streamlined alloy 'dustbin' fairing. This machine, ridden by Sandro Ciceri and Mario Carini, proceeded to set 44 new performance records, which were outstanding for the period, let alone for a bike using a standard engine (except for a larger 25 mm Dell'Orto SS1 carburettor). At the Monza track near Milan the little streamliner was ridden to smash the records for the hour, the 100 kilometres and the 1000 kilometres. In the 1000 kilometres, the Ducati averaged over 96 mph for the whole of the ride. This was pushed well over 100 mph for the hour and the 100 kilometres.

For the early Grand Prix entries, Taglioni first produced a double overhead-cam version of the 125 Gran Sport, except for a new cylinder head assembly, a truly massive casting which housed the complex valve gear. This modification was good enough to boost power to 16 bhp at 11,500 rpm on a 9·5:1 compression ratio. This, however, was not good enough for Taglioni, and it was to be just a curtain-raiser to the main event on the world stage. For his next design achieved what most designers thought impossible to incorporate in a motorcycle engine, let alone

one of just 125 cc. In so doing, he forged what was later to become one of the strongest links in the Ducati legend.

What Taglioni did was to design his new engine around the desmodromic system of valve gear. 'Desmo' has so long been associated with Ducati that it's often assumed that they invented it. That is not so – the desmodromic system's theoretical advantages had been suggested for a long time. What Taglioni did was to make it work – and work brilliantly.

'Desmodromic', coined from two Greek words, means 'controlled run'. The idea was to eliminate one of the chief bugbears of valve operation at high rpm – the phenomenon of valve float, or 'bounce'. This happens when the valve springs are unable to respond fast enough to close the valves back on to their seats. The desmodromic idea was to replace the troublesome springs with a mechanical closing system much like that used to open them, so giving a positive action. Eliminate the springs and you eliminate the bounce and get a higher-revving engine – in theory.

This has been known since the early days of the internal combustion engine, but no motorcycle designer had managed to harness it. Norton had tried (unsuccessfully) with a converted Manx engine. Even the mighty car industry had done little better, with one exception, Mercedes-Benz. But all they had achieved after spending vast sums of money was to build their highly specialized W196 racing car in 1954. Then they retired from racing!

Ducati is the exception in the desmodromic story. From Taglioni's first experiments, they had adopted the desmo system for mass production by 1968 on the 250/350 Mk 3D. By 1980, almost all their current range were to use it.

Taglioni's first desmodromic masterpiece was the original 125 cc single. Nearly square at 55·25 × 52 mm bore and stroke, it ran a compression ratio of 10·5:1 and used a titanium conrod that was double webbed at the top and bottom

In November 1956 this 100 Gran Sport powered
streamliner set 44 new records at Monza

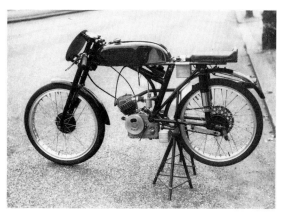

The Cucciolo engine even found its way onto the race
circuit, witness this neat 50 cc racer of 1956

to withstand the stresses of sustained high revs.
The valves were 31 mm inlet and 27 mm exhaust,
and, unlike the later production desmo engine,
no valve springs at all were used. This package
was able to produce 17 bhp at 12,500 rpm and
both five- and six-speed crankcases were available to suit the demands of different circuits, giving a maximum speed on the fastest circuits of
112 mph.

There was also a choice of 27 mm or 29 mm
carburettors – both Dell'Orto SS1 with remote
float chamber. Twin-spark ignition was used,
with the standard 14 mm plug augmented by a
tiny 10 mm one behind the cam drive tunnel.
Rev counter take-off was from the right front side
of the cylinder head cambox. Otherwise, from
the cylinder barrel downwards, the unit was
nearly all Gran Sport – proof of the soundness
of the original design.

Fitted into a single cradle frame with 18 in.
WM1 wheels, the new motor's Grand Prix debut
came after a long period of factory tests. Experimental engines had been run on the test bench
for up to 100 hours at full throttle. Meanwhile,
on the track, testers had hurtled around sometimes exceeding 15,000 rpm with no ill effects –

unheard of at the time. With a profound con-
fidence in the new machine's speed and ability
to keep going, the factory readied the racer for
its first competitive outing.

They picked the 1956 Swedish GP at Hedemora,
which was to be contested by a strong field, led
by the near-invincible FB Mondials and MV
Agustas, ridden by some of the world's top men.
Also in evidence was the new 125 Gilera twin.
In such company, the arrival of Ducati's works
entrant Degli Antoni and his machine provoked
little interest.

However, as soon as Antoni started to warm
up his engine, onlookers knew that here was
something special. This new bike sounded deep,
mellow and powerful. It was a suspicion that was
confirmed in the first practice session, when the
engine note rose to an intense wail like an angry
wasp as the machine swept round the circuit.
Once the race started, Antoni showed just how
superb the new machine really was, setting the
fastest lap, lapping every other rider at least once
and finally finishing the race in record time. How
many other factories have had such a Grand Prix
début, or such a foundation on which to build
a new range of production motorcycles?

Early days in Bologna

21

2 The first 'camshafts'

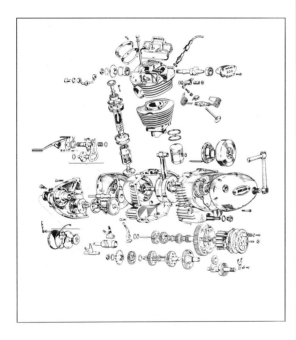

Top **Taglioni's first roadster to use the classic ohc bevel drive system was the 175 (200 version shown)**

Right **The 1957 175S metal tank badge**

In the late fifties, the motorcycle industry was booming and few manufacturers bothered to use glamour as a sales ploy. The typical showroom line-up was a dull affair, with hordes of look-alike machines finished in unimaginative blacks, maroons and military green drab. But in amongst the grey herd it was not unusual to see a gleaming line of bikes tricked out like miniature roadgoing racers, down to clip-ons and double-barrel silencers. The finish was a glaring metallic red and gold, balanced by beautifully polished alloy castings. Inevitably they stood out from the crowd, and a quarter of a century ago Ducati's overhead-cam singles were the objects of fantasy for a whole generation of window-shopping youth.

Sadly, fantasy was never enough to guarantee sales for Ducati, and those British teenagers who lusted for a new 175 or 200 model would probably end up with a worn-out Bantam bought on

hire purchase. It was left to those lucky few who could afford it to appreciate what classics they had bought. Now, with the gift of hindsight, it's easier to see just how special these machines were.

Ducati's new range followed the company plan for a whole generation of similar overhead-cam singles stemming from the successful Gran Sport racer. Eventually, it was to include four different sizes of engine (100, 125, 175 and 200 cc) and a host of variants. When they were first drawn up, they were highly advanced machines. The engine units in particular were astonishingly well designed. Even in terms of today's engineering they are modern and efficient, but over 25 years ago they were outstanding!

The first of these new overhead-camshaft Ducatis were the 125S (a sports model) and two 175s – the 175S and the 175T. These motorcycles were to be the cornerstone of all future Ducati four-stroke design until the chain-driven 350 and 500 cc parallel twins in the mid-seventies. The 125 was to give birth to 100 and 160 cc variants, while the 175 later went up to 200 cc, and as later chapters will show this same 175 eventually spawned the 250, 350 and 450. Altogether, the series had a production life span of 18 years in Italy and continued even longer under licence in Spain.

In spite of this, the early Ducati ohc models never had a whirlwind sales record outside of Italy. In the UK, it was the 200 which had the most success, while in the USA it was the 175 which made the running. The Italian home market was less precise, although much larger, but it was probably the 100 and 175 that met with the greatest popularity.

All three of the original models were based on a design that had been well tried and tested during the racing heyday of the Gran Sport; all of them had an all-alloy unit construction engine incorporating a deeply-finned wet sump. The pistons were forged and the valve gear was driven by shaft and bevel gears. Primary drive

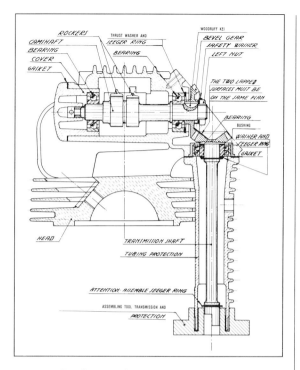

Cross-section drawing showing cylinder head, camshaft and top bevel shaft layout

to the wet multiplate clutch was by gear.

The star of the show was undoubtedly the 175S – with a maximum speed of 84 mph, it was faster than several contemporary 500s! Most of the credit went to its superb engine, capable of producing 14 bhp at 8000 rpm on an 8:1 compression ratio. It was also good for an astonishing 95 mpg. But the chassis, with an overall dry weight of 205 lb and racer-derived handling, contributed to the all-round performance in a way that few could match.

In keeping with the sporting image, the colour scheme was a bright metallic cherry red for the fuel tank, mudguards, toolboxes, chainguard, rear light bracket and headlamp shell. This was set off by the liberal use of metallic gold paint for the frame, swinging-arm, fork legs, fork yokes, spring covers and centre stand. Matching gold flashes highlighted the tank.

The first model had several features which were not retained on later Ducati 175s. Soon to disappear or change were its 'flat' light rim, silencer, exhaust pipe shape and the use of a 'downward'-pointing heel and two-gear lever. The carburettor was fitted with a longer bell-mouth than later bikes and the cylinder head and bevel tube differed in detail. Most noticeable of all, later models used chrome trim on the petrol tanks in place of gold paint.

The touring 175T used the same basic motor and chassis, but its very mildly tuned engine pushed out only 11 bhp at 7500 rpm. As a result, the maximum speed was well down on the sports model, at 68 mph. The fuel economy was a frugal 100 mpg, although this was only a small improvement on the staggeringly efficient 'S'

motor. Detuning consisted of a lower compression ratio (7:1) and fitting a Dell'Orto MB 22 B carburettor with attached air filter. The latter replaced the 'S' model's sporty UB 22·5 BS2 with open bellmouth.

The overall colour of the 175T was dark red, with red and white for the tank. It could also be ordered in black with either a black and white, or black and red, tank. To fit its more pedestrian image, all the tourer's colours were non-metallic.

Of all the three models, the 125S most closely resembled the racer, and although a small ma-

The 1957 175T, the clip-ons strongly contrasting with its 'turismo' aspirations

chine it was unquestionably a true sportster. However, despite steady sales in its native Italy, its export figures never matched those of the 175. This was probably due to there being no capacity limit for learners, which put a premium on ccs. The 125S engine was no slouch though, giving 10 bhp at 85 rpm for a maximum speed of 70 mph and 102 mpg. The finish was appropriately sporty, in metallic blue and gold.

During 1958 and early 1959, Ducati extended the range considerably. The first machine to appear was a smaller version of the 125, the 100 Sport. At the same time, the 125S became the 125 Sport. Both new models were virtually identical and had several obvious differences from the original 125S. They were now fitted with a Silentium silencer, the styling of the paintwork for the fuel tank was revised and a new type of Dell'Orto carburettor was used, fitted at a much steeper incline.

At this time, a touring version of the 125 was also launched. Given the designation 125TS (Touring Special), its engine was rather detuned with a compression ratio of only 7:1 and a lower profile cam. Up to the 1500th machine, the carburettor was a Dell'Orto UA 18 BS, but thereafter an ME 18 BS was used. Together these changes meant that the power was down to 6·2 bhp at 6500 rpm.

The cycle parts of the TS were also revised, with changes that included new front forks and rear suspension units, both of which were to be used much later on the 160 Monza Junior. Also new were the fuel tank (with a filler cap design later used on the 175TS), the headlamp assembly, front mudguard, and touring handlebars that replaced the clip-ons.

The only real difference between the 100 and 125 Sport models was the reduction of the bore to 49 mm to give an actual capacity of 98·056 cc. At the same time, the compression ratio was raised to 9:1 and a Dell'Orto US 18 BS was fitted. Power was 8 bhp at 8500 rpm and the top speed was 66 mph.

The 1958 100 Sport, developed from the 125 version

The 100 Sport sold in large numbers at home, but was never a force in Ducati's developing export market. Today, every Japanese manufacturer produces a 100 cc variant of the 125 design, but in the late fifties, overseas buyers were not ready for this capacity – a classic example of the right ideas at the wrong time.

Since the appearance of the ohc models. Ducati had been making far greater attempts to extend their sales outside Italy. Outside Europe, they were opening dealerships in several new markets, of which the most important were North and South America and the Middle and Far East. So far, none of their attempts with small machines had met with much success, so the factory took the other path and produced an enlarged version of the 175, by the simple expedient of increasing the bore to 67 mm while retaining the 57·8 mm stroke of the original engine. The new machine was then marketed as a 200. Called the 'Elite', it was an 87 mph machine, thanks to the 18 bhp of the new engine. At the same time, as with the 125 when the 100 was developed, the 175 was updated. The original Elites can be identified by their deeply valanced mudguards. Otherwise, they were externally similar to the then latest 175 Sport.

The most striking styling feature of both the 175 and 200 models was the new double-barrel silencer. This was definitely one of the less desirable features, as I found when I owned an Elite with this system; as soon as the bike's outstanding cornering ability was used, the silencer grounded – lifting the rear wheel off the tarmac. Needless to say, I quickly replaced the original fitting with a single silencer, and many other examples of the extraordinary twin set-up doubtlessly went the same way.

Minor differences of the Elite from the 175 were its larger tyres. Pirellis were now being fitted as standard, and the Elite had a 2·75 × 18 front and a 3·00 × 18 rear. It also had Marzocchi rear suspension units with polished alloy top and bottom spring covers, which had convenient three-position adjusting handles. Soon after the launch, the Elite reverted to sports lightweight mudguards, but from then on, until its demise in the mid-sixties, further changes were limited to a new electrical system and alterations to the rear light and the number plate and bracket. Engine details remained identical until 1960.

There is, however, considerable confusion in the history of the 200 series surrounding a so-called 'Super Sports' model. In 1960, the factory did in fact list a version of the Elite called Super Sport, but the only change was to the tank

A tuned version of the 175 Sport was sold in Britain as the Silverstone Super, with a reputed speed of 92 mph

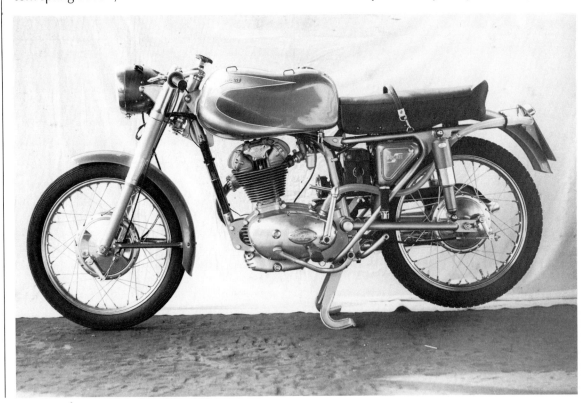

badge, which was the same as the 175 Sport, and the fitting of a single silencer (sense having prevailed over styling). Even though most 200s sold in the UK over the years were in fact Elites, the importers, King's of Manchester, insisted on calling them 'Super Sports'. Also, King's advertising at the time gave the impression that the Super Sports was a tuned version of the Elite, whereas factory records and technical specifications give both machines an identical power output.

What really adds to the confusion is that it was possible to purchase factory tuning parts for the Elite and for the Super Sport. These comprised a three-ring high-compression piston, to replace the standard four-ring pattern, a high-lift camshaft (£6 15s. in the UK), a 27 mm Dell'Orto SS1 carburettor, and finally a pukka racing megaphone in black (£4 5s. for this item). With the full race kit added, including the megaphone, top speed rose to near the 100 mph mark. In the late fifties and early sixties, quite a large number of 200s were converted privately, exclusively for competition use.

At the same time as the Elite was introduced the 175T became the 175 Tourist. Quite why this model was not called the 'Economy' I could never understand, since the only concession to touring was the lower power output and valances on the mudguards. Everything else was definitely Sport, but on an economy scale. The

The 1959 175 Tourist, its mildly tuned engine produced 11 bhp at 7500 rpm, as a result top speed was only 68 mph

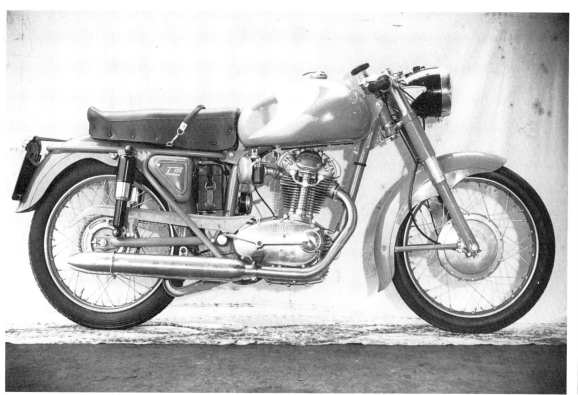

Sporting 1/8-litre, the 125 Sport; this is 1959 version

new Tourist sported the famous and colourful Ducati Meccanica 'big D' tank transfers that were used by the works' racers, these replacing the small metal badge of the 175T, and seem an odd choice for the factory's most basic model. Even stranger was that the Sport had pillion footrests as standard equipment, while the Tourist did not!

Like the 125 series, the 175 had a TS version, but neither this nor its 125 brother were ever exported to the UK. The TS engine was the same as the other models, but there were detail changes to cycle parts. The most important revision was to reduce the brake hub diameters to match the 125 series, front 158 mm, rear 136 mm. The petrol tank was similar in design and finish for both the 125 and 175TS, but the 175's was one litre larger. Both machines had the same handlebars, but a factory optional extra kit for the 175 included high handlebars. It also had a touring single saddle and a parcel carrier.

A 175 which *was* available in the UK was one with a special high-performance conversion. It was originally marketed during 1959 as the 175 Sports tuned Silverstone; by 1960 it had become simply the Silverstone Super. In road trim, with full silencing, the performance was quite simply

stunning, with a maximum of 92 mph, making it surely the fastest 175 roadster of all time! The power increase was achieved with a higher-compression piston, special camshaft and a Dell-'Orto SS1 25 A carburettor. Unfortunately, very few exist today – a great pity, since in its time it was just as outstanding as the later (and better known) Mach 1 and Desmo roadsters.

An even more potent and alluring 175 was offered by Ducati during this period – the 175 Formula III. As early as 1959, in line with their policy of new replacing old, Ducati phased out the 100 and 125 Gran Sport to make way for new Formula III models. One of these was the 175. Although its story really belongs in a later chapter, for it was a pure racer, it was offered with lighting equipment as an original fitment, and with roadster-style mudguards. In my opinion it was one of the most beautiful motorcycles of all time – but it was also one of the most expensive production machines for its size, considering that it was more expensive than a Manx Norton! In 1959, a 175 Formula III cost a kingsize £538 19s. 6d., which was reduced to £521 3s. 11d. the following year and remained so until production ceased in 1961.

Tuned and racing examples of the 125 also appeared in 1959, top of the range, of course, being the racing 125 Formula III (another very expensive choice). The roadsters were marketed like the 175s as the 125 Sports tuned Monza, in 1960 called simply the 125 Super Monza.

New to the UK for 1959 were American-style versions of the 175 and 200, both selling under the name Americano. The smaller machine had previously been sold as a USA-only export model, but the 200 was altogether new. The 175 was heavily restyled around parts from other models in the range, using a fuel tank the same shape and size as the 100/125 models, and the infamous Silentium double-barrel silencer. 'Custom' fittings were high 'Western'-style handlebars, deeply valanced mudguards, crash bars, prop stand and an oversize horn. But its

Top **In 1960 Ducati introduced the 175TS, this time with a more practical set of handlebars**

Above **Touring 125, the TS of 1960**

Above **Stateside influence showed in the 1960 200TS with peanut tank and western bars**

Left **British advertisement for 1960 range. Racing shot is Mike Hailwood's 125 desmo single**

most impressive fixture was the saddle – embossed with more studs than a Hell's Angel's jacket! Most of its special fitting would eventually appear on other models – the crash bar and stand both went to the 160 Monza Junior, 250 Monza and 350 Sebring – but that seat was simply unique. The engine of the 175 Americano was in the same 'soft' tune as the Touring and T models.

The 200 Americano was a far more conventional machine. The fuel tank was a new pattern for Ducati, but was to be used the following year on the first 250 Monza. Other features which differed from the 175 were the silencer (single again!), the shape of the handlebars, the horn, speedometer drive, and of course that seat! The 200 was produced alongside the 175 in 1959, but in 1960 the 175 Americano was discontinued.

Completing the 1959 parade was the new 200 Motocross. Its specification was very similar to the earlier 175 Motocross, except for capacity and the use of a Dell'Orto SS 27 A with remote float chamber and an F 20 filter bent at 45 degrees in place of a 25 mm instrument. The first year's production used an unrestricted upswept black megaphone and a high front mudguard. These were changed for 1960, but otherwise the models were identical. The frame was specially strengthened for off-road use and 2·75 × 21, 3·00 × 19 front and rear knobbly tyres were fitted. Stopping was by large drums on 180 mm conical hubs front and back. Lower gearing was used, and the rear chainguard was raised to accommodate the larger rear wheel sprocket. Off-road style fittings included new handlebars with motocross-type bracing, a sump guard and a slim tank and seat. With the megaphone, the engine gave a healthy 19 bhp, dropping slightly to 18 mph when a restrictive silencer was introduced.

Like the Americano, this model gives a hint of a change of emphasis in Ducati's marketing policy at the end of the 1950s, and in a way oddly foreshadows Japanese bikes of two decades later, with a host of US custom and trail versions on sale alongside conventional roadsters.

It was a policy that was to pay dividends, for the 175 and 200 Motocross models were the forerunners of the later Ducati street scramblers, also known as the SCRs. Over the years, these were produced in large quantities, mainly for the home market and the USA – few UK enthusiasts realize that the factory produced almost as many street scramblers as road bikes in the days of the single.

But if the USA was ready for the new machines, the UK was not. The 200 Americano and

The 1962 200GT, even though it sported tank and side panels from the new 250 Diana, proved a poor seller

Motocross sold only a mere handful of machines and by January 1960, when they had been on sale for just nine months, they disappeared from the UK importer's list. At the time, the range on offer comprised the 125 Monza and Monza Super, 175 Silverstone and Silverstone Super, 200 Elite and Super Sports, plus the competition Formula III racers. The 'tuned' 125 and 175 (Super) models appear to have been UK market 'on-offs', because they were never listed by the factory or sold under those names in any other country. The 'Silverstone' and 'Monza 125' titles were also UK only, in the same way that the 250 Diana was to have the Daytona name applied to models exported to the UK.

This was the range which continued into 1961, the last year in which the Ducati flag was to be borne by its small overhead-cam four-strokes. Waiting in the wings were a new 250, itself a later development of the ohc theme, and an extensive range of small two-strokes. By mid-1962, the 175s had ceased production completely and early that year only one 200, the Super Sports, and one 125, the Monza Super, were listed.

In the spring of that year a new 200 arrived in the UK. Called the 200 Gran Turismo Sports, it was known elsewhere as just the 200GT. It had a new low compression engine and many cycle

Above **1964 200 Elite, with jelly mould tank and double barrel silencer**

parts borrowed from the 250 Diana (the bike that was the Daytona in the UK). The 200 engine had started life as an over-bored 175; from 1961 it became an undersized 250. Although the story of the 250 belongs to a later chapter, owners can easily identify which '200' they have, as they were clearly marked by the factory – stamped 'A' (for 175-type) or 'B' (250) on the bottom fin of the cylinder head and the top fin of the barrel.

Engine differences extend to a number of obvious parts. The 175 had fins running front to rear across the top of the head between the four

Below **A Vic Camp café racer, converted from a standard 200 Elite, with racing tank and seat, with add-on Smiths tach**

head bolt location holes, the 250 casting did not. The 175 had a shorter camshaft and a crankshaft which had flywheels and crankpin of equal width. On the 250, the flywheel and crankpin were extended wider on the alternator side than on the timing side. The clutch housing also differs between the two types. On the 175 it was shouldered and engaged with two bearings on the crankcase, while the 250's was unshouldered and had integral bearings. This type of clutch also found its way on to the 125TS and hence to the later development of that design, the 160 Monza Junior.

Other features of the new 200 which were borrowed from the 250 included the tank, seat, side panels, rear light assembly, suspension units and air cleaner assembly, but it retained the deeply valanced mudguards of the earlier touring models. The whole machine was finished in a deep non-metallic maroon except for the headlamp shell, suspension covers and rear light support, which were black. A white contrasting strip was applied to both sides of the tank. This uninspiring colour match did absolutely nothing for it in the showroom. Neither did the price, for at £229 10s. 0d. it was only £25 cheaper than the recently introduced, and far more glamorous, new 250. By now, this was making even the Super Sports 200 difficult to sell.

Only three of the smaller overhead-cam models struggled on into 1963 on the British market. The 125 was now called the Super Sports, and its two stablemates were the 200 Super Sports (Elite) and 200 Grand Sports (200GT). These survivors were now sandwiched firmly between the two-strokes and the 250, and sales of the old models were very slow through that

In 1965 the last 125 Sport looked like this

year, thanks largely to the success of the 250. After all, why buy a 200 when a 250 is so little more? The results were obvious.

By the end of the year the 125 was no longer being exported to Britain, although it was available from the factory until the mid-sixties. The remaining 200s dropped from production, although this was not to be quite the end of the road in the UK. In 1965 the 200 was back on sale, when a last batch was imported by King's of Oxford, through their Manchester branch. This was a number of Elites with the original twin-barrel silencer which had remained unsold in Germany. Although King's referred to them as 'Super Sports', they most definitely wore Elite tank badges! The winter of 1966–67 saw King's closing their doors as concessionaires and UK imports were then handled by Vic Camp of Walthamstow, London, who had been one of the Kings' dealers. He continued selling off the remaining examples during 1967. With these prolonged death throes an era had closed, but the new age had already begun and sales of Ducati's newer models were at their peak.

3 | Multitudinous two-strokes

Ducati's first two-stroke, the 1961 48 Brisk; hardly an apt name for such a humble machine

Although four-stroke motorcycles were what really established Ducati's reputation worldwide, the factory was also once a producer of nearly as many two-stroke models. Their policy in this diversification was quite simple – to win customers. Like the Japanese after them, but unlike most of their contemporaries, Ducati was early to realize the importance of a 'product line' which starts with models for the first time buyer, then carries the customer on to a succession of more powerful and expensive and, with luck, more profitable machines.

Up to the mid-1960s the Ducati customer could learn on a moped, progress to a small motorcycle and then move up to a large roadster – all with Ducati on the tank. Brand loyalty was a lesson which the factory learnt early, and the strange fact that they did not carry this policy into the seventies inevitably led to them becoming more and more an 'enthusiasts only' marque, and perhaps to their downfall.

Ducati's original involvement with the two-strokes was dictated entirely by this eagerness to woo 'first-time buyer' sales. As the sixties progressed, they were to get more and more heavily involved in two-strokes, until at one point they were a virtual mainstay of production. And yet, in the seventies, production ceased entirely, except for a brief (and disastrous) decision to produce a two-stroke enduro 125. In an astonishing about-turn I was clearly told by senior management during a factory meeting in 1976 that in their opinion it was more profitable to produce only large-capacity machines. Let history be the judge of that, but other makers have learned to their cost that no small machine sales in the first place often means fewer customers for them in the long term. Ducati's production figures for the 1980s were certainly a good deal lower than they were used to, only 7800 units were to leave the factory in the whole of 1981 – though actually a good figure for 500 cc and over machines.

Such troubles were well in the future when Ducati launched their first 'strokers' – both 50s, in 1961. The prospective new Ducati buyer could choose between a three-speed version, the Piuma, or the single-speed Brisk. The Piuma was

available in several versions, including even a Sport (sometimes confused with the slightly later Sport 48). The Piuma was exported to the UK between 1962 and 1965. When it was launched in June 1962, the price was a competitive £68 16s. 2d., and its name was anglicized to Puma.

All these early models had the same engine, differing only in the number of gears and the state of tune; the Piuma had a hand-change for its three-speed gearbox. The simple piston port single had an actual capacity of 47·633 cc and in its basic form it produced 1·5 bhp, which was upped to 4·2 bhp for the Sport. All the engines were fitted with a 6V Ducati Elettronica flywheel magneto which provided ignition and direct lighting.

The 1964 Piuma (Puma) De-Luxe, three-speed with dual seat and fully enclosed chain

Above **1965 48 Piuma Sport, a cross between a moped and a motorcycle**

Below **The 1963 Sport 48 a sportster in miniature. It even had a full duplex cradle frame**

The frames were similar all pressed steel fabrications, but, unusually for utility lightweights of the time, all featured swinging-arm suspension. Most models had 18 in. wheels, but the UK specification Piuma was fitted with 19 in. So were those destined for the USA — Latins were shorter in the leg and generally smaller! America took the bikes with changed names — commonly Falcon. All models except the Sport had 1·2-gallon tanks, the Sport's held 2·5 gallons. The Brisk and standard Piuma had single saddles, while the De-Luxe Piuma (the actual UK market model) was given a dual seat.

UK models were finished in metallic blue and silver, the same colours as the 250 Diana (Daytona) of 1961–64. The frame, mudguards and rear light support were in blue, with silver for the tank, headlamp, rear suspension covers

Only Ducati offer a 90cc *Fan-cooled Engine....

Here's the ultimate in the light weight field! A tough 90cc, 3 speed motorcycle with a fan-cooled 5 & 7 H.P. engine (at approximately 5000 RPM).

"CADET"

The 1965 model Ducati "Cadet" has 18" wheels, chrome rims, streamlined tank, full electrical system, Dell'Orto carburetor with an air-cleaner, side and center stands and chrome luggage rack.

Suggested retail price, F.O.B. New York: **$309.**

Mountaineer 90

The "off-the-road" version for sports and trail riding, also fitted with the efficient fan-cooled alloy Ducati engine has been designed for the sportsman who enjoys outdoor activity . 3.50 x 16 knobby rear tire, dual rear sprocket (converts in a jiffy for road use) and upswept exhaust system will take this "two-wheeled tiger" through the roughest terrain.

Suggested retail price, F.O.B. New York: **$329.**

* WHAT IS 'FAN-COOLING'?

The Ducati 90cc engine is constructed to incorporate a method of forcing a blast of cool, fresh air around the cylinder so that the engine will run cool at any speed. This ensures long engine life and eliminates motor failures caused by over-heating on other engines.

BERLINER MOTOR CORPORATION
Railroad Street And Plant Road,
HASBROUCK HEIGHTS · New Jersey

CYCLE WORLD   5

Right **Berliner advertisement of 1964 launched the Cadet and Mountaineer 94 cc models to Americans**

Below **During the mid-1960s Ducati even put their two-stroke into a range of 3-wheel 'carriers'**

Carriers
DUCATI

and chainguard. The UK Piuma had a two-tone dual seat (blue top with white sides), cowled headlight, valanced front mudguard, and a chromed rear chainguard. All two-stroke Ducatis of this era carried the 'eagle' tank transfers, while model designations were shown by different logos on the side panels.

Following closely on the heels of the Piuma and the Brisk, Ducati launched the Sport 48. Although the engine of this machine was clearly based on the previous models, everything else about its design was quite different, for while they were swimming in the mainstream moped tradition, the new Sport was a pure motorcycle in miniature, and at first sight it was guaranteed to set the pulse stirring, with its sporting image set off by clip-ons, downdraught carburettor, racing tank and seat. Its metallic red and gold colour scheme was identical to that of the then current 175/200 sportsters, and the tank even used the same Bakelite filler cap.

All this was no window dressing either, for the high-revving (8600 rpm) version of the Brisk/Piuma engine delivered the full 4·2 bhp to propel it to a true 50 mph. This was achieved by fitting a new barrel, head and large carburettor (a Dell-'Orto UA 15A with an eye-catching polished alloy bellmouth). The engine was also fitted to the Piuma 48 Sport, but what made its power usable for the first time was the frame of the Sport 48 – a full motorcycle double cradle type unique to this model.

The final details took a little time to settle down, and several prototypes were made which differed from the main production run. Variations extended to a different tank, side panels, mudguards and handlebar layout. The Sport 48 could be ordered with either a kick-start or pedals, but all UK machines were fitted with the kick-start option.

Quite simply, this machine was outstanding. I'm certain that if it had been available (with pedals) during the 'sixteener' boom of the early 1970s, the ten-year-old design would have pro-

48 Cacciatore, known in North America as the Falcon. 1966

vided real competition for Yamaha's top-selling FS1E. Unfortunately, during its period on sale in the UK (1962–65) there was a very limited number of customers prepared to part with £89 19s. 6d. to sample the experience. It was a classic case of unlucky timing for a great little machine.

An 80 cc variant, the Sport 80, was launched at the same time in the UK. Selling at £107 19s. 11d. in 1963, this was to prove an even more crushing sales flop, for there was simply no demand and it was only listed by the importers between December 1962 and April 1963. However, factory production continued until mid-1964 to meet the needs of other markets, mostly Italy, the Middle East and Far East. The 80 was of similar style to its smaller brother, but with a single downtube frame in place of the double cradle, and finished in metallic blue and silver.

The Piuma and Sport 48 both continued to be available in the UK up until late 1965. By this time prices had risen to £82 19s. 0d. for the Piuma and £95 0s. 0d. for the Sport 48.

Even before these models were phased out, they were joined on the production lines during 1964 by six new two-stroke designs. All six had fan-cooled engines and the range consisted of permutations of two capacities (48 cc and 94 cc) and three styles. There were two roadsters (48SL and 100 Cadet), two on/off road (48 Cacciatore and 100 Mountaineer), and to make up the half-dozen, two scooters (both called Brio). The engine units and general specifications were as standardized as possible until a series of revamps for the 1966 season.

The 1964 48 cc engine was based closely on the original Brisk/Piuma design but with a number of detail modifications and tuned differently to suit the different applications. Most potent were the export models still at 4·2 bhp; this engine differed in many details from the home market version. The 'softest' motor was fitted to the scooter and gave just 1·5 bhp. Similar differences were apparent between the 94 cc engines, which had a family similarity with the rest of the range. The fan for cooling on all six models was driven by an alloy plate bolted on to the flywheel magneto rotor.

Frame and styling specifications differed between the models to suit their different roles. The scooter was clearly a completely different concept from the motorcyles and almost all of its fittings were unique. The nearest the Brios ever got to being real Dukes was the 100 Brio's rear light assembly — identical to the Mach 1 and Desmo Sportsters. Although the other four machines used similar, and conventional, cycle parts, there were also many detail differences between the roadsters and the trail machines.

To suit the trail bikes' two roles, they featured dual rear wheel sprockets. This gave an interchangeable gearing of 42 teeth for normal road work and 60 for dirt use. Besides these, they were fitted with knobbly tyres, a high-level exhaust system with heat shield, a built-in sump guard,

1966 version of 100 Mountaineer, now had four-speed footchange, but was still fan cooled

metal footrests, braced handlebars, single saddle and rear carrier. In other respects they were the same as their roadster brothers, relying on the original frame and suspension. However, I rode a completely standard 100 Mountaineer in a trial in Aden (now South Yemen) during late 1964, where it showed a distinct advantage over the motley variety of machines that were pressed into use – anything from a side-valve Triumph TRW twin to a Cotton 250 scrambler. The same bike also went sand racing, and under both conditions it ran faultlessly. With the fan-cooling it could be ridden flat out for long periods without any ill effects.

The first changes to the 'new' line came in 1966 when the 48SL became the 50SL. Fan-cooling was dispensed with and its capacity was increased from 47·63 to 49·66 cc by enlarging the bore to 38·8 mm. The stroke was retained, but the compression ratio went up to 11:1. In place of the original carburettor went a new Dell'Orto UA 18 S. The piston rings were made of a superior material, which allowed them to be thinner, and the piston itself was now forged rather than cast. Unfortunately, no power output figures record the results of these modifications, but the most significant change was easy for the least technically minded rider to appreciate. Gone was the old three-speed box with the awkward hand change that had spoilt an otherwise good range of small motorcycles, and in its place

The 1967 100 Cadet (and Mountaineer) had a redesigned top end and alloy cylinder with chrome bore; capacity upped to 98 cc

was a new four-speed gearbox with a 'proper' footchange.

The styling of the 50SL, however, was distinctly not an improvement. The finished product looked like something of an 'ugly duckling', which was a pity because the engine/gearbox improvements had considerably enhanced the appeal of what was already a good performer. Its colour scheme was the same as the 48SL's – both were metallic red and silver.

Both versions of the Brio, and the Cacciatore, retained the original engine and gearbox until the end of their production lives (Cacciatore in 1967,

Brio in 1968). This is sometimes a point of confusion, because the 48 Brio was renamed the 50 Brio in 1967, when the 100 Brio became the 100/25. But this was true badge engineering, as the only changes were quite literally to the badges. No internal or styling changes were made at all, and even the colours stayed the same, with white for the smaller machine and pale green for the larger.

The Cadet and Mountaineer gained the four-speed footchange in 1966. A year later they were improved again, with engine modifications similar to those already carried out on the 50SL, if a touch more radical. Both bikes were fitted with a completely new alloy cylinder head and chrome-lined barrel, and the bore went up by 1 mm for a displacement of 98 cc. Although the 50SL had also dispensed with fan-cooling, in

The most attractive Ducati two-stroke – the 1967 50SL/1? Twin filler caps was pure styling fantasy

Final scooter effort—the 1968 Brio 100/25

The 1968 Rolly 50 was an unsuccessful attempt to produce a basic commuter moped

doing so it had retained the original iron barrel. The carburettor size was increased to a Dell'Orto UBF 24 BS, a massive size for a 100 of the time, and the same as fitted to the 250 Monza and 350 Sebring!

1967 also saw the wraps come off what many enthusiasts, myself included, consider the best-looking two-stroke Ducati ever produced. Coded simply the 50SL/1, it had all the style of a café racer in miniature with a performance to match that style. In standard trim it was good for a genuine top speed in excess of 60 mph, no mean feat for a road-going 50, and so good in fact that several were converted for 50 cc racing.

The engine of the SL/1 used a cylinder head and barrel of the same design and materials as the new ones that had been introduced for the 1967 Cadet and Mountaineer, but otherwise the engine was the same as the successful power unit of the 50SL of 1966. The styling was crowned by a superbly sculptured racing tank, and it was the first Ducati to feature the twin filler caps that became associated with the original 250/350 Mark 3D Desmo singles of 1968.

For its second season in 1968, the SL/1 was offered with a high-level exhaust system. Other-

wise, it was virtually the same machine with just detail changes to the front mudguard stays, and modifications to the front wheel, which mounted the brake plate and speedo drive on the opposite side of the original.

Around this time, the factory also produced a model which they listed as the 50SL/2 — not an updated SL/1, but a completely separate styling alternative. The engine specification was the same as the SL/1, but gone was the café racer image, and in its place was something akin to a small version of the 100 Cadet — except for the tank, which was an entirely new design. Differences between it and the SL/1 included adding shrouds to the front fork springs, and fitting a different type of seat, side panels, silencer and handlebars.

For all the emphasis on the sporting customer, the commuter moped market had not been forgotten and Ducati's range at this time included an improved version of the Piuma which even had white-walled tyres — it was obvious which market they were trying to attract with this one. Other styling updates on the model included a new square fuel tank. The factory also offered an economy moped with no rear suspension and the single-speed engine that had previously powered the Brisk. This machine was called the Rolly 50 and shared a familiar Ducati styling feature with the 1968 Piuma, for its headlight was a smaller (105 mm lens) version of the Aprilia square alloy-bodied type used on several of the Monzas and Sebrings.

But by this time Ducati's two-stroke production had peaked. The only two-strokes to be available in 1969 were two new models – the 50 and the 100 Scramblers, broadly based on a mixture of previous models and styled in an on/off-road guise. They continued to be available into

1970 before volume production of two-strokes finally ceased. Apparently Ducati's management had lost their way and sales had slumped somewhat because of it – how much this was a pointer to Ducati's eventual decline is obviously a matter for conjecture. It is, however, a fact that the factory's peak production years coincided neatly with the best years of the two-strokes. In 1966, for example, the factory was experiencing a boom in all its operations, from commercial light trucks to stationary engines and outboard motors. All of this was buoyed up by the motorcycle division, which were producing a total of 20 different models, over half of them two-strokes! It's a balance which most English-speaking enthusiasts often overlook, since of all the vast numbers of two-strokes Ducati ever made, only a tiny fraction was ever

Available during 1969–70 the 50 (and 100) scramblers were Ducati's answer to the expanding 'cross' market in Italy

exported from Italy. The greatest numbers made were the 1964/66 model fan-cooled Cadet, 1967 model alloy-barrelled Cadet, 100 Brio scooter, 48 Sport, Piuma De-Luxe and SL/1.

1970 was not to be quite the last time a two-stroke was seen at Ducati, because much to most people's surprise, a brand new one appeared in the middle of the 1970s. The 125 Regolarita Six Day came on to the scene at the same time as the parallel twins and the original 'square' Guigiaro-styled 860GT. Like these projects, it seemed an odd choice, since Ducati effectively killed off their complete traditional four-stroke production ranges (250/350/450 singles and the 750 twins) at a time when they were selling steadily, to concentrate instead on three wildly differing concepts, all new and untried. In this period (late 1975) Ducati may just

have seen the writing on the wall, since none of the new machines sold in any numbers. Had it not been for the 900SS V-twin, originally conceived as a 'once-yearly production special', the factory might well have had such problems then from which they could not have recovered.

While the reasoning behind the introduction of the parallel twins and the 860GT can be partially understood, it is still not clear just why the factory should ever have wanted to make the new 125 two-stroke. Perhaps they had seen the rise of firms like KTM, Italjet and Fantic, all of which enjoyed rapid growth on the Italian

The 1975 125 Regolarita, an expensive lesson for Ducati. It suffered an 'identity crisis'

Developed from the Regolarita, the 1977 Six Days was even more highly tuned, this didn't improve sales though

home market by selling expensive two-stroke enduro bikes to the country's fashion-conscious youngsters. I feel that this must be at least part of the answer, and it is significant that the managing director of Italjet – Leo Tartarini – was an advisor to Ducati at the time.

The Regolarita certainly looked the part, and with a dry weight of 236 lb, and a good frame and suspension, handled well on the rough. The all-new engine had a 12·4:1 compression piston running in a chrome bore, and square bore and stroke dimensions at 54 mm each. Revving at 9000 rpm it produced a peak of 21·8 bhp, and a six-speed gearbox was fitted to keep it on the boil. Whatever the merits of the machine might have been, however, it just did not sell. One journalist said it suffered from an 'identity crisis', a sentiment I would echo, since the enduro flew in the face of just about everything that Ducati's name then stood for.

Only two 125 Six Days are known to have been officially imported into the UK. One was ridden by Pat Slinn in the 1975 ISDT, unfortunately breaking in the process. The factory did, in fact, make an improved version in 1977. New cycle parts and more power didn't help; the gearbox was unable to cope and so development and production ceased, including other variations of the six-speed stroker theme, a custom roadster and a fire-breathing, dirt-racing motocrosser.

The Ducati two-stroke finally rattled and died.

4 | Narrow case

Start of an era, the 1961 250 Diana

Truly outstanding motorcycles are rare and the names of the few really great machines are guaranteed a place in enthusiasts' affections as well as the history books. Ducati's Mach 1 was such a machine. But all too often, legendary names come to summarize an entire range or era — obscuring other less well-known, though still worthy, models in the process. It's a phenomenon that BSA enthusiasts will recognize, and in similar ways the Gold Star and the Mach 1 came to epitomize the ultimate sporting single for their respective marques.

The fact is that while the Mach 1 was the most famous, Ducati produced many other models of the early 'narrow crankcase' 250 singles. Many of these models sold worldwide in larger quantities than the true Mach 1, and their production run was in some cases longer. Lots of owners of singles think that their pride and joy is a Mach 1, when in reality it is one of these more widespread, but less known, variants. The changes that were rung during the lifespan of the popular 250 are such that it is no easy task to put the record properly straight.

Ducati's first 250 single was a racer, based on the 175 Formula III. This machine appeared during 1960, at the request of the Berliner Corporation, Ducati's US importers, and was intended to promote the name of Ducati on the American market. Ducati already had a considerable worldwide racing pedigree after the factory's Grand Prix successes of the late 1950s, but this stood for nothing in the USA, because, unlike present top American riders, only the odd fanatic would race outside the AMA (American Motorcycle Association) events – which meant not leaving their homeland. The AMA rules forbade World Championship-style events. For example, the main class was for 500 cc pushrod twins, 500 cc singles (including ohc engines) and 750 cc side valves. The latter, unlikely sounding category existed specifically because the main domestic manufacturer – Harley-Davidson – happened to make racers of that type!

If Ducati wanted a racing reputation in the USA, then they would have to race under AMA rules. The most logical entry would be a single-cylinder 250, which could have a similar specification to existing roadster Ducatis, and which would be able to compete against machines of the same type in a separate class.

Besides the new motorcycle, Ducati also sent over a top Italian rider, Francesco Villa. This combination of bike and rider soon achieved the desired result, and amassed a formidable reputation with a string of racing successes in just a few months. A lot of Americans now knew that Ducati made quick machinery that won races and stayed together – both of which the 250 did, admirably.

Encouraged by this auspicious start, Ducati went on to build a small batch of production 250 Formula IIIs in early 1961. In April, the UK importers included the model in their range – to special order – as the 250 Manxman, a name coined for the British market and not used by the factory. Very few were actually exported to Britain, unlike the States, where Villa's results ensured that several were sold. One British rider who did campaign a Manxman was Campbell Donaghy of Limavady, Northern Ireland. On it, he experienced a modest success, mostly in the local 'real' road races popular at the time.

The production racer concept was never taken further by the factory – a pity in my view, since it was an excellent basis for development into a real over-the-counter racer. Such a

The Diana (Daytona in Britain) was perhaps the finest machine in its class when launched in April 1961

machine could have been quite the equal of Aermacchi's highly successful, yet less sophisticated, design – which dominated the sales charts of the sixties between the demise of the British singles and the rise of the new wave of Japanese machines, Yamaha in particular. And a successful production racer is always a good advertisement for the road-going versions.

But although the production racer was not to be developed, the roadster side was, and the first of them quickly appeared. One month after the announcement of the racer in the UK saw the start of the factory's most successful product line ever – the 248 cc overhead-cam single. From start to finish, a host of variations on the basic design were made at the Bologna factory over a total period of 14 years.

Ducati's first two mass-production 250s were released together – a tourer, the Monza, and a red-blooded sportster, the Diana. UK enthusiasts should not confuse the first Monza (which was never exported to Britain) with the late sixties model of the same name.

Both of these new 250s had an actual capacity of 248·589 cc with a bore of 74 and a stroke of 57·8 mm, making them well undersquare. The compression ratio was either 8:1 or 9:1, depending on which of several states of tune the engine was in. Maximum power (quoted from the original 1961 handbook) was 24 bhp at 7550 rpm for the Diana, and 22 bhp for 7220 rpm for the Monza. However, both of these figures were measured at the crankshaft and were grossly optimistic in terms of the power available at the back wheel. The factory's contemporary figures show that the real (i.e. rear wheel) bhp figures were in fact much less – 16·4:19·8 for the 250 in its various states – but these are still good for a machine in this class. The carburettor was a Dell'Orto UBF 24 BS with different jetting for the two models, and depending on whether they were for home or export consumption. An SS1 27 A was a performance option on the Diana, and this machine used either an air cleaner or an open bellmouth for the most performance-orientated versions. The Monza had an air cleaner as standard.

The electrical system of these machines was the same as used for the 200s since the beginning of 1960. It was to be continued right through the narrow crankcase 250s, plus the 350 Sebring model, with only minor modifications until the introduction of the wide crankcase models in 1968. A conventional 6-volt system was powered by a 40-watt Ducati Elettronica alternator with a distinctive brass rotor. This charged an SAFA 3L3 6V 13·5 amp hour battery through a 6V-7A static regulator/rectifier unit. The only exceptions to this arrangement were those models which would use a direct (no battery) flywheel magneto system, the USA Diana, Street Scramblers, and most of the narrow-crankcase Mark 3s.

Although the early Monza was never exported to the UK, the Diana was marketed in Britain as the Daytona – a name which was used in no other country. Without doubt, it was this machine more than any other which first established Ducati sales on a firm footing in Britain. There were two main reasons for this: the first was the motorcycle itself, which possessed undeniable

Making its debut at the same time as the Diana was the touring version, the Monza

charm and character; the second was the law. For the first time, learner riders in the UK found themselves under a capacity restriction, and were limited to 250 cc. Quite simply, apart from Honda's sporting CB72 Dream, the Daytona was the best $\frac{1}{4}$-litre machine on the market. It was the Daytona which first introduced me to Ducati ownership – all set to purchase a 175 cc Parilla when an illustration of the Daytona changed all that. Like all those others who bought one, I was not disappointed, and although over 20 years have gone by since we parted company, the memory of ownership is still there.

With the birth of the new 250 models came several improvements and modifications to the existing range. During 1960 the 200 had already been a test-bed for the new clutch housing that was to be used on the 250s, although on the 200 (and 175) only 11 clutch plates were fitted – the 250 used 13. From the introduction of the 250 onwards, the 200 also gained the 250's crankshaft assembly, the longer 250 camshaft, while the head and barrel castings were altered to accept these new components.

The most noticeable styling differences between the 175/200 sportsters and the new 250s were the tank, seat and side panels. The

British advertisement of May 1961 showing the new 250s, the road-going Daytona and racing FIII Manxman

Monza's tank and seat had first been seen on the 1960 200TS, but the side panels (which it shared with the Diana) were new and much larger than those previously used. The near side panel housed a capacious toolbox, while the off-side panel concealed the air cleaner assembly. Both machines used a large rubber tube to connect the air cleaner to the carburettor, although some high-performance options on the Diana dispensed with the cleaner completely and used an open bellmouth.

The sporting Diana was suitably equipped with clip-ons, while the Monza carried higher touring bars, and a touring-type saddle, plus a valanced rear mudguard. Their frames were, however, identical in most other details with the exception of the nearside front engine mounting plate, which on the Monza carried a prop stand

mounting. Tyres on both models were 2·75 × 18, front and rear.

The colour scheme of both bikes was metallic blue for the main frame assembly, which included the swinging-arm pivot, stands, engine plates, chainguard and bottom yoke (and the top yoke too on the Monza). The blue extended also to the rear number plate and light mounting, parts of the side panels and the fuel tank. It was used for the top rear suspension shrouds on the Diana, but these parts were finished in gold on the Monza.

The Monza also used gold on its mudguards, headlamp shell and part of the air cleaner and toolboxes. All of these were silver on the Diana. The Monza was trimmed with chrome plating, which was used for flashes on the fuel tank, and the lids of the air cleaner and toolboxes. These bright finished parts were also pinstriped in red.

A few prototype 250s used the big D tank decals, but all the production machines had the eagle transfers. The prototypes can also be distinguished by a different method of connecting the air cleaner to the carburettor; which was itself an earlier pattern Dell'Orto with the float chamber mounted on the offside, unlike the main production run which was on the nearside.

Besides the tank and side panel decals, all the 250s also carried a 'Made in Italy' transfer at the rear of the filler cap, and a small 'Ducati' in gold on the front of the mudguard. These transfers were used on all Ducati models up to the 1968 season, when some models were fitted with chrome mudguards. On those which retained the painted guards, the transfer stayed until 1972, while the 'Made in Italy' transfer was finally phased out in the late 1970s.

So, they looked good and were well engineered. But how did they go? Well, the Monza was reputed to be good for 80 mph with the rider crouched and around 75 mph seated normally. The Diana with the 24 mm carburettor, full silencing and the standard 8:1 4-ring piston was five miles an hour faster than the Monza. But the factory offered a tuning kit (available in the UK as an optional extra costing £18 10s. in 1962) consisting of a replacement 9·2:1 piston, 27 mm SS1 27A carburettor, new sprockets and a Formula 3 megaphone. Fit this, said the factory, and your 250 Diana was able to top 100 mph. Testers of the day concurred with the factory's claims – *Cycle World* timed the US version (fitted with the above kit as standard) at 104·1 during a 1962 test session at Riverside Raceway.

Apart from the 'special' parts the US version also differed from the normal Diana, whose electrical system has already been described, by having no battery. Instead the ignition and lighting were provided direct from a flywheel magneto of the type fitted to the Scrambler models. The headlight, taillight and mudguards were also from the Scrambler. A final distinguishing feature of the US Diana was the large Veglia rev counter,

red lined at 8500 rpm and fitted centrally between the two alloy top fork filler plugs. Interestingly, this version of the Diana began the widely used Mark 3 designation, for in the States it was known as the Diana Mark 3.

The price of the Daytona in the UK remained almost at a standstill for its whole existence. Starting at £254 6s. 1d. in May 1961, two years later it had dropped slightly, to £249 0s. 6d., where it remained until the last was sold in the UK in late 1964.

Production of this model had already ceased by this time, however, for a very significant move

Exploded drawing of the narrow crankcase 250 ohc engine (in five-speed form)

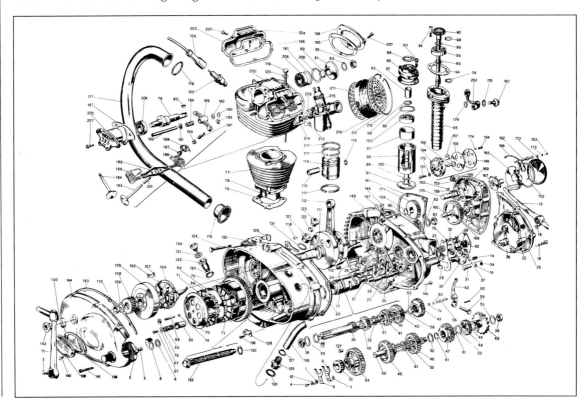

1964 250 Diana Mark 3, USA model.

The classic 250 Mach 1 made its British debut in August 1964

was made during May 1964, with the launching of an updated version of the Monza and a new 250 Scrambler (whose story will be told later). The most exciting news was that these two models were both five-speed, at a time when very few motorcycles had this desirable feature. Completely new models for 1964 were quickly on the way, when the Diana and the Monza were joined by the GT, Mach 1 and Mark 3. And so the legend was born, for both the Mach 1 and the Mark 3 were out and out sportsters in the same mould as BSA's Gold Stars. Today they are considered real classics in every sense, with a devoted band of admirers the world over.

The Mach 1 was unveiled in Britain just before the 1964 Earls Court Show, and instantly caused a sensation – mainly because of its billing as the fastest 250 money could buy (a claim, incidentally, which could be tested for just £269). The 1964 Mark 3 was never exported to the UK, but with the exception of the new five-speed gearbox was the earlier Diana Mark 3 and thus not in such a high state of tune as the Mach 1.

The new 250GT was a far less sensational machine, whose purpose was to replace and fill the gap left by the ending of the 200GT. In many

respects it actually was a 200GT, uprated to 250. Even the camshaft and valves were from the smaller model, giving a power output lower even than the Monza. In the UK Ducati's British importers only listed the 1964 GT during 1965, and the 1965 model was never sold in Britain.

On all the 1964 models the engine dimensions were unchanged. The compression ratios went up with the performance: on the Monza and GT it was 8:1; the Mark 3's was 9·2:1; the Mach 1 had a mighty 10:1 ratio. Other features were also varied to tune the different engines. The camshafts were progressively 'hotter' and were colour coded: black on the GT; violet on the Monza; red on the Mark 3; grey on the Mach 1. The carburettors likewise grew in size, with the UBF 24 BS used for the GT and the Monza, SS1 27 A on the Mark 3, and a colossal SS1 29 A fitted to the Mach 1.

Identifying the different engines is relatively simple, unlike many of the model differences in Ducati's history. All Mach 1s and Mark 3s were stamped DM 250 M1 (Mach 1) or DM 250 M3 (Mark 3) on the top of the crankcase at the front of the cylinder barrel. The Monza, GT and Diana just had a number and DM 250.

Mach 1 was the fastest production 250 of the era, but as standard, it would not match the maker's 106 mph claim

White face 100 mm diameter Veglia tacho was standard on the Diana Mk3

Electrics were also uprated for 1964. Although the battery and wiring were unchanged, the alternator on these models had an alloy rotor and an output of 60 watts. To cope with the extra power, a 6V 10A static regulator/rectifier was fitted. This system was used on the GT, Monza and Mach 1, while the Mark 3 adopted the earlier Diana Mark 3's flywheel magneto system.

On most of the models other differences were largely cosmetic – the majority of the frame and cycle parts were the same. Tyre sizes were identical except on the Mach 1, which was fitted with a 2·50 × 18 front. Another minor feature, introduced on the Mark 3 and Mach 1 from the start, though not on the other 250s until later, was the adoption of ball-ended control levers.

The Monza was the same as the original four-speed version in everything except the gearbox and the paintwork. In place of the blue and gold, metallic cherry red was used on the fuel tank, a choice that blended well with its chrome. The side panels, however, were no longer chromed.

Despite the GT's broad similarity to the 200, it did have three main differences – the saddle, handlebars and colour scheme. The saddle was also seen on some Mach 1s, but the handlebars

were only ever used on this one Ducati model. Best described as 'raised clip-ons', they were non-adjustable, but nevertheless gave a comfortable riding position. The colour scheme was a distinct improvement over the earlier 200 version. In place of the drab dark maroon was a smart black and silver/ivory. The GT was also supplied with a front crashbar and propstand as standard equipment.

The Mach 1 departed far more from earlier practices and design than its sisters did. As well as the engine modifications already detailed, the piston was a new Borgo 10:1 forged 3-ring design. The Mach 1 also received a higher-lift camshaft and larger valves, with a 36 mm exhaust and 40 mm inlet. At the same time the inlet port diameter was increased to match the 29 mm carburettor. To cope with the extra stress on the valve gear, the material of the valves was improved, the collets were changed for a new type and thicker-gauge valve springs were fitted. The Mach 1 also adopted the shim adjustment for the rockers that had been used on the Formula III racing machines, the rockers themselves being solid.

A little-known fact is that the uncompromis-

1964 250GT had 5 speeds, and an even lower state of tune than the Monza

250GT again, 1964 version featured these touring, swan neck clip-ons

ingly sporty Mach I could be supplied from the factory with high touring-style handlebars. Ducati even got round to print a colour promotional leaflet showing both versions of the Mach 1 with an identical colour scheme in silver and Italian red.

Surprisingly the touring version of the Mach 1 still retained the full rearset foot controls. These comprised a heel-and-toe gearchange lever in the best Italian tradition, with an arm locating the linkage rod from the gearbox selector. The footrests were solid, with no rubbers, but were knurled and had larger diameter ends to prevent the rider's feet from slipping off them. Because the brake pedal was rearset, the rear brake cable was much shorter than standard. To avoid fouling the footrest, the brake pedal itself was curved, as was the kick-start lever, actually the weak link in the entire design. Compared to the standard Ducati fitting, this one only had about half the travel, making it an extremely awkward and frequently unsuccessful device to use. If one was to be unkind, it could be said that this was a very good reason why a lot of Mach 1s were converted for racing.

For 1965, the Mach 1 and Monza remained

unchanged, but the GT and Mark 3 were considerably updated. The Mark 3 was now given the Mach 1's engine and carburettor, and it also got the Mach 1 fuel tank – needed because it had a special indentation underneath to allow for fitting the larger 29 mm carb. The old Scrambler-style mudguards were replaced by those from the Mach 1 and the foot controls and rear number plate/light assembly also came from the Mach 1, while the handlebars were from the Monza. Mach 1 toolboxes were also fitted, although these were given the appropriate 'Mark 3' distinguishing logo. A new seat (which later found its way on to the Mach 1) was specially designed for the new Mark 3. No change was made to the old direct flywheel magneto electrics.

The Mark 3's colours were similar to the Mach 1, with the exception of black in place of red for the frame, swinging-arm, chainguard, engine plates, bottom yoke, fork shrouds, centre stand and number plate/light bracket. Pinstriping was yellow for both the tank and side panels, whereas the Mach 1 used yellow on the tank and red on the panels.

Meanwhile, the GT had received the Monza's

larger inlet valve together with the Monza's cam-shaft; at the same time, the carburettor specification was brought into line. To simplify production, the raised clip-ons were replaced by a conventional top yoke and high bars, once again parts that came from the Monza. Both machines, like all the 1965 production, now had ball-end control levers.

Left **Real forte of the Mach 1 was out on the race track; Bob Baldock at Brands Hatch in 1965**

Below **1966 250 Diana Mark 3, by now its engine specification was pure Mach 1**

1966 saw the GT and Monza undergo a completely drastic styling change that was to prompt a major motorcycle industry crisis involving three countries and 3500 bikes – the subject of the next chapter. The Mark 3 continued unchanged except for a reversion to conventional foot controls. Likewise the Mach 1 was the same as the 1965 machine, although UK models reached Britain with a larger dual seat, originally designed for the Mark 3.

1966 was to be the Mach 1's swansong before it was phased out in favour of the Mark 3. Thereafter, the European Mark 3 was identical to the 1966 Mach 1 (gone in name but not in fact), while the US market still received the 'original' Mark 3. Finally, in 1967, all Mark 3s were produced with alternator/battery electrical systems. (The UK model was now selling at £287.) In Europe, the Mark 3 had clip-ons, but in the States even the 1967 model had high bars and the 'extra' kit of black megaphone, racing flyscreen, new jets and the Veglia tachometer and bracket (although this had moved off-centre to the right-hand side with a revised bracket from 1964 onwards).

But by 1967 much of the impetus had been lost, and the factory were already preparing for the future and the introduction during 1968 of the first of the new generation of wide-crankcase singles – including the exciting prospect of Desmo roadsters for the first time.

1967 250 Mark 3, after the Mach 1 was dropped, was also offered in Europe but unlike American version, a battery was fitted

5 | Square style

340 cc Sebring (350), 1st series resembled early Monza, year 1965

There have been several bizarre episodes in Ducati's short history, but the oddest affair of all must surely have been the development of the 'square'-styled singles, which led to the so-called 'Hannah incident'. What happened to these machines dominated Ducati's progress during the late 1960s, and it was to influence the factory's thinking for some considerable time. Above all, it made them extremely concerned that no one importer should ever be allowed to dominate the plant's output again.

The story of the 'square' version of the narrow-case singles began in the USA, where, during the mid-1960s, Ducati's market had expanded so far that it accounted for a large percentage of the factory's total production. As a result, the American market came to exert a considerable force over company planning and policy, affecting not only the numbers they built but also the types of machines they designed.

One early example of this was the development of the 250, originally a racing showpiece for the AMA races. Oddly enough, despite Ducati gaining their American reputation on the racetrack, the factory soon found that the USA importer wanted strictly non-sporting models. Probably the only exception to this was the 250 Diana Mark 3, and even this was supplied with high-rise bars — most out of place on such a sporting mount. The uncompromisingly sporty Mach 1 250 was never exported to the States at all, which was the main factor contributing to the model's short production life.

Because of the special needs of this large and expanding market, Ducati conceived a whole crop of US models. Production of these ran alongside the home market and other export machines, and their design was broadly similar. Others were built specially for the American distributor only, but later found their way to more countries. One of the first American-market machines was the 250 Monza, which dated back as early as 1961. And as has already been told, many of the Ducati two-stroke models were destined for the USA.

But when the American market really began to expand Ducati took a look at their existing range of four-stroke singles, and in the middle of the decade several new machines made their appearance one after the other. The first of these major 'Americanized' four-strokes was the original 160 Monza Junior. This came out for the first time in 1964, and in the original Series 1 version used as many of the then current 'round style'

Above **2nd series of Sebring (also 1965) saw tank and seat from 250 Mark 3 fitted**

Below **Definitive 3rd series Sebring, the 'square' style mass-produced version of the type contained in the infamous Hannah shipment**

DUCATI
350
SEBRING
for Public Services

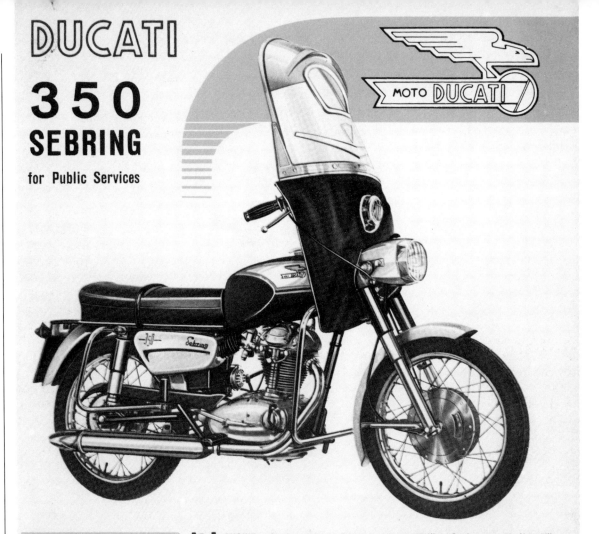

MOTO DUCATI

4 strokes

340 cc.

Timing by over head valves, bent 80°, controlled by an over head camshaft.
Gearbox in unit with the engine, 5 gears.
Maximum speed km/h 125 (78 MI/h).

Consumption for 100 kms. lt. 4.5 (63 MI/Imp. gal. = 52 MI/U.S. Gal.).

MOTORCYCLE

ENGINE - Single-cylinder - Bore mm. 76 (2.9921'') - Stroke mm. 75 (2.9527'') - Compression ratio 8.5 to 1 - Carburetor Dell'Orto UBF 24 BS with quiet air inlet in the toolbox - Air cooling - Forced lubrication by gear pump. - Oil sump in engine crankcase - Ignition by distributor - Lighting by battery recharged by alternator flywheel, 3-light headlamp, tail light with stop light, horn, siren, rear and front side flashers - Transmission: by gears; by chain with special cushion drive - Speed control by pedal with gear shift - Starter by articulated pedal - Clutch by multi-plate discs running in an oil bath.

FRAME - Highly resisting steel tubing, of very smart appearance - Front and rear legshields with 2 central stands - Windshield - Front suspension with telehydraulic fork with steering damper - Rear suspension with swinging fork with hydraulic adjustable shock-absorbers - Spoke type wheels, with chrome plated steel rims, normal profile 18'' x 2 ½'' - Wheels with removable axle - Expanding brakes: front, hand operated; rear, foot operated - Drums diameter: front, mm. 180 (7.0866 in.); rear, mm. 160 (6.2992 in.) - Tyres: front, 2.75'' x 18'' ribbed; rear, 3.00'' x 18'' knobby.

Weight (unladen)	. . .	. . .	Kg. 125.	(lbs. 275.578)
Oil sump capacity	. . .	Kg. 2.	approx. (lbs. 4.409), corresponding to lt. 2.400 (0.5279 Imp. gal. = 0.6340 U.S. gal.)	
Petrol tank capacity	. . .	. . .	lt. 13.	(2.8597 Imp. gal. = 3.4342 U.S. gal.)

DUCATI MECCANICA S.p.A. - CAS. POST. 313 - TEL. 49.16.01 - BOLOGNA (ITALIA)

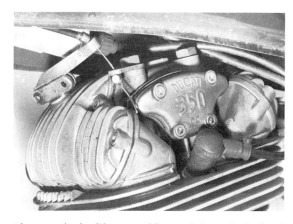

Close-up of valve lifter assembly on Sebring cylinder head

250 Monza parts as possible. It was followed the next year by the 350 Sebring, which once again had conventional Ducati styling. It even looked a little staid in following earlier designs but with the standard US-type raised handlebars.

The 160 had an actual capacity of 156 cc, from a bore of 61 and a stroke of 52 mm. It was based on the earlier 125 ohc engines, having most in common with the 125TS, the compression ratio of this engine was 8·2:1, using a 4-ring Borgo piston. The 160's carburettor was a Dell'Orto UB 22 BS and its electrical system was powered by a 6V 28W flywheel magneto, which charged a 6V 7AH battery. Other parts of the bike were a combination of 125TS, 200/250GT and 250 Monza components. Uniquely, however, it had 2·75 × 16 front and 3·25 × 16 rear blocked tyres. A second series version was produced in 1965 differing only in minor details from the first year's production.

Like the Monza Junior, the 350 Sebring borrowed heavily from earlier, existing models. The first and second series were substantially the same, with the exception of the fuel tank (the first of the original 250 Monza type, replaced by the 250 Diana/original GT pattern). The overall

styling included round mudguards with a valanced rear guard and the headlamp and side panels were taken from the 1961 to 1964 models of the 250 Diana, GT and Monza.

The Sebring's engine capacity was 340·237 cc, achieved by taking out the old engine design to a new bore and stroke of 76 × 75 mm. It was fitted with a 3-ring Borgo piston with a compression ratio of 8·5:1, and used a Dell'Orto UBF 24 BS carburettor, giving a fairly soft performance. The Sebring had alternator electrics, with a 6V 60W unit charging a 6V 13·5 AH battery.

These machines were recognizably similar to many of those the factory was producing for other markets, but then, in 1966, Ducati decided to do it all differently. That year saw the introduction of a new look for all their American export models – the so called 'square' styling. These were produced with one intention: mass US sales. The new range included an updated 160, the Monza Junior Series 3; two 250s; the Monza and the GT; and a revamped 350, the Sebring Series 3. They had a complete group identity, with many shared parts including the tank, seat and side panels.

Mechanically, the new 160 was very much the

Far left **Bizarre role for the Sebring was this 1966 version for 'Public Services'**

Below **1966 250 Monza featured same styling as the larger Sebring**

160 Monza Junior was introduced in late 1964 mainly for USA market

2nd series of 160 in 1965 saw first use of the square styling which was to end so disastrously for Ducati

same as before. Some of the third series had narrow $\frac{1}{2} \times \frac{3}{16}$ in. chain and sprockets, and were also fitted with an oblong alloy-bodied rear light. But most had a wider $\frac{1}{2} \times \frac{5}{16}$ in. chain and sprockets, and a round rear light made by CEV (also used on the 250 Monza and 350 Sebring of the period). All 160s were delivered with a crashbar and carrier, with both centre stands and propstands fitted as standard.

For some inexplicable reason, the Series 3 160 was supplied incorrectly geared: the gearbox sprocket should have had 16 teeth, not 15 as fitted, the standard rear wheel sprocket had 46 teeth, and the resulting gear ratio meant that the engine could be over-revved in top. Maximum speed with the correct gearing was around 65 mph.

The 250 and 350 were also mechanically much as before, but now had the new square-styled look and were also fitted with touring and convenience accessories – crashbars, carriers and twin stands. For their size (and for Ducatis) the performance was very poor, less than 80 mph flat out. And yet this was deliberate design, for simple modifications could transform them. A favourite improvement was to fit Mark 3 valves,

springs and piston, with a 350SCR (green and white) camshaft. The inlet port was then taken out to match either a 30 or 32 mm Amal Mk1 concentric carburettor. To illustrate the potential of this combination a tuned Sebring engine lapped the Isle of Man in the 1973 Manx Grand Prix at over 93 mph – faster than any other Ducati single.

The colour scheme of the 160 and 250 was black and silver, or they could be ordered with a metallic cherry red tank replacing the standard silver. The 350 was supplied in a black and silver finish, or with metallic green tank and side panels (this green colour scheme was also specified for a very limited number of 250 Monzas). All had eagle tank transfers and 'Made in Italy' just behind the filler cap, while the front of the mudguard carried a small 'Ducati' transfer. The side panels had transfers for the appropriate capacity and model name and the final trim consisted of coach lining in black for the silver-finished models, or gold for the red or green finishes.

After all the effort Ducati had put into their American machines, the results of the 'square' styling exercise were to prove a nasty shock. One can only presume that both Ducati themselves and the Berliner Motor Corporation (Ducati's US importers) had believed that they were on the right track, but events were to prove them quite wrong. The results of disastrously poor US sales were to reach a head after only a few months, in the spring of 1967, when a complete shipment carrying almost 3500 Ducatis to the States was refused by Berliner.

At that time, Berliner was extremely powerful as a major supplier of imported motorcycles. Not only did they import Ducati but they also held the agency for Associated Motorcycles of Woolwich, London, makers of AJS, Matchless and Norton. Faced with this crisis Berliner sent a letter to W. A. Smith, then chairman of AMC, telling him to find a home, and quickly, for a certain shipload of Ducati motorcycles. The

terms of the letter made it crystal clear that until this happened there would be no more of AMC's products required. As AMC were themselves facing financial disaster at this time, the problems the letter posed Smith need hardly be emphasized. How much Berliner's demands played a role in AMC's collapse is not known, but it is certain that they did not help matters.

The shipment that caused all the trouble consisted of 500 Sebrings, 300 Monza 250s, 1800 Monza Juniors, 400 Mark 3s, 300 Cadets and 100 Brio 100 cc scooters. With a need to find a solution quickly, by 1968 a financial agreement that

Final 3rd series, the 1966 160 Monza Junior

involved a leading merchant bank had been finalized and the entire consignment became the property of Liverpool businessman Bill Hannah. The exact financial sum involved in the transaction is not known, but at the time it was reported as being £$\frac{3}{4}$ million.

Who was Bill Hannah, and why had he purchased the bikes? Scottish by birth, he was an entrepreneur who had built up a sizeable financial empire that included large car showrooms. Hannah was most definitely an extrovert, taking pleasure in showing pictures of his large mansion and driving his Iso Grifo (Italian body with an American V8 engine) – which was always parked in a prominent place. Besides the Ducati deal, other involvements had included importing reconditioned Honda Super Cubs and marketing a fire-escape ladder while in the motorcycling world. He is perhaps best remembered for his

road-racing sponsorship during the 1960s, such as the Hannah Honda of Bill Ivy and the Hannah Paton works team, riders of which included Billy Nelson and Fred Stevens.

With this background Hannah was well placed to market the Ducatis and, whilst visiting Italy for the Italian GP in September 1968, he discussed a more permanent arrangement for importing spares and even some more bikes from the factory. A few spares were consquently shipped, but no bikes, although a written quotation was sent for 250 and 350 Mark 3D models (Desmo, wide crankcase). It is hard to know whether the factory actually did intend to supply further motorcycles or not, but when the American shipment first appeared on the UK market (a month before his Italian GP trip) Hannah advertised it as 'only the first batch – not a flash in the pan'. However, although the factory could hardly ignore large orders, it took Hannah a long time to sell off the first huge batch (until 1972) and Ducati would then have had to charge for any replacements at a price related to current models of the time.

Besides the factory, Berliner, AMC and Hannah, one other party was involved in the incident – although only indirectly – the official UK Ducati importer, Vic Camp. For almost the whole of the time while he held the British Ducati concession he had the threat of the Hannah bikes hanging over his own efforts, so much so that the total number of Ducatis imported by Vic Camp was just a fraction of the one huge Hannah consignment.

The other problem caused by the affair was for UK Ducati owners. Almost overnight existing Ducati bikes lost the 'exclusive' tag and the name was quickly tarnished. Spares for new Ducati owners were often erratic, partly because Hannah Ducatis soon outnumbered those which had been imported by the official agency, and partly because Vic Camp was none too keen on supplying the spares for the 'Hannah bikes'. In fact, this was the reason why I got involved with the

1800 160 Monza Juniors were sold off in Britain in 1968–71. Unfortunately as it left the factory it was undergeared leading to several premature engine failures

business side of Ducati motorcycles in the first place.

Having owned and raced various Dukes for over ten years, I 'retired' from racing in 1969, but was soon getting more and more requests for parts and help. Many owners just wanted someone who was interested in them, since large numbers of Hannah Ducati customers found a total lack of anyone who understood them and their bikes.

Just why the Hannah Ducatis were so unpopular and took so long to sell was no mystery. Almost any Ducati enthusiast will say that the styling of the 'square' Monzas and Sebrings that made up the bulk of the Hannah bikes was completely unsuited to the machines – no surprise that they did not sell. One wonders how it came about that the factory and Berliner both got their act so wrong. It certainly seemed to be an exercise dreamed up by some sort of marketing adviser who knew little about motorcycles and without any recourse to the opinions of past owners. One thing is perfectly clear, and that is that Ducati were extremely sore about Berliner's role in what happened.

But in spite of the body blow dealt them by the refusal of Berliner to accept the Hannah consignment, Ducati did not immediately cease assembly on the 250 Monza and 350 Sebring lines. Both models were produced again in 1968, now fitted with the newly introduced wide-crankcase engines. But even with the adoption of the later power units the demand was still not there, and Ducati finally accepted the fact, with the result that the models were dropped – this time for ever.

Not content with just designing the models contained in the Hannah shipment, Ducati also went ahead and produced the 125 Cadet/4 during 1967. Many of its components came from the two-stroke 100 Cadet, including the frame, forks and wheels, but it was powered by a pushrod ohv four-stroke of 121·33 cc (also styled in street scrambler guise called the Motocross). The

Monza Junior engine, a development of the 125, was in reality a frugal ride-to-work mount, not a sportster

Cadet/4 was a cheap-to-produce commuter bike with a maximum speed of 59 mph, and its fuel consumption could be up to 110 mpg, depending on conditions. Its styling and conception followed the Monza and Sebring range, but by the time it appeared these other models had already been adjudged failures. Berliner in America refused to take on the Cadet/4, and so it was offered for sale elsewhere. This time, however, there were no takers in the UK either, and the nearest the model got to either market was having a handbook printed.

After this whole ill-fated affair the factory did not develop the new 125 any further, other than to produce a small batch that sold during 1967 and 1968, mostly in mainland Europe.

Meanwhile, the UK market was dominated by the Hannah machines, a situation that continued up to the beginning of 1972. The first models to be sold out completely were the two-strokes and the 250 Mark 3s – significantly, these were the most 'traditional' of all the Ducatis in the shipment. Most of the Mark 3s were the usual USA version with flywheel magneto and no battery or horn (despite the latter being legally required in Britain). However, about a quarter of the 400 in the batch sold to Hannah had the European specification electrics, with 60W alternator, battery, full wiring and switches.

Without doubt these were outstanding buys, with examples being sold by Elite Motors of Tooting, south London, at £249. The price included the large Veglia tachometer, plus the optional megaphone and jets; so just by adding clip-ons

they could be converted into the Mark 3 as sold by Vic Camp, but for a lot less money. My brother Richard and I both thought this was exceptionally good value and we each purchased one in May 1969.

Both machines were used on a daily basis for

The Thompson Suzuki T20 was well-known in Britain, but the same firm also built these customized 160 Monza Junior and 350 Sebring models in 1969

The strange pushrod 125 Cadet/4 of 1967; its owner seems to be saying, 'I'd rather be fishing than riding . . .'

a long time with no problems, and in fact mine, XML 962G, was ridden to the SUNBAC high-speed trials at Silverstone in 1970, where it obtained a first-class award. Later it was entered for the 1970 Thruxton 500-miler endurance event. Besides being truly standard, with not even a fairing (which we were later to regret when the weather broke during the race), our fully road-going Mark 3 had cost less than £250, an amazing sum. Against a number of works sponsored and specially prepared machines, my everyday transport finished as the seventh 250!

This was not to be my only connection with the Hannah bikes, however, for one day in early 1972 my Ducati spares business was getting short of some particular items. Imagining that Bill Hannah had perhaps half a dozen bikes and hopefully a few spares left, I arranged to see him. This was my first direct contact with his organization, since up to this point I had managed to obtain parts elsewhere.

At the Liverpool car showrooms there was no

sign of the Ducatis, but when Mr Hannah took me to a large building next door I was amazed to see rows of them. My expected half a dozen was multiplied by maybe 40 times! Looking closer, I found that almost all had been robbed of bits, and although some were pristine many others were going rusty.

I left Liverpool the owner of all that remained of the Hannah Ducati consignment. With these machines the pressing spares problems of British Ducati owners were solved, and from some of these bikes grew the basis of a line of Mick Walker Ducati racers. Each of the 'square' singles was completely stripped — a task which took over one year. With this came a final sad end to Ducati's bid to capture a larger slice of the huge US market.

6 | Street scramblers

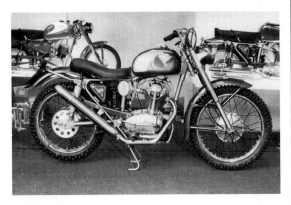

Top **Show time, the 1960 200 Motocross flanked by 125TL (left) and 175 Sport**

Right **200 Motocross was a cross between a real dirt racer and what's known today as a trail bike**

Years before the Japanese motorcycle marketing machine made the 'on/off-road' dual-purpose bike into a whole new motorcycling genre, Ducati were producing bikes of this type in their thousands. When they first turned a wheel the term 'trail bike' was something for the future, so Ducati called them 'street scramblers', a term that was to linger on until the last of the range In 1974 – but most owners abbreviated the name to SCR. And yet this successful formula, which became a mainstay of the Bologna factory through the 1960s, was reached almost by accident.

Ducati's involvement in off-road motorcycles goes back a long way in the company's history – to 1951 in fact. In that year, a prototype of what was later to become the 65 cc ohv model gained an award for Ducati in the ISDT – 'T' for trial (now known as the ISDE – 'E' for enduro). It was the only machine in its class (under 75 cc) to achieve an award.

5 SPEED*

ALL 1965 DUCATI
250 OHC MODELS
HAVE **5** SPEEDS!

* SCRAMBLER — 30 H.P. — Alloy engine — Special Saddle — H.D. 19" wheels — Ball end levers — Extra gearing and cables — Jet black and Chrome finish.

* MONZA — Alloy engine — Dual-seat — Large full hub brakes — Center stand — Safety bars — Red, Black & Chrome.

* DIANA — 30 H.P. — Alloy engine — Special cam — High Comp piston — Tachometer — Folding foot pegs — Dual-seat — Red and Chrome.

It rely for technical spech and notes of nearest dealer.

* *Suggested retail price, F.O.b New York*

Berliner Motor Corp.
Hasbrouck Heights, N. J.

As 1965 American advertisement shows the 250 Scrambler enjoyed a level of popularity at times above its roadster brothers

By 1958, Ducati's interest in off-road competition had generated a production bike, the ohc 175 Motocross, whose development as part of the firm's contemporary range has already been mentioned. This was a machine to go out and win races on, and in a curious way it was virtually the high point of all Ducati's off-road production. For not only was it the first of a new line but it was also one of the few that actually looked and performed like a real racer.

As the fifties turned into the sixties, it was clear that Ducati had taken the off-road motorcycle to their hearts, and right up to the demise of the single the factory continued to produce SCRs of various capacities — 125, 200, 250, 350, and finally even 450 cc. All were built in large numbers, mainly for the US and Italian markets. Very few

examples ever made it to the UK during the long period that SCRs were available.

And yet as time went by it became clear that Ducati's concept of the SCR had moved away from the racing aspirations that might have been expected. Instead, the idea seemed to be to produce a general-purpose machine rather than a competition motorcycle. The definitive Italian design of the SCR concept saw it firmly as a 'huntin', shootin', fishin'' bike, which could also be ridden around during the week as everyday transport. Many of the factory's advertisements in the Italian press of the time showed the bikes allied to this type of activity.

With each new model this became more and more evident, with fewer and fewer concessions made to true off-road fittings. The culmination of this policy was to lead to the production of motorcycles that had become so civilized that they were hard pressed to even leave the tarmac! For proof of this, compare the 1958 Motocross to the 1974 SCR. The 1958 model had a special frame, suspension, wheel hubs and brakes, racing carburettor and tuned engine. The 1974 designs were virtually stock roadster Mark 3s, except for very slight cosmetic styling and detail alterations.

Quite why the factory chose this course is not clear, although they certainly achieved the desired object of mass sales. But without doubt, after 1965 — with the exception of the 1971 450 R/T and R/S — Ducati were selling general-purpose machines, not scramblers that could be raced.

When the first 175 Motocross made its debut, the state of the art in off-road machinery was light years away from what it has since become. The 175 was followed by a 200, which gave 19 bhp at 7500 rpm and was the equal of race-winning 250s. A typical competitive machine of the day — the Dot 250 scrambler — produced 17·5 bhp at 5700 rpm, and most British 250s were similar.

And yet Ducati sold very few of either the 175 or the 200 Motocross. Its quality alone was not

1966 250 Scrambler, now with battery and Pirelli MT street tyres

enough to guarantee sales. Unlike today, few riders outside of road racing circles had even heard of a Ducati – but the main stumbling block was the price. The Dot sold for £198 7s. 0d. BSA's C15S scrambler cost £183. The Ducati's price was almost £300 – £299 8s. 0d. This was even more expensive than BSA's 500, the Gold Star B34 in scrambles trim, at £282 11s. 2d.

Both the 175 and 200 used a special 'one-off' braced frame, with massive gusseting around the headstock and double downtubes underneath the engine unit, making the frame into a full-loop cradle type, unlike the roadster models, which had no tubes underneath the engine and relied on the crankcase as part of the frame. The Motocross's swinging-arm was also stronger than the roadster's, with a completely different design around the rear suspension support and rear wheel spindle/chain adjuster fitting. Also at the rear the frame took a different loop from the back of the tank to the upper suspension mountings. There was an additional bracing loop under the seat, between the suspension mountings and running over the mudguard.

Other 'special' fittings were the conical brake hubs and forks, which differed from the ordinary

road bike version, and the Motocross used a 21 in. front wheel with 19 in. rear. It was fitted with a battery/coil ignition (and lighting) set that used an early Ducati Elettronica alternator/rectifier system.

For 1960 the factory produced a less powerful variant of the 200 which was not exported to the UK, no doubt due to the lack of sales of the previous version. A fully upswept silencer replaced the pukka racing megaphone fitted to the original 175 and 200, and the front mudguard was enlarged and placed nearer the tyre as on a conventional roadster. One thing that it did retain was the earlier model's frame, and the new bike was still capable of being raced successfully even if it did have less edge over its rivals.

The next 'off-road' bike that Ducati made was the first of the true SCRs, a 250, that went into production as the 200 was discontinued. It was designed at the request of the Berliner Corporation, Ducati's US importers, who asked the factory for a version of their then-new 250 – suitable for 'street riding, road racing, short-track racing and scrambles'. A tall order indeed – and to meet it, Ducati designed their first 250 Scrambler. This new model went on sale in the States in August 1962. Finished in the same metallic pale blue as the Diana (Daytona), it sold for $669. These early bikes were four-speed, but in 1964 the 250 gained a new five-speed box, a black and silver paint job and a new shape petrol tank.

The engine was a version of the then-current 250. Its actual capacity was 248·589 cc from a bore and stroke of 74 and 57·8 mm. This 250 had a compression ratio of 9·2:1 and was fitted with Dell'Orto SS1 27A with air cleaner. It was safe to 8000 rpm. Ignition and lighting were by a Ducati Elettronica brass flywheel magneto of 6V 40W.

The 250 was greatly changed from the old 200 and most of the radical differences were in the cycle parts, where the 250 adopted mainly 'production' components. The front forks now used were completely standard – the same as the other 250 models. The rear suspension and frame were also absolutely stock, with the exception of the rear shock absorbers. These were similar to the roadster Marzocchi items with three-way adjusting handles, but the spring rate was changed and, like the Monza's, they were fully enclosed. For American flat-track racing a pair of solid replacement struts were available as factory listed spares. The brakes hubs were now standard roadster parts, with the front drum 180 mm diameter and rear 160 mm. The tyres were proper Pirelli Motocross type, but fitted now to 19 in. rims on both wheels.

The 250SCR used a lot of parts straight off the American Diana Mk 3, including the lighting and ignition system, carburettor (except for air cleaner), mudguards and most of the engine components. The SCR did not have such a high compression ratio or such a large carburettor as the Mach 1, which was introduced in the same year, but it was fitted with the same solid rockers as the Mach 1's, using shim adjustment. The camshaft was a unique fitting for the Scrambler and was colour-coded white.

Other detail differences included a metal guard fitted inside the gearbox sprocket enclosure to avoid damaging the crankcase if a chain broke or jumped the sprocket teeth. The sprockets themselves were suitably adapted to give lower gearing, with a 14 tooth front and 55 tooth rear, and the chain was $\frac{1}{2} \times \frac{5}{16}$ in. In addition, a large range of alternative sprockets were available, allowing owners to experiment for themselves with the gear ratios. Options listed were 14, 15, 16, 17 and 18 tooth gearbox sprockets, 42, 45, 50, 55 and 60 tooth rear wheel sprockets.

In conjunction with the flywheel magneto ignition system a different points backplate and advance/retard mechanism was fitted. On the first 250SCRs the advance unit was fixed, with no bob weights or springs. The later pattern was identical to the one used on the four-speed Diana Mk 3, 160 Monza Junior and five-speed US-specification narrow crankcase 250 Mk 3. The differences were that the elongated adjusting holes in the backplate were shorter than on battery ignition models, and the advance/retard unit cam had a shorter lift period.

The exhaust system was one-piece, with a straight-through pipe of the same diameter as the exhaust pipe on standard 250s ($1\frac{1}{2}$ in.). The standard ring-nut and gasket were used, together with a special fixing strap that mounted on the frame lug where a pillion footrest would normally have gone.

The valves were the same as the 1962 to 1964 Mark 3, but the hairpin valve springs were of different thicknesses for the inlet and exhaust. This was an arrangement that was also used on the 250 Monza and 350 Sebring. The inlet spring was the same as on the Mach 1, while the exhaust was an earlier version from the 175/200 engines.

The chainguard was an abbreviated version of the roadster fitting, and the propstand was borrowed from the 250 Monza or the 350 Sebring. Actually this was very fortunate from the rider's point of view, because the propstand was one of the very few that could be operated from the saddle without fear of either burnt boots or hands. The rider's footrests were a pair of the folding pillion-type fitted to many other Ducatis. They were mounted on extended support arms which then bolted on to the frame. From engine number 87422, purpose-made footrests and supports were introduced – for the very good reason that the old pillion-type rests used to fall to pieces when the bike was raced! The rear brake pedal, kick-start and gearchange lever were all stock parts. Handlebars were motocross braced types with standard controls, although they were fitted with a more comfortable type of rubber grips.

1965 saw the 250SCR almost unaltered – although like the Monza and GT roadsters it gained ball-end levers. The rear light was repositioned from its conventional place on the rear of the mudguard to the top of the mudguard, fixing directly to the rear of the saddle. The saddle itself was also reshaped, to obviate the type of injury that could be sustained by the unfortunate rider who made a heavy, front-end landing on a 1964 bike.

The 1966 model saw Ducati moving even further towards the concept of the SCR as a general-purpose motorcycle. This bike had almost completely lost the real 'scrambler' image. Out went the motocross tyres and the QD lighting set. In came a battery, roadster lighting and roadster-type tyres. Almost the only genuine scrambler part left was the straight-through open exhaust pipe – a strange mixture.

The electrical system was taken directly from the original 160 Monza Junior – even down to the layout. The new system used the SCR and US Mk 3's flywheel magneto system, but incorporated a 6V 7AH battery with a diode in the circuit. The advantage of this system over the earlier SCR's was that larger front and rear lights could be carried, together with a horn if required. Previous SCRs had no provision for an electrical horn at all.

Despite the roadster bias a speedometer was still not fitted, and there was no provision in the headlamp shell for fitting one. In 1966 all 250 and 350 models, including the SCR, gained a dummy air scoop on the 'speedo drive' mounting plate, but on the 250SCR no gears were inside. For the first time on an SCR an ignition switch was fitted (once again this was a 160 item). The solid metal

Prototype wide crankcase 350 Scrambler, year 1967

folding footrests of the 1965 model were retained, but the toe-and-heel roadster gear-change lever was at last discarded on the SCR, never to return.

The colour scheme of all the five-speed narrow-crankcase 250SCRs was a standard black and silver with yellow pinstriping on the fuel tank, the mudguards, headlamp shell and the 1964/65 rear tail-light and support (black on 1966/67 models).

During 1967 extensive testing had been taking place for the next generation of singles — later known as the wide-crankcase variants. Unknown to many enthusiasts the first production batch were SCRs — 350 versions, in fact. The wide-crankcase design was intended by the factory to give the singles a new lease of life, which in many ways they undoubtedly got, although

the biggest failing of the design in the long term was the retention of the 6-volt electrics. Strangely enough, a 12-volt alternator was produced, and available as a spare part, so could easily have been incorporated had the factory thought it worthwhile. It is even believed that some Australian models were fitted with this alternator as standard equipment.

The rest of the wide-crankcase design package was certainly right. The new frame did handle better and the engine design finally got rid of previous weak points, such as kick-start gears, main bearings and (in the larger crankpin sizes)

First widecase models produced were 350 Scramblers like one pictured here in early 1968; sold in USA as 350SS

big end problems. The connecting rod was also less prone to breakage than before. Of course there had to be a snag, and there was – in this instance – too much weight. This is the main reason why the narrow crankcase models are more suitable for road racing.

The first 350SCRs were released in early 1968 in both Italy and the USA. Besides the design changes to the engine and frame, which were common to the rest of the wide-crankcase models, the new 350 introduced a lot of changes to the SCR range itself. Gone forever (except for a brief revival in the 450R/S and T/S) was any pretence at producing a competition-orientated off-roader. In its place was a much more civilized motorcycle that also included a full road-going specification for the first time.

The 1968 350SCRs, like their Mark 3 and Desmo contemporaries, were no sluggards, being the fastest in standard trim of all the wide-crankcase models produced. The engine was nearly square with a 76 mm bore and 75 mm stroke, giving a capacity of 340·237 cc. It ran a compression ratio of 10:1 and was safe to a maximum of 7500 rpm. As standard, the SCR came with new high-performance camshaft coded green and white (just about the best cam to go road racing with!), a new high-compression piston (later used for the new 350 Mark 3 and Desmo) and the Dell'Orto SS1 29 D carburettor taken off the Mach 1 model. All this performance

1971 350 Scrambler, by now very much a huntin', fishin' and shootin' go anywhere bike

potential was to be somewhat wasted by fitting a shortened version of the familiar Silentium road-going silencer.

Besides the new frame, unlike its roadster sisters, the SCR received completely new front forks. These were longer and more robust than the pattern previously used. The wheels and tyres were identical to the 1966/67 250SCR, as were the brakes. Other features of the first 350 model included rubber gaiters both for the front forks and the rear suspension units. A totally new design of fuel tank (with 2½-gallon capacity) and a new saddle made their appearance. Both were to become standard features on the next generation of SCRs. New 'high-and-wide' or cow-horn handlebars replaced the old braced type.

The new 250 version of the wide-crankcase model made its début just over a month later, and in its cycle parts was clearly a straight 250 adaptation of the 350SCR. But apart from the general wide-case design improvements the engine specification was exactly that of the narrow-case models, having the same compression ratio, camshaft and valve sizes. Even the carburettor was exactly the same – right down to the various settings.

Colour schemes of the 1968 250 and 350SCRs originally continued with the black and silver; on later models either white or red replaced black as the main colour on the petrol tank and mudguards.

1969 saw very little change to either of the SCRs, although the chromium-plate tank-side panels replacing the previously painted ones were obvious. Less obvious, but more important, the specifications of the carburettor and silencer were altered, conforming with changes made on the Mark 3 and Desmo models. To replace the long-serving SS-type carburettor, Dell'Orto introduced the all-new square-slide VHB. The older carburettor was becoming increasingly expensive to manufacture, and it had also shown some reliability problems. When used as a purely racing instrument, wear of the slide assembly was not important, but when fitted to everyday machines, it was critical. The VHB was to prove much more long-lasting – although less of a pure performance and precision carburettor – than its predecessor. The only real criticism that could be levelled at the VHB (although many enthusiasts said that it did not look as good as the SS) was that it had an extremely heavy throttle action when fitted to multi-cylinder bikes. Needless to say, this did not cause any loss of sleep at Ducati.

In line with the enforced carburettor change, a new style of air filter was adopted. The other change, to the silencer, was that the design now had a sharp cut-off at the rear of the unit in place of the traditional round cone. As with the carburettor change, this was 'planted' on Ducati, since both components were bought in from outside suppliers. It was not only Ducati who fitted the new-shape silencers, there were other Silentium customers too, including Benelli, MV and Aermacchi/Harley-Davidson.

The next major addition to the SCR range was for the 1970 season, when the new 450 model was introduced. Unlike the 350 and 250 engines, which were similar to one another in many respects, the 450 engine was entirely different, to the extent that all major parts were new, including the crankcases, the complete crankshaft assembly, barrel and piston, and the cylinder head casting. To its credit, Ducati still managed to incorporate many of the 250 and 350's smaller components, to give an excellent interchangeability of parts – a feature of most Ducati designs until well into the early 1970s.

The new engine had an actual capacity of 425·5 cc from a bore of 85 and a stroke of 75 mm. With a compression ratio of 9·3 : 1 and a VHB 29 AD carburettor, it gave 27 bhp at 6500 rpm. Most of the other specifications were identical to the 1968 350SCR. Both the 350 and 450 engines had a valve lifter, although none was used, or needed, on the 250.

Quite a number of other changes were

included in the 450 version of the SCR. The frame was braced with extra gussets along the top tube under the fuel tank. Wider sprockets and chain were used, increasing in size from the previous $\frac{1}{2} \times \frac{5}{16}$ in. to $\frac{5}{8} \times \frac{3}{8}$ in., but despite this the transmission still retained the same effective cush drive that had given such sterling service since it was introduced on the original 175 in 1957. Because of the new chain size, a new range of alternative sprockets was offered. This time the ratios owners could choose from were: 12- (surely a recipe for jumped chains) or 13-tooth gearbox sprockets; 33-, 35-, 37-, 41- or 43-tooth rear wheel sprockets.

The 450SCR was sold by Berliner in the USA as the Jupiter; this was a stock SCR, and it was only marketed under the Jupiter title for the 1970 season. The sole colour offered was yellow.

1970 also saw changes to the existing range of SCRs. The old method of mounting the speedometer in the headlamp shell was discarded. Instead, the bikes gained a new instrument console, with a chrome binnacle to house the speedo and a matching one for a rev counter, which was fitted to all the 1970 models, including the Mark 3 and Desmos. The new instruments were made by CEV, replacing the old type made by Veglia which had been used since the original 175s. Another superficial change was that the mudguards were now painted in the main tank colour, with a black stripe running centrally

1971 125 Scrambler used a five-speed Spanish Mototrans engine and Amal carburettor, but was still too expensive to sell in worthwhile numbers

along both the tank and the mudguards.

1971 saw a change to the SCR line-up, with a brace of new models that were interesting not least for their diversity – the 125 Scrambler and the 450R/S (called the R/S in Italy but R/T elsewhere, depending upon where it was sold).

The new 125 used a Spanish-produced engine, which had a five-speed gearbox and Spanish Amal 375/20 carburettor. The exhaust was also a Spanish version of Ducati's earlier round-cone Silentium type. But these components were all installed in cycle parts made and assembled in Italy – in effect, a mixture throughout of the earlier 125 and 160 designs but with 1971 production parts. Whatever the merits of this combination might have been it met with very few takers, mainly on the grounds of price. Even with its Spanish engine assembly the 125 cost almost

as much as the 250SCR, and after a very short time it was dropped from production.

The other 1971 machine was perhaps one of the most interesting motorcycles Ducati ever put into production. Although it used a stock 450 Desmo engine unit, virtually all the rest was a complete 'one-off' design – which must have cost Ducati much time and money to put together. Once again, the Berliner Motor Corporation played a major role, for without doubt it was at their request that Ducati undertook the exercise. Even with all the problems Ducati had experienced with their American market, they

Developed from the 450R/T Desmo, the 450T/S was an exclusive, dirt-styled trail bike, sold mainly in Italy during 1971–72

Final 350/450 Scrambler produced in 1973–74 looked like this sharing many parts with Mark 3 models

still realized the importance of their US sales.

The new bike was first shown at the 1970 Bologna Show, together with the first 125SCR. When first shown it was fitted with direct lighting equipment, which it retained but in QD form for the production machines. The prototype colour scheme was also used for production machines, and featured a silver frame and swinging-arm assembly. Tank, mudguards and side panels were yellow, with the familiar SCR central black stripe, plus a further black stripe running under the Ducati logo on the tank.

The amount of work that went into producing this, the most special of all the SCR family, was impressive in its attention to detail. The engine was mainly stock 1971 production 450 Desmo, but with many special cycle parts. It was fitted with a Dell'Orto 29 mm VHB carburettor, and owners were also given three extra optional main jets. A compression release valve was fitted to the engine at the rear of the bevel tube, in the same place as it was possible to fit a second (10 mm) spark plug to other 450s. This modification called for a special oil-drain tube. The

exhaust pipe was a pukka motocross component, which tucked neatly out of the way round the back of a frame tube. Final drive was by $\frac{5}{8} \times \frac{3}{8}$ in. chain, and as supplied the 450 has a 12-tooth gearbox sprocket and 50-tooth rear wheel sprocket. Options on this were 11, 13, and 14 tooth.

Racing number plates were standard equipment and ignition and lighting were powered by a Ducati Elettronica 6V 40W flywheel magneto (brass flywheel, three-wire stator plate).

The front forks were proprietary Marzocchi units, but were a special motocross design, with 7 in. of travel. The stanchions were a hefty 35 mm, and used two oil seals per leg protected by rubber dust covers held by chrome clips. Sliders and fork yokes were beautifully polished alloy castings.

The frame was completely different from any other Ducati and had taper roller steering head bearings of 26 × 52 × 15 mm instead of the steel balls with cups and cones fitted on other Ducati singles. It also used a bolt-on rear loop, together with a strengthing brace under the seat. The top mounting for the Marzocchi 320 mm rear suspension units had four adjustment positions.

Like the frame, the swinging-arm was also a 'one off'. Snail-cam adjusters were fitted to tension the chain and the pivot had screw-in grease nipples, one either side, in place of Ducati's usual push-in type. A chain guide was also fitted, and this was bolted to a lug with two holes on the swinging-arm.

Both wheels had Borrani alloy rims; the front fitted with a 3·00 × 21 in. Pirelli Cross tyre, with a 4·00 × 18 in. Pirelli Cross MT74 at the rear. Both mudguards were plastic, with the front carried on an alloy bracket, and both were rubber mounted.

The petrol tank and saddle were more special parts. The tank had a screw-on type filler cap and was retained in the same way as on the later Mark 3 and Desmo models; it was held to the frame with two Silentbloc bushes at the front and a mounting rubber at the rear. A propstand was fitted; this was mounted on a special bracket which also located the rider's footrest. Two types of footrest were used, both were spring loaded and both did not carry rubbers. The first type were round and interchangeable, while the second came as a left- and right-handed set and were flat. A quicker-action Tomaselli Super Pratic Olimpic twistgrip was fitted, and the handlebars also carried special clutch and brake levers with quick-action adjusters. Besides the engine unit one of the few production parts used was the front brake and hub, from the 160 Monza Junior. Finally, a comprehensive sump guard and a chain oiler were fitted, completing what must surely have been one of the most special production Ducatis ever.

From then until the last few SCRs were produced in 1974, very few changes occurred to the established range, and then only to the larger models. When the 250 was finally discontinued late in 1974, it was virtually the same as the 1970 model – even down to its black and yellow colour scheme. The only alterations in the last year were the adoption of a Spanish production engine unit – to conserve the limited supplies of Italian engines for the Desmo and Mark 3 – and a change for the silencer back to the original round cone type. It also used the black rubber Mark 3/Desmo-type instrument mounting, but like the other SCRs it never received the electronic ignition system fitted to later Mark 3s and Desmos. Unlike any other SCR, except the 125, this final 250 had a Spanish 26 mm Amal Mk 1 concentric carburettor – obviously supplied as a package to the Bologna plant, together with the engine units.

The final 350/450SCR were really for most purposes thinly disguised 1973/74 Mark 3s. The only concessions were the tank, seat, wheel rim size, handlebars, gear pedal, footrest rubbers, mudguards (the front was a cut-down Mark 3 item) and the swinging-arm. The side panels were those used on the 1972 'Silver Shotgun' Mark 3

and Desmo, painted in a different colour scheme. Except for these detail changes, and a round cone silencer like the 250's, everything else was Mark 3. The colour scheme was metallic gold, like the same year's 750GT, but with black side panels and contrasting silver flashes for the 450 and overall black with contrasting gold flashes for the smaller bike.

1974 was the only year when the SCRs were officially exported to Britain – although there had been a few direct imports over the years where customers had brought their own. The bikes supplied comprised around 50 of the 250 versions, together with 35 or so 450s. The British importers, Coburn & Hughes, called the 450 the Mark 4, reasoning that they could more easily sell it as an improved version of the successful Mark 3 – which led to more confusion in the company's marketing history.

The SCR story ended when, like the Mark 3 and Desmo single-cylinder models, production ceased at the end of 1974. By then they had virtually merged with their roadster brothers.

Like the 1971 125, the 1974 250 Scrambler used a Spanish-made engine and carburettor, it also used Telesco forks from the same country

7 | Spanish cousins

Barcelona-based Mototrans started building Ducatis under licence in the late 1950s, initially straight copies (like this 200 Elite), ultimately bringing out its own designs owing little to Bologna

Any motorcyclist who visited Spain through the 1970s and on into the 1980s could hardly have failed to notice the popularity of a particular make of motorcycle; and at a glance, the casual visitor would have labelled them as Ducatis. Ducatis by another name, however, for these were Mototrans machines from Barcelona. In fact, the Spanish factory went on producing the overhead cam singles – and other models – for longer even than their originators in Italy. The story of the Spanish Ducati connection starts in the late 1950s, when, after a series of triumphant racing victories by Ducati machines, Mototrans began making Ducatis under licence in the very city that had been the scene of their greatest successes.

Ducati's victories at Barcelona's Montjuich 'through the streets' racing circuit were achieved to much popular acclaim, dominating the scene at the end of the fifties and into the sixties, with wins in 1957, 1958, 1960, 1962 and 1964. They were to win again in 1973, and it was perhaps the last two years that were the most famous of all their victories. In 1964 they fielded a special 285 cc prototype, while nine years later another prototype was a forerunner of the eventual 860/900 series – essentially a round-crankcase 750 Super Sport with prototype 860 barrels and pistons. Both machines won their races overall, and in a record number of laps.

As was so often the case in Ducati's history, racing success soon turned into public demand.

1971 250 24 Horas featured a different bore and stroke from its Italian cousins and totally different cosmetics

To meet it, Ducati arranged for road-going machines to be manufactured in Spain under licence, and many of the machines subsequently produced by Mototrans under this agreement were to be straightforward copies of the Italian originals. But most of them saw a large amount of independent development and modification work over a long period, which produced models that were special in their own right, including a version of the single with an electric starter. The Mototrans factory also produced some completely indigenous designs, and even had a very active and enthusiastic competition race shop. This was responsible for several gems, including 125 and 250 four-cylinder racers in the mid-sixties! Although these unfortunately never appeared outside Spain, being ridden exclusively in home events, the parent factory evidently considered their development important, since Ducati works rider Bruno Spaggiari was 'on loan' to the Mototrans plant for a number of years.

The first roadsters that Mototrans produced were built in 1957; straightforward Spanish copies of existing Italian Ducati's then new 175 overhead cam design. But during the mid-sixties what had been a relatively small firm grew into a large organization, with mass sales all over Spain. By 1967 they had expanded their range to include a number of two-strokes – based on the Italian 48 and 98 cc engines – and had increased the number of four-strokes to include five models. These consisted of the 160 Turismo, 160 Sport, 200 Turismo, 200 Elite and 250 De Luxe. No models had undergone much local modification.

The most heavily modified were the two 160s and the 250. In my opinion, the 160s in particular

1972 125 Sport, a 160 version was also made in a similar style

were a vast improvement on the styling of the Italian model. Indeed, if such a thing is possible, they looked every inch more like real Ducatis than the real Ducatis! The 160 Sport was virtually a larger version of the original Italian 125 Sport, while the Turismo had an engine that was more lightly tuned, deeper-valanced mudguards, a large fuel tank based on the style of the Diana/ Mach 1, touring handlebars and a more comfortable saddle. The 250, on the other hand, had very similar styling to the Italian four-speed Diana – but an engine that was vastly different from its Italian cousin. Mototrans' changes to the specification included using a different cylinder capacity and a shorter camshaft – identical in length to the cam used in the Italian 175 cc machine.

During this period all the four-stroke Mototrans models used alloy wheel rims; a nice feature and a worthwhile improvement over the Italian steel ones. And unlike the Italian factory, Mototrans used not Dell'Orto carburettors but Amals.

The Spanish connection with the British Amal factory is a similar story to Ducati's own, and Amal carburettors were first produced under licence in Spain at about the same time. The company responsible for their manufacture was called Talleres, which translated means simply

'works', with a plant in the Basque region of northern Spain. Spanish Amals were a hallmark of the majority of the Spanish Dukes, and even found their way on to some of the later Italian SCRs. The only exceptions to the rule were either when supplies were short or on the very early models, which were straight copies of the Italian originals – such as the 200 Elite and 175TS.

Mototrans also often retained earlier Ducati features long after they had been dropped by the Italian factory; this included production of the narrow crankcase design until well into the 1970s. Not only this, but they did not introduce a five-speed version until 1970 and the advent of the infamous 24 Horas (24 hours) model. The 200 cc and 250 cc narrow crankcase engines were themselves (with the exception of the clutch housing layout) based on the original 175 of 1957. This differed from the Italian factory's development of this design, which after 1960 was based on the then new 250 model. Keeping the old design was also the reason for Mototrans' use of the shorter camshaft on all models except for the 125 and 160, since it was designed to fit the Italian 175 castings. Another odd result of this policy was that the external engine covers, tim-

1972 250 24 Horas gained a poor reputation in Britain, being renamed 24 Horrors!

Left **250 Road, it together with a 350 version was sold in America in the early 1970s; this one is a Spanish home market variant**

Below **City bike, Mototrans manufactured several versions of just such a bike; 1976 Mini 3, with fan cooled 48 cc power unit**

Left **The Pronto was produced in 50 and 100 and offered Spanish commuters a lively little bike, the 100 in particular. First deliveries began in 1974**

Below **Looking every inch a miniature trials bike, the 75TT Senda from 1975**

ing case, selector box and clutch/primary drive cover on all models – even the 250 – were the same as on the 125/160.

The specifications of the different engines were thus broadly similar. The 160 had a precise capacity of 156·992 cc from 62 × 52 mm bore and stroke. Both versions used the same piston, which gave an 8·5:1 compression ratio on the TS, but on the Sport a shorter barrel was fitted to raise the compression ratio. Both engines also had the same carburettor – an Amal 275/20 – although on the Sport an open bellmouth replaced the TS's air filter. The Sport had a higher lift camshaft, and the result of the various tuning modifications was to raise its peak power to 10 bhp at 8500 rpm, against the TS's 8 at 7500.

The 200s likewise had similar specifications – a 67 × 57·8 mm bore and stroke gave a capacity of 203·783 cc for both the Elite and the TS. The sportier Elite had an 8·5:1 piston rather than the TS's 7·5:1, and exceptionally for the Spanish machines it had a Dell'Orto carburettor – a UBF 24 BS with open bellmouth. The TS had an Amal 375/22 with air filter, and its softer engine produced 14 bhp at 7200 rpm, while the more powerful Elite had 18 bhp on tap at 7500 rpm.

The 250 had a bore and stroke of 69 × 66 mm and an 8:1 piston. Peak power was developed at lower revs than on the other models – 20 bhp at 7000 rpm – with its 376/25 Amal.

All of these models retained Ducati's earlier four-speed gearbox, and had 6-volt electrical systems; the electrics were based on a Motoplat alternator and Tudor battery. All had 180 mm front and 160 mm rear brakes on full-width alloy hubs. On the 160s these were laced into 17 in. wheel rims with 2·75 front tyre and 3·00 rear, but on the other bikes 18 in. wheels were used, although the tyre widths were the same. All models also used Silentium-pattern round-cone type silencers.

This range carried on successfully for some time, but by 1970 it was considered due for an update. Major changes that year were to drop both the 160 and the 200, and to replace the 250 with a new design that capitalized on the 24-hour racing successes on the Montjuich Park circuit.

The 160s went in favour of 125s – at first glance these were nearly identical except for a smaller bore, but the big change was that the engine now had the five-speed gearbox. This engine was actually supplied by Mototrans to Ducati in Bologna, complete with Amal carburettor, for assembly into the 125 Scrambler. (Although this was the first known case of the Barcelona factory exporting their products to Italy, other examples of this reversed trade occurred, including complete 250 Street Scramblers and 350 Mark 3 engines in 1974.)

The most important model introduction was Mototrans' all-new sportster 250. In many ways, it was to the Spanish plant what the Mach 1 had been for the Italians – a no compromise 'road racer'. It was obviously completely different from the old 250 cc De Luxe in concept and style, and these differences extended to fundamental engine changes. To start with, the new 250 had five gears and a revised kick-start mechanism to go with the new cluster. It had a new 10:1 piston and revised valve gear, complete with a new cam; the triangular cam cover carried a glass inspection plate. Two years after its introduction Mototrans set the seal on the sporting nature of the 24 Horas when they dropped the original model's dual seat in favour of a racing hump and increased the size of its brakes.

These Spanish 250s differed fundamentally from their Italian counterparts. Some of the major engine peculiarities included a different bore and stroke and the actual capacity. The gearbox parts were also different, as was the clutch, for the Italian machines used seven friction plates and six steel, while the Spanish Ducatis had one less of each. Other detail differences were the cylinder head internals (except for the interchangeable valve springs, the rockers and the various cylinder head gaskets); however,

The 1976 300 Electronic, a strange mismatch of parts and only just bigger than a 250 in actual engine capacity

both the centre crankcase and cylinder base gaskets were different.

The Spanish bikes had several special ancillaries, too, ranging from alternative proprietary components to minor design variations between the two factories' parts. The carburettor fitted to the 24 Horas was again a Spanish Amal, a 376/27 with open bellmouth. The silencer was a completely new type – in fact, a black racing megaphone that featured a detachable end cone to quieten the noise generated to a low enough point for normal road use. This had compartments packed with steel wool! Also new was the complete front fork assembly, except for the steering damper. New front and rear wheels were used, which meant a different rear wheel sprocket and cush drive assembly. Minor parts differences extended to the nearest gear lever, brake pedal and footrests, rear light and number plate mounting. The petrol tank and mudguards were made in fibreglass and the saddle was a special fitting.

The finish and trim of the 24 Horas reflected the sporting dreams of many of its customers: predominantly it was painted a flamboyant non-metallic red with white lining. The fuel tank dis-

played the familiar eagle transfers on both sides, together with a transfer showing the Montjuich victories' list in capacities and years. Another transfer, in the triangular toolboxes simply said '24 Horas 250' on a white background with a blue lining running around the outside in the shape of the Montjuich Park circuit where the 24-hour race was held.

Of all the Mototrans machines without a doubt it will be this one which is the best known to UK enthusiasts. This is partly due to the fact that it is the only one that was ever exported to Britain in any numbers, but more particularly because of the notorious reputation it gained on arrival. Its official title in the UK was the 24 Hours, but it soon gained another one – a pun on the original Spanish – the 24 Horrors.

This unfortunate name was bestowed on the model by a British customer who had purchased a new one from Vic Camp, the then importer. Very shortly afterwards an advertisement appeared in *Motor Cycle News* classifieds: 'Ducati 24 Horrors for sale'. It went on to say that this undesirable yet new motorcycle was being sold for scrap outside Vic Camp's showrooms the following Saturday morning!

Unfortunately for the machine's reputation the story was such a good one that it went down in folk lore to haunt the 24 Horas – for 24 hours a day ever since. But to nail this one finally, the truth behind the story was that the material used on the cams and rockers was drastically inferior to that in the normal Italian engines. This led to a series of early failures with this vociferous customer's machine, and what blew the whole incident out of proportion was the importer's handling of the problem – hence the advertisement and the tales ever since.

There was little question that the cam and rocker durability was poor, and in my own experience when stripping a brand new 24 Horas down for spares, the material used was not up to the standard of the Italian cams and rockers. However, normal Italian rockers and early 175/

200 camshafts could be substituted for the original Spanish parts to cure the problem, but the real Achilles heel was the habit of its Motoplat alternator rotor to shake its taper flange rivets loose. In defence of the model I would definitely say that many of the cycle parts of the machine were an improvement over some of the earlier Italian Ducatis – in particular, the forks and the wheels. My last serious race was on a 24 Horas in a production race at Snetterton in 1972, and from that experience found the bike to be superior to the Mach 1 in both the road-holding and braking departments. On top speed it was only down by about 5 mph on a Mach 1 and, for everyday convenience, the layout of the kick-starter to avoid the rearset footrests was improved over the Bologna model.

On balance I think that the 24 Horas has been over-criticized. During a season's racing in 1972, besides my own use, my 24 Horas was also raced in various events by Mick Taylor of York, including outings at the TT production race and Silverstone British Grand Prix. Except for fitting Italian rockers and cams before we started, the machine was completely standard, and in all that time and hard use I cannot remember any problems whatsoever, not even with the dreaded rotor.

The first 24 Horas in the UK was imported by Vic Camp in August 1971. This machine, registered KGJ 823K, was the early type with dual seat and smaller brakes. All the others imported

The 1977 350 Vento looked like a Spanish version of the final Bologna desmo single, but was actually not a desmo

sported a bump-stop seat and larger brakes — twin-leading-shoe at the front. Total imports of the model were around 150. Vic Camp also imported five 250 De Luxes. These were in a black and silver finish, but apart from this and the valanced mudguards, they were very similar to the Italian 250 Diana (Daytona).

Two other Spanish models were exported to Britain at the same time, both two-strokes. Their engines were of 48 cc (47·6 cc from 38 × 42 mm), cooled by a fan mounted on the flywheel magneto — a derivative of the Italian two-stroke engines — and both had hand gearchanges with three speeds. The 48 Cadet was clearly based on the 100 Cadet, but with a new tank and toolbox to replace those on the Italian model. It was finished in red and white. Strangely enough, on this model the exhaust system existed on the left-hand side. The other bike was called the Mini 2. In every respect but the power unit this was completely different from the Cadet and best described as a 'monkey bike' in style. It had 12 in. wheels and 3·00 × 12 in. tyres front and rear.

As with the 250 De Luxe, it is believed that only a handful of each of the two-strokes ever went to Britain. In 1972 they sold for £143·63 for the Cadet and £146·02 for the Mini. By comparison, the 250 De Luxe cost £341·11, while the 24 Horas was £352·52.

Also in 1972 a number of Spanish 250s and 350s were produced for the US market. Called

At last a 250 Ducati with 12-volt electrics, the 1978 wide case Strada; nice style too with Italdesign lettering

the Road, the bikes were similar to an Italian street scrambler of the period, but with flat handlebars, alloy wheel rims and a more sporting appearance; finish was in black or orange. The main reason for their appeal in the States was the high price of the Italian factory's wide crankcase models at the time.

The Spanish product's price advantage over the Italian was probably also the reason for their exports to Vic Camp in the UK. However, when his Ducati concession was taken over by Coburn & Hughes in November 1973, the new importers made it plain that their main interest was in the

twins being produced by the Ducati factory in Bologna, and so the Spanish singles were to be seen no more in Britain. Nevertheless, during the mid-seventies, when the Italian factory was in the process of discontinuing singles production and switching over to the twins, 'new' models were still being conceived in Barcelona, and by 1978 the range consisted of five two-strokes and five four-strokes (including two twins).

The 'strokers consisted of a mini-bike, with road and trail models both in two capacities. The new Mini 3 was an updated version of the Mini 2, which with its fan-cooled engine had proved an ideal workhorse in Spanish towns and cities, with large parcel carriers front and rear. The only changes were minor styling and detail points, and it was attractively finished in white (including the seat) with a red frame. But the most interest-

Final variant of the Senda, here's the 1980 bike. A real dirt bike even though it was only a 50

350 Forza electric starter motor location for 1978/81, thereafter repositioned on top of crankcase at the rear of the cylinder barrel

Floating rear disc brake layout on the 1979 350 Vento

ing model was a trail bike called the 50TT Senda (pathfinder) styled like a miniature Bultaco or Montesa trials machine and with an engine unit that looked very like the later four-speed alloy-barrelled Italian Ducati two-strokes of the late 1960s.

Incidentally, Mototrans also supplied rivals Bultaco with 47·6 cc three-speed engine units for installation into the latter's Chispa 49 miniature trials bike!

The Senda had been introduced in 1975 to widen Mototrans' model appeal. It was also produced in a 75 cc version — identical in all but capacity. Both machines used a chrome-lined bore in the alloy barrel and had four-speed footchange gearboxes. They were fitted with trials tyres — $2\frac{1}{4} \times 19$ in. front and 3×18 in. rear — plus a high-level exhaust system. The frame was finished in silver, with a red tank and side panels, black fork yokes and sliders and headlamp shell.

The balance of the two-stroke range was made up by a conventional roadster, the Pronto. This had been introduced in 1974 to supersede the old Cadet 48. Unlike its predecessor it was produced in two capacities, 50 and 100. Like the

Senda, both Prontos had hard chrome cylinder bores and four-speed footchange gearboxes. In fact the smaller Pronto utilized the same power unit as the 50 Senda. The '100', however, reverted to an engine with the dimensions of the 1967 Italian 100 Cadet, with a capacity of 97·691 cc, and bore and stroke of 52×46 mm. Using an 11:1 compression ratio and a 25 mm Amal concentric carburettor, this offered 10 bhp at 6500 rpm, giving a top speed of 65 mph. Electrical power was provided by a Motoplat flywheel magneto with a 6V 50W output. Later versions of the Pronto (post-1976) featured minor styling and technical improvements, including more extensive finning on the cylinder barrel and head. The engine was mounted in full motorcycle frame in miniature, with a neat yet strong double cradle frame assembly, Telesco telescopic front forks and full-width alloy brake hubs of 110 mm front and rear. Dry, the bike was a lightweight 143 lb. Included in the standard specification were square chromed plastic direction indicators and 17 in. wheels and tyres. Of all the small Mototrans two-strokes, the 100 Pronto was the most attractive of the various designs of the sixties and seventies.

A fresh variation of the familiar single-cylinder theme appeared in 1976 with the new 300 Electronic. It had a unique (for a Ducati) capacity of 256 cc. This was achieved with bore and stroke figures of 66 × 75 mm. Remarkably long-stroke compared to its other brothers and sisters, the 300 Electronic also included in its specification a 9:1 compression ratio, giving 20 bhp at 6500 rpm, with five gears and a 30 mm Spanish Amal carburettor. Maximum speed was a decidedly lethargic 80 mph. Its styling was a strange mixture of sporting and touring; the result was a rather ungainly looking bike that ended up as a sales failure. Its only claim to fame was its capacity and Motoplat electronic ignition system. Production ceased during 1977.

For 1978 the four-strokes consisted of three singles – a 250, and two 350s – and a pair of parallel twin 500s, touring and sport models. The 500s were more or less straight copies of the then current Italian GTL and Desmo Sport with minor changes to trim and fittings, while the singles were yet another stage in the Spanish Ducati's development.

Of all the models the most interesting without doubt were the pair of 350s. The Forza (force),

Mid-1978 Mototrans unveiled their first completely autonomous design, the Yak 410 owed nothing to Bologna

a touring mount, featured an electric start for the first time on any Ducati single; the starter motor was mounted at the front of the crankcase. However, the star of the range was the Vento (wind). This was an update of the last of Italy's singles, the 1974 yellow Desmo. Produced only as a 350, the Vento (and Forza) was, however, not a Desmo, despite appearances. Even so, it was in my opinion Mototrans' best bike, and it is my feeling that had the Desmo singles continued in Italy, they would have developed like this.

The bike was the epitome of the sporting single in its ultimate development, from its clip-ons, rearsets and racing saddle to its alloy wheels with triple discs (on all but the original version). Its engine was a high compression (10:1) version of the 340 cc unit fitted to the Forza. Both machines had points ignition and five-speed gearboxes. While the Forza had a 30 mm Dell'Orto PHF 30 carburettor, the Vento's was a full 32 mm – a PHF 32 (although it used an Amal originally).

One Vento, imported to Britain by an enthusiast, caused a stir wherever it went, including the Isle of Man for the TT, where its owner received many favourable comments. Unfortunately, the Vento was to remain a 'dream only' machine as far as most enthusiasts outside its homeland were concerned – a great pity when the supply of singles from Italy had ceased.

By comparison, the 250 was a much less interesting machine, although still a worthy follower in the singles' tradition. By 1978 Mototrans had finally discarded the old narrow crankcase design and adopted the wide crankcase dimensions. So the new 250 Strada featured the later-type engine unit, with the Italian bore, stroke and cubic capacity, respectively 74 mm, 57·8 mm and 248·58 cc; 9:1 pistons were fitted. As with the other 1978 models, the new engine specification meant that the outer engine cases were now of the conventional Italian type rather than the 125/160 pattern used previously.

Another major change on all the four-strokes was the adoption of the eccentric chain adjustment system pioneered by the 860GT model in Italy. All the 1978 four-stroke range also used Telesco front forks and rear suspension – fittings which had been introduced for the 250 Street Scrambler that Mototrans supplied to Italy in 1974. Cast-alloy wheels were introduced on the Vento and the 500s, as were disc brakes. The Vento's three discs were all 260 mm in diameter, while the Forza had a single 260 mm disc front brake – all of Brembo manufacture. The Forza's rear drum was 200 mm, while the Strada retained the original early single-leading-shoe 180 mm polished-alloy front brake and matching 160 mm rear unit.

The four-stroke models had metal tank logos and side panel badges in the style of the original Italian square-sided 860GT. The Strada and the Forza's tank and side panel design were identical

throughout. Rear lights on all models except the Vento were the same as the Italian 860/900 touring models, and the Spanish tourers were fitted with indicators; the Vento used an Italian Mach 1 style oblong alloy-bodied rear light. Mudguards on all except the Vento were stainless steel; the Vento's were painted. Paintwork on all the machines were black except for the tank and side panels, which were blue on the Strada, red on the Forza and green on the Vento.

In mid-1978 Mototrans unveiled their first completely autonomous design, called the MTV Yak 410 (MTV for Mototrans); this owed nothing

By 1980 the Strada had gained a disc front brake

to Ducati in Bologna. If anything it looked more Japanese inspired than European, with its appearance very similar to many Oriental trail bikes; the Suzuki SP370/400 series in particular.

The Yak 410 was a complete break from the past and although an ohc single it was far removed from the traditional Mototrans/Ducati design. Actual capacity was 406·61 cc, with a bore and stroke of 86 × 70 mm, which with a 9:1 piston gave 39 bhp at 8500 rpm. Drive to both the ohc and primary drive was by chain, certainly a break with tradition! Showing the design to be a typical one of the late seventies were such items as its six-speed gearbox, electronic ignition and 12-volt electrics, both Motoplat products. The battery was a 14 amp hour Japanese Yuasa item. Unlike most Mototrans bikes a 34 mm Dell-'Orto was used in place of a Spanish Amal carburettor.

Maximum speed was a quoted 84 mph, with other more minor details including leading axle motocross-type long-travel front forks, plastic mudguards, left-side gearchange, gas rear shock absorbers and a matching speedo and rev counter. Finish was white for the fuel tank, side panels and mudguards, with a bold 'MTV' logo emblazoned on the tank side. In place of those areas that would have previously sported chrome plating, a black finish was used, with very few items finished in either polished alloy or chrome plate.

Final version of the 350 Forza with repositioned electric starter and cast alloy wheels

Zundapp provided the power for the 1982 MTV 50 Sport, its up-to-the-minute styling hid a disappointing performance

Towards the end of 1981, Mototrans ran into financial problems, which forced an end to all production. Many thought that this would be the end of the firm and the finale to the Ducati single.

However, this was not to be the case, and in the summer of 1982 machines once again began to leave the plant. Once again there were two small two-strokes; the MTV 50 Sport, a mini café-racer with cast-alloy wheels and a cockpit fairing. The second was the 50 Cross, a young man's replica-motocrosser. These were powered not by updated versions of the sixties Ducati engine but by identical Zundapp engine units from Germany. This again showed Mototrans clearly moving away from the Italian ties which it had closely held for a quarter of a century, at least until the arrival of the Yak 410 five years earlier.

The 50 Sport looked every inch a boy racer, with its single monoshock rear end, full double-cradle frame, racing-style tank and seat unit, abbreviated mudguards, clip-ons, bikini fairing and rearsets. It even had a matt black racing-style expansion chamber! Although both wheels had 120 mm drum brakes, these were of the cast type, giving the small bike very attractive lines.

Colours were a pale ice-blue for the bodywork, with black frame parts.

The 50 Cross was for the aspiring dirt-bike rider, just what the 50 Sport was for a young tarmac racer. It too had a monoshock, but otherwise, except for the power unit, it was an entirely different bike from its road-going brother, having all the modern motocross/enduro features including an up-and-over motocross exhaust system, enduro competition number plates and plastic mudguards. Finish was in white and black or, lime green and black. No attempt had been made to hide the Zundapp name, which was clearly evident on the engine side casings. This unit had a capacity of 50.0 cc, with a bore and stroke of 39×41.9 mm and a compression ratio of $9:1$. Power output was 2.9 bhp. However, appearances sometimes lie; customers must have expected more from those looks! The Zundapp engine was in fact the 1980 specification unit fitted to the Zundapp GTS50, very much the touring model in the German manufacturer's line-up, so the performance was disappointing. Two important changes from the standard German specification were the use of Motoplat igni-

Also Zundapp powered, the 1982 MTV 50 Cross was for the aspiring dirt-bike rider

ƆUCATI
VENTO 350

1981 Vento, triple discs, cast wheels and superb looks

tion and Dell'Orto carburettor, replacing the Bosch and Bing components respectively.

The three four-stroke singles all continued in updated form. The Forza now had its electric starter mounted at the rear of the cylinder, and had gained gold cast-alloy wheels. The Vento's wheels were painted black rather than silver, and the machine was finished in bright red with yellow pinstriping, but otherwise little of importance had changed. The Ducati single's spirit was to live on for a short while longer.

8 | Last and best?

Good as the original Ducati single's design was, its long production history had obviously shown the factory some areas where it was capable of improvement. Towards the end of the sixties they had started to look for these with a vengeance, with the result that a new family of singles soon emerged. These new Ducatis are commonly known now by the feature which most distinguished them from the previous singles models, and are called simply the 'wide crankcase' Ducatis.

The characteristic wide crankcase engine first appeared in prototype form at the Cologne International Motorcycle Show in West Germany during the late summer of 1967. This was shown as a 350 styled in Mark 3 form. Except for different paintwork on the tank and side panels, the new production Mark 3s, launched in June 1968, were essentially the same as this prototype. But these were not in fact the first examples of the wide crankcase design to find their way into a motorcycle showroom; that honour belongs to the 350 Street Scrambler, the story of which has already been told, and which first went on sale in May of 1968.

Including both 350 and 250 versions of the SCR, the complete range of new models comprised four 250s and four 350s. The introduction of the 250 Monza and 350 Sebring was a story in itself, as has already been related, but the other four new models were just as interesting. In both capacities, the Ducati customer now had a choice between a Mark 3 and a Mk 3 Desmo. For the first time in history the theoretically so promising desmodromic valve system was on offer on a mass-production machine.

Engines apart, the Mark 3 and Mk 3 Desmo versions were virtually the same bikes – and even the engine differences between them were minor, apart from the very special heads of the Desmos. The only thing which obviously distinguished one from the other at a distance was the finish. The Mark 3 was finished in a flamboyant Italian racing red, which extended to the tank, toolboxes, fork yokes, top spring covers, frame, stand, chainguard and rear light housing. The Desmo was a more conservative black, except for the tank and toolboxes – attractively picked out in a deep metallic crimson. Slightly less obvious were the 'D' transfers on the side panels of the Desmo and its use of chrome plate, on the headlamp shell, mudguards and tank sides, in place of the Mark 3's silver paint.

What distinguished these new roadsters from any and all other machines in the world was the Ducati aura. Both were in the mould of the Mach 1 and the earlier Mark 3s – every inch traditional Ducati sports models. A road-tester of the period summed things up nicely when he wrote: 'There is only one thing like a Ducati – another Ducati. The little Italian overhead-camshaft singles have an appearance and performance which is entirely their own.'

As well as the flair and practical virtues of the earlier models, these new bikes incorporated many important improvements, although this was done in a manner that provided an extremely good interchangeability of parts. Most of the more commonly used items were the same, and it was really only in the area of major 'lump' components that the changes were made. Important service replacement parts, such as the contact breaker points, condenser, fork oil seals, piston rings and swinging-arm bushes, were all identical to those on previous Ducatis.

Of course, the most significant changes were

World premier for the wide crankcase single, the prototype 350 Mark 3; Cologne Show, September 1967

to the engines themselves. Besides gaining the new, wider crankcase, which gave the range its name and added considerably to the strength of the assembly, they also had new crankshafts. To start with, these were given 27 mm crankpins, but the diameter was progressively increased to gain strength – first to 30 mm, and finally to 32 mm in 1974.

The over-square 250 engines had a capacity of 248·6 cc from 74 × 57·8 mm bore and stroke, and used 10:1 pistons. Despite the increase in the crankpin size and the displacement and power of the engine the small end bush remained the same as it had always been since the inception of the 175 in 1957 – and this was even the same on the 350! Both engines used the Dell'Orto SS1 29D carburettor, but on the Desmo the main jet was a 115, rather than the Mark 3's 112. Peak power on the Desmo came in at 9500 rpm – 1700 higher than the Mark 3 at 7800.

Specifications of the 340·2 cc version of the engine (76 × 75 mm bore and stroke) were almost the same as the 250, with once again a 10:1 piston. However, the 350 piston was completely new, with larger valve pockets than the

Sebring, to suit the higher compression ratio. The cylinder barrel was also lengthened slightly to avoid having to use the thick alloy spacer that had been a feature of the earlier narrow crankcase Sebring. Carburation details were like the 250, except that a 14/2 needle replaced the 250's 14/3. Both engines were lower-revving than their smaller brothers; peak power on the Mark 3 was at 7500 rpm and on the Desmo at 8500 rpm.

Of course, the really significant difference between the engines was in the valve gear. The valve spring models used the same head casting and components as on the five-speed narrow

crankcase machines, while the Desmo's were almost completely new. It retained only superficial parts – covers, bearings, nuts and washers, for example. But the main casting was quite different, as were the camshafts, rockers, valve guides and collets, rocker shafts and bushes, the nearside cam end cover, with, 'Desmo' emblazoned on it.

The actual design of the desmodromic system for mechanical valve opening and closing was very similar to the one that Taglioni had devised for his early racing machines. The main difference was that the roadsters' valve closing was assisted by springs, unlike the racers', which had none at all. However, the springs used were very much lighter than the ones on non-Desmo models; in fact, they were the ones from the 125/ 160 roadsters. As with several of the design's less

1969 350 Mark 3D (desmo) pictured with high bars, normally had clip-ons

critical components, borrowing from existing models gave both Taglioni's production staff, and Ducati owners, a far easier time when spares were needed.

As with the earlier five-speed models, all the wide crankcase engines' camshafts were colour coded for identification: the 250SCR was white; the 250 Mark 3 was grey; the 250 Monza was violet, and the 250 Desmo was white/blue. The 350's were similar: green/white for the SCR and Mark 3 (later Mark 3s usually had a softer cam), and blue/white for the Desmo.

Other engine changes affected the bottom end of all the models. An important alteration was to the kick-starter gears – always a weak point of the narrow crankcase models. The new design was to prove outstanding and became known as just about the most bullet-proof part

of the new engine. At the same time, the internals of the selector box were improved – particularly the shaft to the gearchange lever. So strong was the new design that this part was used for all the right-hand gearchange V-twins. As well as this the gear cluster was also modified, including both the layshaft and the mainshaft.

Although the selector box and timing covers remained unchanged, the large clutch outer casing was altered to incorporate newly added timing marks. The main bearings were enlarged and the sealed gearbox bearings on the offside of the engine were sealed on both sides, rather than

1971 saw a major re-styling exercise on the desmo models now finished in metalflake silver; this model was nicknamed 'Silver Shotgun'

450 Mark 3 of 1972, Ducati's most successful attempt to make a touring single

on only one as before. In line with the wider crankcases, the main clutch pushrod was increased in length and the pushrod seal design was improved. Also, the clutch cable was changed. Where the old one had a solderless nipple at the engine end, the new one had a fixed nipple and a proper built-in adjuster. This allowed the factory to redesign the clutch arm extending from the engine, lengthening it to lead to a better clutch action. At the same time, a built-in guard was incorporated to protect the crankcase from the result of a chain breaking or jumping its sprockets. On the narrow crankcase engine this usually led to the clutch arm support being broken away from the crankcase.

Several major cycle parts were retained from existing models, notably the suspension (both front and rear) and the wheels (2·75 × 18 in. with 180 mm drum brake front, 3·00 × 18 in. with 160 mm drum brake rear). The exhaust system, a Silentium 'round cone', was a familiar pattern, although this was only used on the 1968 production. And the rear light, steering damper, headlamp brackets and instrument assembly had all been used before. The clip-on handlebars and levers were almost identical, although they had

been modified to obviate an annoying tendency of the earlier type to wear around the pivot points of the levers. The front mudguard was also virtually the same.

Just about everything else, from the frame onwards, had been substantially improved or completely redesigned. With the new frame came different front engine mounting plates, a new chainguard, a revised swinging-arm, tool-boxes and rear mudguard. The saddle was new, as was the 13-litre fuel tank. In a pure flight of styling fancy, this was fitted with twin filler caps – although both these were the same pattern that had been used for some years. This strange feature only lasted for the 1968 production.

The centre stand was a much wider and sturdier affair, and the rider's footrests and brake pedal were improved. To make seat removal easier, it was retained by sliding it on to two prongs welded to the frame, so that it only needed two fixing bolts at the rear. Also the tank mounting was improved; whereas the old bolted fitting has no flexibility and no protection for the paintwork, now the front of the tank was supported by special rubbers, which fitted into sockets formed in it. Longer bolts went through these to secure it, while at the rear the old fixing via a plate and spring was used as before. For the first time on a Ducati a steering lock was fitted as standard. And although the fork assembly was the old type, the oil filler plugs were changed for conventional hex-head types rather than the Allen socket head of earlier forks.

At this time the electrics were also uprated. A new alternator and regulator box were fitted, as well as a complete new loom. The headlamp was another new part, and to cure a problem with the previous set-up a new three-pole ignition switch was mounted under the headlamp shell on the nearside of the machine. The old four-pole switch mounted on top of the shell had allowed rainwater to enter – until it finally killed off the switch!

The first the British market saw of the new

Ducati models was in late 1968, when a small number was exported to Vic Camp. *Motor Cycle News* put a 250 and a 350 Desmo through their paces and both were received favourably. In their road test, particular praise was reserved for the riding position and a smooth and flexible power output with no vibration. The new frames were found to be 'rock steady' around corners, and in summing up the tester stated that 'the wide spread of power makes the Ducati incredibly easy to ride'.

This report appeared in January 1969. By then, in Italy, detail changes were already being made for the 1969 production programme. The main event was to be the launching of a further development of the single-cylinder line – the 450. This was to be far more than just a simple boring-out exercise on the smaller engine, and in many ways it was a quite different power unit. In particular it had a taller barrel and longer conrod – the extra barrel height made it necessary to fit a new shape of exhaust pipe. Obvious external differences were modifications to make it possible to fit a wider chain and sprockets, and extra gusseting to strengthen the frame top tube. Also, on the early 450s, the speedometer and rev counter (where fitted) were housed in chrome mountings. These were CEV instruments rather than the traditional Ducati-Veglia clocks.

Changes for the rest of the range in 1969 were the adoption of the new Dell'Orto VHB square

Same model, same year, but with touring extras and valanced mudguards

1973 Desmo and Mark 3 updated. This is the 350 Desmo, drum brake version

hump of the single racing saddle. It was also used for the racing fibreglass front mudguard.

The new-look Ducati quickly became known as the 'Silver Shotgun'. To complement its sporting appeal it had Tommaselli clip-ons and quick-action twistgrip, a large Veglia racing rev counter, rearsets, Borrani alloy rims, a Grimeca double-sided single-leading-shoe front brake and 35 mm Marzocchi racing-type front forks with polished alloy yokes and sliders plus exposed chromed stanchions. The rear suspension units had stronger springs than those fitted previously, to match the new forks. With the new handlebar set-up came new levers, although the Aprilia horn/dip-switch button was still used. And a new steering damper knob was fitted, which had a smaller diameter than the old one – the same 1957 pattern that had remained right up to 1970. Usefully, the rear brake pedal folded to allow the standard kick-starter to be used – avoiding one of the petty annoyances that plagued the Mach 1. The old oblong alloy-bodied CEV rear light seen on so many earlier models went in favour of a round unit, although the brake light switch was identical to the other earlier wide crankcase models.

Like the original 750GT, with which it was roughly contemporary, this model was a definite break with several Ducati styling traditions. And it was a definite stepping stone to the last of the singles – the blue and gold Mark 3s and yellow Desmos. The 'Silver Shotgun' was produced up until the end of 1972, and many of its parts were to be found on the models that replaced it.

Another version of the 450 was produced during the same period – very similar to the 1969 to 1971 450, it was in touring trim. This model was known as the 450 Mark 3, while the proper name of the 'Silver Shotgun' was the Mark 3 Special. The tourer was finished in the same colours as the 1969 Desmo – metallic crimson and black; additionally a few examples were produced in white and black. It gained new stainless mudguards and the updated round rear light.

slide carburettor in place of the SS1, and a change to the new pattern Silentium silencer. Some machines kept the old SS1 carburettor on into 1969 , but no 450s were fitted with this type. The all-red finish of the 1968 Mark 3 was dropped and now, besides the metallic crimson paint, three other colours were on offer – non-metallic blue, yellow and white.

The Mark 3 and the Desmos continued unchanged during 1970, but in 1971 a major styling exercise was carried out. The objective was to make the range look more modern, and a new styling was offered in all three capacities – although first seen on the 350 Desmo. The colour was a striking metalflake silver with a black frame, chainguard, centre stand and rear light support. The silver extended right across the fuel tank, on to a pair of side panels, almost double the size of those they replaced, and over the

The engine and chassis were as before, except for the fitting of a concave piston that dropped the compression ratio to around 7·5:1. But the most noticeable change was to the riding position, which together with a soft engine and a good cruising range made it, in my opinion, Ducati's only really successful tourer. The range was achieved by fitting a special, large 4-gallon tank, allied to frugal 80 mpg. The ride comfort came from a superb new saddle and sit-up-and-beg handlebars. Introduced on this model for the first time was a new rubber housing for the twin CEV instruments – later used on 1973–74 Mark 3s and Desmos.

Selling at £460 in the UK, the tourer was only a little more than £40 cheaper than the sports machine. Very few of either were exported to Britain – only around 20 of the tourer during 1972 and possibly less still of the 'Silver Shotgun'. Such low sales figures, in fact, opened the door to a revision of Ducati's export policy, and were to lead to the appointment of a new UK importer.

A 'de luxe' version of the tourer also appeared, at least in prototype form. This featured panniers, crashbars and deeply valanced mudguards. The speedo was mounted in the headlamp shell and the tacho was deleted from the specification.

1973 ushered in a new period of change at Ducati. Not only was a new factory being built on the site of the previous one (work had started on this the year before) but not since the mid-sixties had there been such an abundance of new models, not such an interest in modifications to the existing machines. Indeed, it was some years since a range of such size and diversity had been available all at the same time. For 1973 Ducati's model range included new versions of the 750 twins – the GT, Sport, and SS production racer – plus updated Mark 3 and Desmo singles in all three capacities.

The most obvious and striking change was also the most superficial – the new paintwork. The orange-yellow-finished Desmos stood out from the crowd like a beacon, while the blue and gold Mark 3s were just as striking, if with a slightly more restrained character. But just as significant, and of far more worth, were the changes to engines and cycle parts.

Chief among these was probably the adoption of the then very innovative electronic ignition system. This was energized by an additional coil on the existing alternator unit and fired by a transducer and pick-up unit. On both the Desmo and the Mark 3 the ignition system was either by Ducati Elettronica or by Motoplat. Most bikes were fitted with the former, and in practice the Motoplat system produced a weaker spark. This meant that bikes that had it often lacked the easy starting virtues of the Ducati ignition. Electrics were further improved with a Japanese Yuasa 12VAH battery. The alternator was rated at 80-watts, and had an electronic rectifier and regulator.

All the engine units were fundamentally much as before, with capacities remaining at 248·6 cc, 340·2 cc and 435·7 cc. The compression ratio of the 250 models had been reduced to 9·7:1, while the 350's remained at 10:1 and the 450's was 9·3:1. All models had Dell'Orto VHB carburettors of 29 mm choke size, but with different settings.

1973–74 Mark 3 produced in 250, 350 and 450, also in 1974 as a 239

Early 1973 mock-up of 450 Desmo disc, note the different tank decals and front forks from production models

a quick-action flip-up filler cap and larger-bore fuel taps.

The electrics saw several minor revisions. The front brake light switch on the Mark 3 models (a Lucas item) was now incorporated in one of the front brake cables, which had its outer section in two pieces, and the stop/taillight was the round-unit CEV first fitted to the 1972 singles. Both the Desmos and the Mark 3s used a 150 mm Aprilia headlamp with a chrome-plated shell, mounted on Verlicchi brackets that incorporated rubber shock-absorbing pads.

Instrumentation and controls were also new, or borrowed from other existing models. The instruments' rubber surround was the same as on the 1972 Mark 3 450 tourer, and this was also used on the Desmo range. The instruments themselves were most commonly British Smiths, although about ten per cent of the production had CEV speedometers and rev counters. Drive to the rev counter was from the top cam drive bevel cover – which like the V-twins was a combined casting, unlike the separate cover and drive of earlier models. This was introduced in an effort to cure oil leaks.

The Mark 3s came with either clip-ons (which unlike the Desmo versions had welded lever clamps) or touring handlebars (fork tubes were different lengths). Also, in common with most of the Desmos, they had black plastic and nylon Verlicchi twist grips with rubber Verlicchi handlebar grips. A choke lever was mounted on top of the front brake lever fitting and, on the 350 and 450 only, a valve-lifting lever under the left-hand control clamp.

The Desmo version had full rearsets and clip-ons. The hand control had separate lever clamps so that the rider could adjust them to the most comfortable position – this was something that could not be done on the Mark 3. On the drum-braked version these controls were made by Tommaselli. Apart from the colour the tank and side panels were the same as the Mark 3, although the seat was completely new. Like the

Another major difference was an option on the Desmos – an improved braking system. All three capacities were offered with a choice of either the original double-drum front brakes, or an 11 in. front disc. The disc and the caliper were by Brembo, and the bikes to which it was fitted were also given Ceriani 35 mm front forks, rather than the original 35 mm Marzocchis. Tyre sizes on all the Desmos were 3·25 × 18 front (the Mark 3's were 3·00 × 19), and 3·50 × 18 rear (3·50 × 18 on the Mark 3).

Of course, there were numerous other detail changes. These extended to new fuel tanks and seats and fibreglass side panels (although some still had the earlier metal ones). They also gained new mudguards – the Mark 3's both in steel with chrome stays at the front, the Desmo a fibreglass front and steel rear – and both came equipped with Borrani alloy rims. The fuel tank now had

Mark 3 the seat only bolted at the rear, with the front held by two pins, but the shape and style were different; it was made of fibreglass and extended at the rear to house one of the Mach 1-type alloy-bodied rear lights. The rearset footrests were parts that were also used on the 'Silver Shotgun', and these had no rubbers. The same type of footrest carried over into the sporting V-twins – the 750 Sport and SS and then the 900SS.

The first time I came into contact with the yellow Desmo singles was in February 1974, at the Ducati factory in Borgo Panigale, Bologna. I was on a visit to sort out various parts problems, and with me on the trip were John Nutting of *Motor Cycle Weekly* and Ray Elliott of Coburn & Hughes. Coburn & Hughes had taken over the British Ducati concession from Vic Camp in November of the previous year, but at that time were only importing the Mark 3 singles and the 750 twins.

As soon as I saw the yellow Desmo I was convinced that this was *the* Ducati – and asked why Coburn & Hughes were not interested in these machines. The reply was that there would be no market for them in Britain – but there was at least one buyer, because along with the spares I had gone to collect I also loaded up a 350 Desmo (disc brake) for myself. My subsequent enthusiasm convinced Ray that he should be importing the Desmos and that they would sell. Coburn

1974 350 Desmo considered by many as the best of the late singles

& Hughes remained unconvinced – until the bikes arrived in the dealers' showrooms, and then they could not get enough to satisfy the hunger of the bike-buying public. In August 1974 the UK prices of the Desmos were £599 for the 250 and £669 for the 450 (apart from my own, only six other 350s were ever officially exported to Britain). The Mark 3 versions were considerably cheaper, at £519 for the 250 and £549 for the 350, and it was, no doubt, this price differential that had made the Desmos look hard to sell.

But happily there is always a market for a masterpiece. Looking back at all the Ducatis I have owned and ridden, that 350 was the nicest of all, with the exception of my first Ducati racer, the 175 Formula III. It was one of a rare handful of motorcycles capable of feeding a message back to the rider all the time it was being ridden and making man and machine one.

The only real thing I would have preferred on my Desmo were the forks and dual front brake of the drum brake version – in my opinion the 35 mm Ceriani forks of the disc version just did not suit the bike as well as the Marzocchis. In all other respects I could not fault the bike in doing what it was built for – pure, enjoyable sporting riding – although customers who bought one for a ride-to-work plodder might have been disappointed, except for the frugal fuel consumption!

As it is, the yellow Desmo signifies to Ducati

The author's own 350 Desmo before being loaded onto the truck for transport back to England, February 1974

239 prototype pictured at the factory February 1974, intended to get round the French tax system on bikes of 240 cc and over (ignore side panel decal!)

enthusiasts what Ducatis are all about: style, speed and stamina. Those yellow masterpieces had all three virtues in abundance, and even when I first saw one standing in the factory it looked as if it was already hungry for the open road.

There was one new model in the singles range for 1974, and this also made its way to the UK by the end of the year – the 239. The 239 was actually a French-market model, built by Ducati to beat the French tax laws, which placed a much higher duty on motorcycles of over 240 cc. It was made in both Desmo and Mark 3 trim and, in fact, was probably the best of all the last of the Ducati singles. They were quite different from the normal 248 cc '250' – not only were they as fast, but they had a superior specification, with a number of changes. The cylinder head, barrel and valves were all different, and a new 72·5 mm slipper-type piston was used. The bike had a Dell-'Orto PHF 30 mm carburettor with a special manifold, and a silencer based on the 860GT type made by Lafranconi.

A few detail changes were made to the rest of the range. What was to be the last batch of the 350 Mark 3 was fitted with Spanish Mototrans-built engines (identified by no 'Made in Italy' insignia on the small clutch inspection cover), and a number of them were fitted with lower profile camshafts as used on the Sebring and Monza, for example. The crankpin on the 250/350 engines had already been increased to 30 mm diameter, and now took its final step to 32 mm. Two types of piston were used on the 450, and those that used the type fitted to the 860 engine had a smaller small end bush (20 mm as opposed to 22 mm).

The real reason for the introduction of the 239 on to the British market, and for all the minor specification changes, was that by the end of 1974 the singles were being phased out of production. Paradoxically, the British importers' demand was increasing, with the result that they were actually having to 'pinch' other countries' shipments. It is a sad fact that it seems to have been when the singles were almost at their last gasp that their appeal grew. They had been there for the taking for many years, but to many riders their benefits and classic charm were only just beginning to be appreciated.

Any of this was just too late to ensure the singles' continuing production, and during 1975 the last of a famous line were sold off throughout the world. In many enthusiasts' hearts they have never been – and probably never will be – replaced by any other motorcycle. And yet the spirit was not quite dead, for Mototrans of Barcelona existed to carry on the tradition, if not the name.

9 | Carving the racing image

Ducati's first star rider, Gianni Degli Antoni, with the 100 Gran Sport, 1955

Ducati's initial involvement in competition did not come from road racing, as many might think, but from speed record attempts and trials.

After the factory's abortive involvement with the aviation company Aero Caproni to produce a complete two-wheeler in early 1951, when the plan was to use Ducati's Cucciolo 48 cc pull-rod ohv engine in a Caproni frame, both companies decided to go their own ways. (Caproni, like Ducati, did in fact build complete bikes in the fifties and early sixties under the Capriolo name.) Ducati, meanwhile, soon realized how important it was to advertise their own brand name, in March 1951, and with this in mind the factory came to an agreement 'to sponsor' veteran rider Ugo Tamarozzi. They would assist him in various speed record attempts during that year. These took place quickly in late spring, followed by further runs in November, a final one taking place on 16 January 1952 with an unstreamlined record-breaker powered by a suitably tuned Cucciolo engine. It resulted, over that period, in the amazing feat of wrestling away all the records held by Victoria, who at the time were a leading German company producing 50 cc machines. Tamarozzi also competed successfully in the 1951 ISDT, held in Italy that year, again using Cucciolo power; he gained a bronze medal for himself and the factory.

More success followed in off-road competition when, in 1954, the factory sent two riders to take part in the ISDT held in Wales. Both returned

Taglioni designed the 100 Gran Sport, forerunner to the whole family of ohc bevel drive singles

home to Italy with coveted silver medals, having ridden the smallest machines entered, two Cucciolo-based flyweights. These caused eyebrows to be raised in astonishment in an era when everybody's idea of a 'six-days' bike centred around the much larger and heavier traditional British singles of 350 or 500 cc.

At around the same time Ducati took their first steps in the directions of road racing, participating in long-distance road events such as the Giro d'Italia and the Milan-Taranto. Unfortunately these early efforts did not achieve the instant results of the record attempts or trials, meeting instead with a distinct lack of success.

Although the factory's management (at the time headed by Dr Giuseppe Montano) had correctly perceived the importance of racing, it was quickly realized that, to secure the much-needed publicity that Ducati's planned expansion required, just taking part was not good enough; they had to be the victorious marque. So Ducati recruited the brilliant Ing. Fabio Taglioni from rivals FB Mondial and gave him a simple brief: to make the dream of racing success a reality. That he did this and more is now history – he set Ducati on course to becoming one of the most highly respected marques, producing some

of the finest sporting motorcycles of all time. Taglioni was not slow to grasp the urgency of the need for a race-winner, and his first design for Ducati, the 100 Gran Sport, was introduced to the world's press on 5 March 1955, shortly before its début, which was to be the annual Giro d'Italia later the following month. The details of this new design were related in Chapter 1.

During the preceding year the Italian long-distance road events for the popular 100 cc class had been dominated by Laverda from Breganze. They, like most of the other manufacturers of the period, used ohv engines, so it came as a nasty shock that the newcomer's design was a bevel-driven ohc, giving it an instant advantage on technical merit over its rivals. Besides the Gran Sport, Ducati also entered a number of the less technically advanced 98 cc pushrod '98 Sport' models. Unlike the opposing factories Ducati had none of the established stars of the Italian lightweight scene to call upon, only relative 'unknowns' from the Bologna area. These included Gianni Degli Antoni, Italo Fantuzzi, Leopoldo Tartarini, Giuliano Maoggi and

125 Grand Prix, a dohc production racer developed from the Gran Sport first sold in 1958

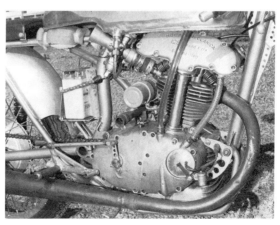

Above **Cylinder head gear train exposed, 125 Grand Prix**

Below **The 175 Formula III cost more than a 500 Manx Norton in 1959**

Francesco Villa. The team was headed by one Bruno Spaggiari.

Four of these competitors are particularly noteworthy. Antoni had the distinction of being Ducati's first star to rise from the pack and the honour of gaining the factory's first ever Grand Prix victory, the 1956 event at Hedemora in Sweden. Spaggiari proved to be the 'stayer', as this loyal enthusiast raced the Bologna products in the fifties, sixties and through into the seventies, finally finishing 2nd two years running in the Imola 200 classic of 1972 and 1973, behind Paul Smart and Jarno Saarinen. Villa and Tartarini went on to achieve fame in another way, as motorcycle manufacturers in their own right; Villa under his own name, Tartarini under the auspices of Italjet.

In all, 37 Ducatis lined up for the start of the 1955 Giro d'Italia. Although prior testing at Modena Audodrome had shown how quick the Gran Sport design was, how would it fare in such a long, gruelling race? And how would the mass of novice riders stand up to one of Italy's premier

events? The results amazed even the most ardent of Ducati's followers. From the original 37 starters, only nine retired (eight of whom were mounted on the pushrod 98S). For an event of 2113 miles (3400 km), this was a very low figure. But the real excitement was from the second stage onwards, and centred on Antoni as he roared away from the rest of the pack to lead his class. After nine stages he comfortably cruised home to record an impressive début for the new bike at a speed of over 61·5 mph (98·90 km/h). Besides this he finished 5th overall, in the process beating a number of larger machines – including some 500s! He even got home in front of the Benelli-mounted 125 cc class winner. The final results for the 100 cc class of the 1955 Giro d'Italia showed: 1st Gianni Degli Antoni, 2nd Franco Villa, 3rd Italo Fantuzzi, 4th Bruno Spaggiari, 5th Giuliano Maoggi, 6th Ettore Scamandri – all Ducati mounted.

Following this highly successful and impressive début, the Gran Sport piled up a vast number of successes over the following three years. So much so that Ducati's domination of the 100 cc category in long-distance events led to the Italian Federation scrapping the class completely. A parallel can be drawn between this and Britain's BSA Gold Star, which had such a victorious run in the IoM Clubmans TT that it eventually saw the event killed off. However, the successful efforts of the 100 Gran Sport had not been entirely wasted, as it went on to sire a whole family of roadster singles, culminating with the 436 cc introduced in 1969.

Meanwhile, Taglioni had been hard at work developing a full Grand Prix version for the 125 cc class (see Chapter 1). At first this had a dohc cylinder head and five-speed gearbox, followed by six speeds and a Desmo head. The new bike finally appeared with Antoni aboard at the Swedish GP in 1956, achieving a superb race victory. Antoni returned home to Italy with the winning bike, where unknown to him disaster awaited. In his very hour of glory, with a real chance to be David against Goliath in the factory's World Championship début (the Swedish

Mike Hailwood's 125 desmo single at Silverstone, 17 April 1959

GP that year was not classed as a championship event). Antoni took his 125 Desmo out for a test session at Monza where the Grand Prix was to be held. Tragically, he crashed on the Lesmo curve and died from his injuries.

This was a double disaster for Ducati. Antoni was their star rider and thus held a very special place in the hearts and minds of all the factory personnel; his untimely death threw all Ducati's Grand Prix efforts out of gear. The next season, 1957, proved this to be only too true and was a disappointing one for the Ducati team. Their dominance in the long-distance events had caused other factories to lose interest, while the fatal accidents in the Mille Miglia car race of the same year had effectively caused the Italian authorities to ban all forms of motorized marathon racing over public roads. This brought an era of Italian racing history to an untimely end and thereafter only short-circuit events were allowed. A combination of the Antoni accident and the factory's need for Taglioni to develop

A 220 dohc cylinder head, one of a handful built following Ken Kavanagh's successful Australian tour, winter 1959–60

new road machines caused Ducati to miss a whole season's Grand Prix racing, with one exception, a successful return to Sweden, where, in the GP (this time a championship event), team riders recorded a convincing leaderboard dominance in the 125 race, with the first five positions going to Ducati-mounted riders.

Not all was darkness in 1957, however, as Ducati made their mark in two other branches of racing; Italian Formula II/III class racing (winning both) and the Spanish 24-hour endurance classes. The Spanish event was without doubt an important move by Ducati. Not only did it effectively replace the now banned long-distance road events at home but it was also to prove just the first of many visits to the Iberian Peninsula over the next quarter of a century – the scene for some of the factory's most famous victories. But the objective of the first entries was to help establish Ducati's off-shoot in Spain, the Barcelona-based Mototrans factory, which at that time was just setting up in business, mainly assembling parts shipped in from Bologna. Without any doubt the '24-hour' endurance races, held over the tortuous Montjuich Park

Isle of Man TT 1959, Brian Clark (right) with 175 Formula III

circuit in the city of Barcelona, were not just one of the best-known motorcycling events in Spain, but were also the most important in terms of sales for the victorious marque.

Ducati's Barcelona début in July 1957 was to prove equally as successful as their 1956 Swedish GP or the 1955 Giro d'Italia successes. Paired with Spaggiari was a newcomer to the Ducati team, Alberto Gandossi (who in the following year just missed taking the 125 cc World Championship title). The machine they used was a 125 cc version of the 100 Gran Sport and had originally been prepared, back in Bologna, for the Milano-Taranto road event, which was cancelled following the Mille Miglia débâcle. The team of Spaggiari/Gandossi covered a total of 586 laps, to win the event outright after 24 hours at an average speed of 57·66 mph, covering 1385 miles in the process. Ducati 125 Gran Sport models filled the next two places, with the all-Italian team of Farne/Mandolini in 2nd place, while 3rd spot went to local Spanish competitors Relets and Roda.

Ducati were doubly lucky. They had given the newly formed Mototrans a tremendous start and found an outlet for their well-developed long-distance racers. The 1st, 2nd and 3rd which they gained can be compared to a British factory taking the first three places at the TT in its heyday.

1958 heralded what was to be an entirely different year in the Grand Prix events for the Ducati team. With Taglioni's latest 125 Desmo single, 1958 was Ducati's year on the World Championship trail.

A variety of riders rode for Ducati that season, including Gandossi, Spaggiari, Romolo Ferri, Villa, Luigi Taveri, together with British riders Dave Chadwick, Sammy Miller and youngster Mike Hailwood, who was Ducati mounted after father Stan Hailwood had been so impressed with the Ducati's outstanding speed in the TT. Mike was riding the Ducati in time for the Dutch TT, finishing in 10th spot on one of the production valve spring dohc 125 Grand Prix. One outstanding performance was that of Alberto Gandossi, who except for a fall at the Ulster GP would surely have recorded Ducati's first world title. It was not to be, however, for although he remounted to finish a brave 4th both his and the factory's hopes of the championship had gone.

As the season passed, it was found that the Ducati Desmo singles were unbeatable on the fastest circuits; but their rivals, MV Agusta, had the supreme riding skills of the experienced Carlo

A 175 Formula III at Hall Bends, Cadwell Park, September 1959

Brian Clark, September 1960, Scarborough Gold Cup, Mere hairpin, with FIII now converted to 198 cc

Ubbiali and second string Tarquinio Provini to compensate for the MV's inferior speed.

In spite of this, by September, when the Italian round was to be held, it was all over. MV Agusta were World Champions again. But a shock was in store at the very circuit where MV wanted most to celebrate their world title in style – Ducati spoiled it all by gaining the first five places, to give MV a nightmare homecoming. The 5th of September must therefore go down alongside Paul Smart's 1972 Imola victory and Mike Hailwood's triumphant 1978 TT comeback ride as one of the high spots of Ducati's racing efforts over the years.

1958 was also a highly successful season for the less well publicized, but nonetheless important, sports machine category. In this class, at the same Monza meeting as the Grand Prix, Villa joined the 125 Grand Prix winner Spaggiari on the winner's rostrum with his victory in the Formula III race, in which he beat a pack of Benellis and Morinis to the flag. And, in fact, all three classes of 125 cc racing in Italy that year were won by Ducati machines.

At the end of 1958 the factory's management decided to tone down the racing effort, for both financial and development reasons. Consequently, the following year was not a particularly successful one for Ducati in Grand Prix racing – even though Mike Hailwood recorded his first Grand Prix victory, the Ulster, aboard a 125 Desmo. He also set up new race and lap records, the latter at 84·75 mph. For the TT, which was held on the short Clypse course, Hailwood was booked to ride the new twin, which at its début in the previous year's Grand Prix at Monza gained

Above **Close-up of 1961 250 Formula III engine, when delivered machine came complete with lights and even a centre stand!**

Below **Welshman Mick Manley 220-mounted leading another rider at a very wet Crystal Palace, 1961**

Pair of 250 Ducatis in pit area prior to start of 1963 Kuala Lumpur Grand Prix

middle of 1958. His first races were in Canada at Harewood, Ontario, in 1959, where he gained 6th and 7th places aboard a new Ducati 175 Sport, purchased for $350. It was Farne who performed the initial work on Tunstall's machine. This consisted of fitting different valves, springs, piston and camshaft and producing a megaphone to his own specification. Showing the great comradeship of the time Tunstall and Farne clashed several times at the old Laconia track and at other circuits throughout North America. Tunstall recalls lying second behind Farne at Laconia during one event in 1959 until an ignition wire broke, thereafter sitting by the roadside and watching the Italian win with ease. Tunstall continued riding his faithful 175 well into the sixties, before replacing it first with a four-speed and then with a five-speed 250 Diana, even competing several times at Daytona.

Other leading Americans racing 175s, 200s and later 250s during the early days were Ron Dahler, Jimmy Hayes, Chuck Andrews, Gerry Karns, George Rockett and Ray Hempstead. Perhaps the most noteworthy result during this period was George Rockett's 4th place in 1964 at the opening round of the World Championship, the US 250 cc Grand Prix held during Daytona race week. Race winner was Alan Shepherd on a works MZ twin. Rockett (and Frank Camillieri) were both later assisted by Reno Leoni, who, like Farne before him, had been sent by the factory from Italy in 1964 to assist the Ducati sales effort. Unlike Farne, Leoni stayed and has been resident in the States ever since. Although the official importers were none too keen, many Ducati singles were successfully raced throughout America. This was due, in no small part, to the tuning ability and enthusiasm of men like Leoni and Tunstall.

Ducati's success in America was not only limited to the north, with riders in countries such as Argentina and Peru flying the flag in South America with great success for almost a decade.

An interesting development of the Grand

a 3rd spot in the successful first-five leaderboard scoop. However, at the last moment Hailwood decided to use his faithful single for the race, finishing in 3rd position to add to his Ulster victory and the other 3rd places in Germany and Holland. On British short circuits he was unbeatable that year, winning everything and taking the ACU 125 cc Gold Star in the process.

A notable competitor on a 175 Formula III was Ducati employee Franco Farne. Farne had been sent by the factory to the USA in 1958 to assist their new importer, the Berliner Motor Corporation, as a 'sales representative'. It was Farne's job to travel to various fledgling Ducati dealers across America, instructing them on the finer points of how to correctly set-up Ducati motorcycles in order to best promote the marque. It was also his task to show his American hosts just how quickly a racing Ducati could perform. For this purpose the factory had shipped over a 175 Formula III (and a 125 Desmo). Most of Farne's racing across the Atlantic was on the 175 (the 125 was mainly a showpiece).

One of the first 'private' Ducati racers in the States was Sydney Tunstall, who had left England for Canada in February 1957, remaining in that country until moving to New York State in the

1963 Singapore Grand Prix Ducati rider Ng Yeng Heng 250 Formula III (1), Doug Curran race-kitted Diana (40) and an unnamed Honda rider

Prix was a 220 cc version; this came about through Australian 'Continental Circus' rider Ken Kavanagh, who in 1959 had campaigned a couple of Manx Nortons and a very rapid 125 Ducati Gran Prix production racer. Resident in Italy, Kavanagh decided to return home for the first time since 1951 and friends down-under, including his old motorcycle club, begged him to bring back machines and race in the various meetings that took place around Christmas time. Taking advantage of his trip, Ducati asked Kavanagh to attempt to find an importer for their products in Australia, noting at the same time that it would be bad policy to be seen riding a Norton! His 125 was already just about the quickest 'private' $\frac{1}{8}$-litre bike in Europe featuring an inclined six-speed motor and full duplex frame, but what he needed was a 250. However, at that time the largest Ducati was the 175 Formula racer, yet Taglioni after a few calculations

said that 'maybe' he could get enough power out of a modified 175 to beat the Aussie opposition, which at that time consisted of mainly specials based on the Velocette MOV and a couple of NSU Sportmax, owned by the Hinton brothers and Jack Forrest. Within two weeks the '220' was built from a 175 with its bore increased to 69 mm, giving a capacity of 216·130 cc, which on a compression ratio of 9:1 gave a maximum power figure of 28 bhp at 9600 rpm. Other details included a 29 mm Dell'Orto SS1 carburettor and, on this prototype bike, four speeds (later increased to five). But its most obvious feature was the twin camshaft head based on the lines of the 125 Grand Prix. This was an experimental item that just happened to be sitting in Taglioni's office. It had never previously been fitted to an engine and the biggest problem was designing and making suitable camshafts. This original prototype stemmed from a joint idea of Kavanagh and Giorgio Monetti and was built in the factory race shop by Farne, Spaggiari and Villa, with assistance from mechanic Recchia. The only 'test' the bike got prior to shipment was a quick 400-yard blast up the road outside the factory. The prototype's finish was red and bronze, with an unpainted polished alloy dolphin fairing. The frame and engine number were the same – 552.

Kavanagh's two machines (125 GP and 220) were crated and taken from Bologna to Genoa, there embarking with the rider aboard the Lloyd Triestina motor ship *Australia*, leaving Genoa on the 14 November and arriving at Melbourne on 18 December 1959.

Running on a mild alcohol mix (with an 11:1 piston) the début of the 220 was on 1 January 1960 at Phillips Island, some 50 miles south of Melbourne. After winning the 125 race ahead of MV-mounted Bob Brown, Kavanagh was also leading the 250 when a combination of ignition and carburation troubles forced him out.

The second meeting was at Fisherman's Bend, an airport on the outskirts of Melbourne, at the end of January. Again he won the 125, this time ahead of Tom Phillis, also Ducati mounted, just prior to joining the Honda works team. This time the 220 went perfectly, winning without trouble.

The third meeting was at Longford, Tasmania, but here the 125 and 250 races were run together. Kavanagh, therefore, elected to ride his 125, convincing Eric Hinton to leave his NSU in

1965 250 Mach 1/S developed from 1964 Barcelona race winner, was far too heavy for serious short circuit use

Sydney and race the Ducati. Hinton proved his decision correct by winning the class aboard the 220.

Next time out a broken piston caused an early retirement. Following this, his last race in Australia ended with another win – the last in his long career.

Soon after he returned to Italy, being unable to find buyers for either machine in Australia; eventually selling his 125 to Jim Redman in Bologna after the Rhodesian had failed to purchase a new 125 Grand Prix at the factory. This he rode throughout 1960, including a 13th in the TT, until Redman was offered a Honda contract following the death of Bob Brown in the West German GP. The 220, meanwhile, was sold to Geoff Monty for £420 before eventually passing to Barry Davis in late 1964, its ultimate fate being recorded in Chapter 11.

In addition to the Ken Kavanagh prototype, five other 220s were built, and in addition a couple are believed to have been converted from 175 Formula IIIs. One such machine was campaigned by English rider Brian Clark, although he found his own Formula III, converted to 198 cc, to be quicker.

Brian started riding the 175 in early 1959, and at the TT that year he was lying around 10th when he came off. At the end of the year his sponsor, Tom Lambert, approached Alan Mullee, the sales manager for Ducati Concessionaires Ltd, about a five-speed gearbox. 'OK, but the engine has to go back to the factory,' was the reply. Whilst at the factory it was fitted with a twin cam head; which is how this Formula III was almost unique in having five speeds and a twin cam head, as the factory had these on hand to build the batch of 220s.

Brian Clark's modified engine arrived back in England at the beginning of April 1960, but straight away a problem arose when he went to fit it. Quite simply, with the new twin cam head the engine would not fit his frame. (He found out later that the factory used a different frame on

Earls Court Show November 1966, development of Mach 1/S, with lighter Oldani brakes. A sister bike was clocked at 116 mph in roadster trim by an American magazine

the 220.) With the aid of a hacksaw and welding tackle it was made to fit. After a minor problem the modified engine, still in 175 form, proved its worth by winning the 1960 Scottish 200 cc Championship and recording many excellent placings against the likes of the NSU Sportmax in the 250 class. He also finished 11th in that year's TT.

During the winter of 1960/61 the machine was fitted with a 66 mm piston (175s had 62 mm as standard) manufactured by Hepolite, bringing the capacity to 198 cc. For the 1961 TT Clark was entered by Irishman Tom Chaillon on a brand new 220. However, the machine proved troublesome in practice, with the small end bush seizing three times, so it was back to the faithful 198, on which he finally managed to qualify on Thursday of practice week. Even so, Brian decided to use the 220 for the race, resulting in a lap two retirement due to the clutch falling apart. After the TT things greatly improved – including a 2nd place behind Dan Shorey's NSU Sportmax at the Scarborough International, setting the fastest lap. Finally, at the beginning of 1962 Brian Clark went over to the Aermacchi camp.

Of the production 220s, besides Kavanagh's performance, another successful rider was Welshman Mick Manley, who piloted his gold-painted machine to runner-up spot in the 1962 ACU Star (British Championship). By this time the factory had dropped out of direct participation, except for the Barcelona 24 hours and an American trip made during 1960 by Francesco Villa aboard the prototype 250, which resulted in a small production of a 248 cc version of the 175 Formula III being made, still with four speeds. Known in the UK as the 'Manxman', this pukka racing 250 had a short but hectic career on several continents.

In both North and South America the 250 Formula III performed with credit. Sadly only an odd example ever reached Britain, but amazingly one of its happiest hunting grounds was in the Far East – in Malaysia and Singapore – with British riders. Now long forgotten, the early sixties events such as the Malaysian GP, rated almost at the top of the list, were vital to the fledgling Japanese race teams of Honda, Yamaha and Suzuki with their desire to become household names across the world. During the period 1961–64 the Malaysian Peninsula was a hotbed of racing and Ducati provided in many cases the main opposition to the howling Honda twins and fours, and Suzuki/Yamaha strokers.

The reason the Japanese considered this area vital was twofold: not only was it close to home, but interest in motorcycling was at a peak with crowds often far higher than at European or American events (a reported 125,000 were on hand to witness the 1963 Malaysian GP).

The single-cylinder Ducatis should have been completely overwhelmed by such big guns, but when reliability counted in such events as the 180-mile GP, their ability to complete the distance non-stop enabled quite astonishing results to be obtained as the faster machinery often faltered and fell by the wayside. The highlight of this was RAF serviceman Fred Dingle's magnificent 2nd place to Motohashi on a works Yamaha in 1964. The local Ducati agent was so delighted that afterwards he gave the RAF rider the bike!

Strictly speaking this was a special, a prototype five-speeder, one of three or four shipped from Italy that year. An engine from one of these was fitted into Dingle's existing 250 Formula III of 1962 vintage, sporting Oldani brakes front and rear and 19 in. rims and tyres.

The Kuala Lumpur GP was another noteworthy Ducati performance with a team finish of 4th, 5th and 6th. Run in atrocious monsoon conditions over 180 miles, all three Ducatis finished on the same lap as the winner. The Ducati riders were Nobby Whales, Fred Dingle and Doug Curran. In the supporting 250 cc race Ducati took the first three places, with the same three riders. At any one time up to six riders were officially entered by the local importer, with three British and three local riders being provided with a mixture of machinery; all 250s comprising converted Diana's, Formula III or the five-speed specials. Doug Curran recalls that of the three the Formula IIIs handled and braked best, but the special five-speeders were the quickest, easily outpacing any Mach I based racer.

Barcelona was a continuing commitment for Ducati. In 1960, for example, eight 175s were entered in the 250 class, with Spanish and Italian pilots. Riders Francesco Villa and Amedco Balboni won at an average speed of 59·25 mph, with 603 laps completed. This was against formidable opposition such as British riders Peter Darville and Bruce Daniels on the MLG-entered BMW R69S. This pairing won the event the previous year on the earlier R69 model – both BMWs were 600 cc class machines.

Ducati were back at Barcelona again in 1962, this time with a prototype Mototrans 250. But perhaps Ducati's most famous victory came in 1964 (the year of the Mach 1 launch), in which they entered a '285' prototype based on a 248 cc unit with its bore increased to 79 mm, the stroke remaining at 57·8 mm. Its actual capacity was 283.317 cc! At the time, the rules allowed factory 'prototypes' in the event, although these had to be based on a production bike. Actually, the Ducati was far removed from anything like a standard machine and was definitely a special, expressly constructed for long-distance events. It was also much heavier than normal with massive 220 mm Grimeca brakes – a four leading-shoe front and twin leading-shoe rear. The winning 285, which was ridden by Spaggiari/Mandolini, set a new distance record for the 24 hours, covering 635 laps in the process. Ducati also fielded a 250 version, which finished 2nd in its class and 5th overall. Both these machines were identical except for their bore size.

Following this victory, the Italian factory produced a small batch of 250 and 350 racers based on these bikes for normal short-circuit events – at least this is what the bikes were intended to be used for. The tales of two of these bikes were particularly notable. The first of them went to Ken Watson, a British short-circuit rider, who had also competed in the Manx Grand Prix aboard a 500 Manx Norton. I first met Ken while we were both in the British colony of Aden (now South Yemen); he was a civil plant engineer, I was an RAF regular. During our time together I came to know the local Ducati importer very well, and this led us to hear the news that the factory was

Factory 450 Desmo ridden during 1970 by Bruno Spaggiari

launching the first of the new five-speed 250 roadsters, including the Mach 1, plus a pair of racers. Unfortunately, being stuck in such a remote part of the world, we had no way of knowing that instead of the racers being a lightweight pukka short-circuit racing version of the Mach 1, they were in reality heavy endurance-type machinery, complete with lighting, centre stand and chainguard.

Ken travelled all the way to Bologna, after arranging through our importer friend in Aden to purchase one of the 250s direct from the factory. To his surprise he was confronted with a very different bike to the one he and I had imagined back in Aden; but undaunted, although a little disappointed, he handed over rather a large amount of lire, put the bike and himself on the train at Bologna railway station and headed back to England. After stripping off all the roadgoing equipment, he found the bike still far too heavy for serious short-circuit going. In fact it was much more suited to the Isle of Man, where in the 1965 250 Manx Grand Prix Lightweight race he finished 9th, gaining a replica.

Besides Ken Watson, another British purchaser was the importer Vic Camp, who had taken delivery of an identical 250, intending to sign up a star rider to race this together with a 350. Things did not quite work out like this, however, for after both Derek Minter and Dave Degens had tested the bikes at Brands Hatch, Camp discovered that here were two bikes that were completely uncompetitive for British short circuits. When this became apparent he asked the riders to 'rev them until they blow', hoping this would enable him to return the bikes to the factory; but this proved impossible because neither machine would break, even though revved way above normal figures, showing just why they stayed together with such reliability in Spain. Nonetheless, Camp did manage to get the factory to take them back, receiving in exchange a couple of road bikes and some race-shop parts

that could be used to make his own converted roadster-based racers (of which more in the next chapter) more competitive.

A 350 Mach 1/S was also shipped to the States in 1965 for Berliner to reap the benefit of a class win . . . at Sebring in Florida, hence the reason the factory's first production 350 got its name. The rider was Franco Farne. Ducati did not make a serious single-cylinder racing iron again until 1967, although a factory 250 sporting Oldani brakes briefly appeared in practice for the 1966 Manx Grand Prix, ridden by Derek Chatterton. However, it never made the race and was shipped straight back to Italy. This was in fact a development of the Mach 1/S, but had smaller Oldani brakes and a different tank and saddle. Tested in the USA, one in roadster trim, clocked 116 mph.

In 1967, Bruno Spaggiari raced factory 250 and 350 machines, which, with Desmo heads, achieved leaderboard placings at most of the Italian international and national events until the end of the sixties, when they were sold off; and in 1971, a 450 version appeared. These three models were the later wide crankcase machines with a number of special parts including dry clutch, close ratio gears and straight-cut bevels, and in line with factory policy were used at an early stage in development of the incoming roadster models. The ex-Spaggiari 350 was purchased by British importer Vic Camp for his rider Alan Dunscombe to use on British short circuits in 1970/71, and afterwards it was sold to club rider Tony Nash from Romford, before passing to its present owner Ian Griffiths. This machine was modified by Camp with a Lockheed/Pagehiln disc front brake, which it still retains.

But these few factory-built racers were just a drop in the ocean. Most of the glory since the late fifties has been gained by thousands of competitors worldwide on their various race-knitted road-going Ducati singles, together with standard bikes used in production events and a handful of special-framed racers.

10 | Privateers in the UK

Terry Grotefeld, Brands Hatch Good Friday 24 March 1959, prior to his first race. Race-kitted 175 Sport

Most of the many racing Ducatis have not been purpose-built competition machines at all, but specially race-kitted roadsters. From the introduction of the Bologna factory's first ohc production roadster, the 1957 175 Sport, large numbers of this and each succeeding model have been stripped, tuned and raced. This happened for two very good reasons – cost and suitability.

Although Ducati occasionally produced a pukka racer for sale – including the Gran Sport, Formula III, 125 and 220 Grand Prix, and the 250 Mach 1/S – these were usually ruled out for all but the very well-heeled, simply on grounds of their price. As a result, the roadsters, which, after all, bore the same lineage, looked like an attractive alternative to the budget-conscious amateur racer. Thousands of such competitors bought the early 175s, 200s, and the later 250 in its various guises. With the introduction of the wide-case singles Ducati had race entries in every capacity, up to the single's maximum 450 cc (i.e. the 500 class). The enthusiasm of their owners was not misplaced, for these machines could really be made to go.

As early as the late 1950s, the Ducati name had become more closely associated with the racing fraternity than with any other sector of the market. This was wholly due to the achievements of Ducati-mounted riders in Grand Prix and long-distance events. Privateers in many countries soon realized that although they could

Practice for the 1959 Ultra lightweight TT, A. J. West, 125 Ducati Sport

never afford a factory-built racer, they could go racing relatively cheaply. In many ways these became what the Norton International and BSA Gold Stars had been earlier.

The same thought seemed to have repeated itself around the globe, so that soon race entry lists increasingly featured the Ducati name. In Europe, North or South America, the Far East or southern Africa, the results were the same; the overhead cam singles from Bologna triumphed even against machines that had been built specially for the track and at many times the cost.

The first models to figure in the results table were the 125 and 175 Sport, soon joined by the 200 Elite. The transformation from roadster to racing iron was surprisingly simple. Purely road-going equipment was removed, or exchanged for racing items, usually consisting of a larger Dell-'Orto SS1 carburettor, Formula III piston and camshaft, an open megaphone and a close-ratio gear cluster.

In Britain three early converts to the Ducati camp included Rex Butcher, Horace (Crasher)

Crowder and Terry Grotefeld. The latter's converted 175 Sport still exists, albeit with a 250 five-speed engine, but sporting the NSU front brake originally added in 1961.

Around the same time that Grotefeld was fitting the NSU stopper to his trusty 175, the first production 250 Ducatis were appearing. Almost instantly these made the many 175s and 200s obsolete, although in a few countries, such as Italy itself, Scotland and Ireland, separate classes that existed for the smaller machines ensured their survival.

Very soon after the new 250 line was introduced a factory race kit was offered for the sports model, the Diana (in Britain, Daytona). This kit consisted of a 27 mm SS1 Dell'Orto carburettor, a 9:1 forged 3-ring piston and a megaphone, plus a selection of carb jets and two rear sprockets. For the USA, the Diana was available with these parts as a standard option, giving it (when the megaphone was fitted) a true 100 mph potential. In Britain the race kit was only on sale for after-market fitting, with a 1962 price of £18. Prices

Aberdare Park, August 26 1961. Terry Grotefeld 10th in 250 final – machine and rider no longer raw novices

at this time for the 175 and 200 cc racing parts included £6 15s. for a Formula III camshaft, and £4 5s. for the megaphone. By 1963, some excellent results had been obtained.

Even so, it was not until the following year that the machine that had perhaps more race potential than all the others appeared – the legendary Mach 1. Here at last was the ideal roadster-cum-racer. Although in truth, its fiery nature probably made it a less than suitable everyday bike, the Mach 1 was an ideal racing motorcycle. The specification showed this well. Not just a five-speed version of the earlier models, the Mach 1 engine owed far more to the needs of the track than to road riding, with its huge valves, extra-strong hairpin springs, high-lift camshaft, forged 10:1 piston and a massive 29 mm Dell'Orto SS1 29D remote float carb. With a Mach 1 there was no need for an extra race kit, this came as standard. Just strip off the sparse road equipment, fit a rev counter, add a megaphone . . . and go racing.

As soon as the Mach 1 was launched in Britain, in September 1964, two of its first customers did just that. The early results gained by Brian Jefferies and Mick Rodgers quickly prompted Vic Camp, the London dealer who had supplied their bikes, to realize that simply by taking a standard Mach 1, removing the various road-going parts (which would find a ready resale market) and adding a fibreglass tank, fairing and seat, plus megaphone and rear oil flap, he could offer a 'racing' 250 Ducati for sale.

The first of these conversions, based on Jefferies' machine, was sold during the winter of 1964/65. The earliest versions had virtually no special preparation at all, and even retained the standard steel front mudguard. All the fibreglass-ware was manufactured for Vic Camp by a company named Duguid Bros., and it was this firm which subsequently produced all the other fibreglass fittings that found their way on to the Vic Camp racers in the years to follow.

Despite such window dressing, and although

Scotsman Jack Gow, foot of Bray Hill, 1960 TT, where he finished 25th on his bog standard 125 Sport, lights an' all

the Mach 1 was impressive for what it was, its standard state of tune was still not strong enough to offer a serious challenge to rivals like the Greeves Silverstone, Yamaha TD1 and Aermacchi of the period. So, while Brian Jefferies had been campaigning his Mach 1 in open events (including making his, and Ducati's, début in the 1964 Lightweight Manx Grand Prix, held in the first week of September), Mick Rodgers had pitted his against other roadsters in the Production class, where its potent power unit and race-bred handling gave it more than a fighting chance. His first victory came with a class win on 25 September at Silverstone in a BMCRC meeting.

By now, owners and dealers were finding out just what a potent machine the Mach 1 really was. In South Africa, for example, several of the speedy little Dukes had shot to prominence in local events in 1965. They included James Whyte, John Gibb, Noel Mayer, and Peter Aitken – all riding converted Mach 1s.

In Britain the 1965 season opened with Brian Jefferies still as Vic Camp's main runner. How-

Across the Atlantic, Sydney Tunstall at Mosport, Canada, September 1960, 175

ever, as the season progressed, Camp realized that a bigger draw was needed to enable more racers to be sold – a big name and a 'special' bike. This resulted in several approaches and eventually led to the experienced Tom Phillips joining the team. Phillips made his first appearance on Camp's new machine near the end of 1965, at an important Snetterton national event. He finished an impressive 2nd behind Derek Chatterton, who was Yamaha-mounted. Chatterton himself was shortly to turn to Ducati for his raceware, albeit in the form of a homebrew special, as recounted in the next chapter.

Meanwhile, Brian Jefferies had returned to the Manx Grand Prix, but his luck was out. After wrecking his motor when the head of the inlet valve came off after missing a gear in practice, and falling in a later practice circuit, he retired early in the race itself with a broken footrest.

Despite this, several other Ducati entrants finished. Ken Watson on his Mach 1/S made a creditable 9th, Paul Ludlam came 36th, Bob Baldock was 49th, and Bob Eldridge-Smith 51st.

North of the border, Jack Gow became the 1965 Scottish Road Racing Champion aboard a 175 Silverstone. The season saw him ride to a win at every one of the races held.

Unlike Brian Jefferies, Mick Rodgers had a highly successful year with his Mach 1, proving it by far the most successful 250 cc production class machine in Britain during 1965, with a virtual monopoly of wins throughout the year. At Snetterton's Norwich straight he was regularly timed at between 102 and 104 mph. Even so, it was Jefferies, not Rodgers, who partnered Dave Chester on a Mach 1 in the international 500-mile race, held at Castle Combe that year. In fact, Vic Camp entered two Mach 1s, the other being ridden by two *Motor Cycle News* staffmen, Robin Miller and Sean Wood.

Conditions during the race were abysmal with rain throughout. The *MCN* riders were ruled out following a multiple crash involving Wood and other riders, but Jefferies and Chester lasted to finish 8th in their class. In fact, they were the first non-works and standard machine home, since all the machines that beat them, Bultaco, Cotton, Honda, Montesa and Ossa, were factory entries.

Following the signing of Tom Phillips demand for the Vic Camp racers increased, resulting in both a price rise and a change of appearance for the 1966 season. The 1965 price had been £299 – £30 more than the Standard Mach 1 – but for 1966 this had risen to £319 10s. The changes to the specification included a twin plug head (with a 10 mm plug put in at the rear of the bevel drive tube), a modified clutch (consisting simply of drilled lobes on the clutch housing), air scoop slots drilled for improved cooling of the front brake, Girling suspension units, Dunlop triangulated tyres, a modified rear seat loop, 30 mm Dell'Orto carburettor and a new-style saddle, tank, mudguard and fairing in fibreglass.

John Daly, 250 Daytona at Brands Hatch, April 1 1962

most lasting memory of the event was the bitterly cold weather – it even snowed that day! Earlier, on 13 March, Camp's own runner, Tom Phillips, had made a successful start to the new season with a 5th place ahead of Derek Minter on the works Cotton Telstar, but behind race winner Tommy Robb (Bultaco), Dave Degens (Aermacchi), Peter Inchley (Villiers Starmaker) and South African Martin Watson (Bultaco).

In the Production class Mick Rodgers's performance of the previous season had convinced Clive Thompsett to purchase a Mach 1, which carried him to victory on his very first outing on 5 March at Brands Hatch. The season was to be marked by some tremendous battles between Thompsett and Rodgers, with no clear winner. Another notable Ducati performance was in the 500-miler, held back at its original home, Thruxton. The pairing of Welshman Charlie Crookes and Peter Morgan finished 23rd overall (8th 250) on a four-speed Daytona. Surprisingly, the much more experienced and better-equipped pairing of Ken Watson and Tony Wood on Vic Camp's Mach 1 could only manage 25th (9th 250).

My first visit to the Manx Grand Prix resulted in the broken conrod mentioned earlier. The incident happened on the second lap of the circuit in the first practice session, at one of the fastest sections of the course, halfway down Sulby straight. The result could have been much more serious. As it was, after sliding 400 yards, I was still in far better shape than the bike; one side and the engine were written-off. The conrod had broken near the small end, destroying the piston, crankcases and part of the gearbox.

Rather than waste my visit, I was fortunate that another Ducati enthusiast who was a spectator on his four-speed Daytona, offered me his engine for the rest of the practice week – and for the race as well. Somehow, this standard unit survived, and I finished 50th at 60·47 mph. At the other end of the field, Ken Watson on the Camp bike normally used by Tom Phillips blasted round to gain 2nd position at 85·19 mph. As usual, no

Colour options for the fibreglass were red, blue, white, or yellow.

In reality, most of these modifications were of limited value, because apart from the twin plug head and 30 mm carburettor the engines were still standard. Just how much so was revealed to me when my own new 1966 Camp racer snapped a conrod in Manx Grand Prix practice that year. Impressed by Tom Phillips' performances at the tail end of the 1965 season, I had placed an order with Vic. I collected my new machine in February 1966 from Walthamstow, trading in my 175 Formula III, plus £219 10s. for an all-red Mach 1. Another racer collecting his new Mach 1 the same day was Geoff Bunting, tragically killed some five years later at Barcelona.

After running it in at a Cadwell Park practice day in March, my first race on the Mach 1 was at Silverstone in early April. Unfortunately, the other Ducati could touch Camp's bike, and the next finisher was Paul Ludlam in 34th spot, followed by 40th man D. J. McMillan, 44th M. A. Hunt, 45th M. J. Hemming and 46th Bob Baldock.

With the engine blow-up, my own efforts were over for the rest of the season, and although an Aermacchi had been considered, this was now out of the question. During the winter of 1966/67, Vic Camp had taken over from Ducati Concessionaires (King's of Manchester) as British importer. At the same time another racing Ducati dealer, Ted Broad, finally sold his Ducati interest to Camp to enable him to concentrate his efforts on Yamahas. By chance, also simultaneously the Mach 1 had become the Mark 3, but the only change this had on the bikes Camp sold was the name, since both the specification and the £319 price tag stayed the same.

Price effectively ruled out a new Aermacchi for me, and following the expensive Manx Grand Prix experience the remains of my Mach 1 were sold off and replaced by a much older machine. This was a four-speed Daytona-based machine dating back to 1962, and an early race at the final Snetterton national of the year convinced me that although the engine was sound, something more modern was necessary. This turned out to be a new 250 Mark 3 engine unit with flywheel magneto ignition and Dell'Orto carburettor, one of a small batch imported in mid-1966 for use in Formula IV car racing.

London dealer Vic Camp built many racers from standard Mach 1 models. Here's the 1965 version

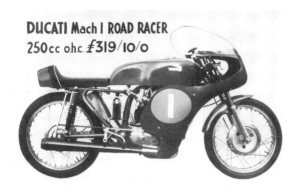

DUCATI Mach I ROAD RACER
250cc o.h.c. £319/10/0

1966 Vic Camp Mach 1 racer

The new engine was fitted into the Daytona chassis, but even so the bike was basically uncompetitive. At the Easter Monday national at Cadwell Park in 1967 I was overtaken by Tom Phillips (Camp's rider) on the straight approaching the Mountain. Although I was able to stay close to Phillips through the twisty bits, the other Ducati just flew away from mine everywhere else.

I discovered that Vic Camp himself was in the paddock, so I approached him hoping to find out what Phillips' motor had inside that mine did not. He was reluctant to part with such valuable information, although he eventually agreed to tell me after I had reminded him about the expensive blow-up of the previous year. Finally, all was revealed, with the promise that I would be allowed to buy identical parts. The special fittings consisted of a titanium conrod, which was double webbed at top and bottom for strength, a 11·5:1 slipper piston and a works camshaft.

With these, and a 32 mm Amal Concentric Mark 1, I soon found that for the first time the roadster-based Ducati's performance approached that of the pukka racers like the

Greeves, Cotton, DMW and Yamaha. With peak power at 10,500 rpm, instead of the usual 8500 rpm, the only mechanical parts to suffer were the standard Mach 1 hairpin valve springs. These lasted an average of four short circuit meetings before valve bounce would set in at maximum revs. To combat this, Camp's own special 250 used coil valve springs specially made for him by the German, Helmut Fath. However, although these eliminated valve bounce, they caused much more rapid wear on the cam gear, dramatically lessening the life of the hardening of the rocker and camshaft. Worse still, many of these conversions were sold to racing customers whose standard bikes never suffered the problem of valve bounce in the first place.

Through April, May and June 1967 my results had improved in line with the bike's new-found zest, even managing to lead a 350 race on my first-ever visit to Mallory Park. The event was a national, against the cream of the country's AJS

The author running-up his brand new Vic Camp Mach 1, Cadwell Park, March 1966

7Rs, Manx Nortons and Aermacchis – all were trounced by a mere roadster 250!

This success was not to last, however, as two visits to the Isle of Man proved. First came the Southern 100 in July, which became a nightmare, with battery problems causing an early retirement. My second visit to the Manx Grand Prix ended even more disastrously than the previous year after fierce contention in the Lightweight race, in some of the worst weather ever to hit the event. The start was delayed until 11 am, only to be held with continuous heavy rain and gale-force winds lashing most of the course and low mist covering the mountain section. I finally finished 42nd with a race average of 69·54 mph,

although the best Ducati was H. M. Cummings in 20th spot at 75·45 mph.

However severe the problems of the race they were nothing to what followed, when several hours after finishing I heard that the garage housing my Ducati and several other competitors' machines had caught fire. My rather special Ducati was badly burned, and with it went the spare engine, tools, paperwork and racing spares. As if this was not enough, it turned out that the garage owner was not insured!

Elsewhere, 1967 was providing mixed fortunes for Ducati riders. At the Thruxton 500-miler, Ken Watson, again on a Camp machine, was partnered by Charlie Sanby, but their chances were upset by battery troubles. Mick Rodgers was more successful with Pete Kilner; his 1964 Mach 1 stayed the course.

This year also heralded the Camp team's first venture abroad, to Spain for the Barcelona 24

The 350 Sebring Vic Camp prepared for Derek Minter to ride in the 1967 Brands Hatch 500 mile endurance race

Hours with Ken Watson and Tony Wood riding – but the visit proved disappointing and marked Wood's last ride for Camp.

1968, the following year, saw the Bologna factory begin production of the wide-case models, but racing continued on the narrow crankcase types – except for the factory's own works efforts. By then Tom Phillips had left Camp, who during the previous season had seen Phillips joined by Geoff Bunting and Cadwell Park specialist John Kirkby. Now Paul Smart was number-one jockey – usually on the 350, but occasionally on the smaller bike.

In line with his other racing versions of the production roadsters, Camp now even offered a machine for the 50 cc class based on the then current SL1. In the state of tune offered, the

Sydney Tunstall displays silverware won aboard his single; date 1968

Camp 50 produced 8 bhp at 9500 rpm, providing a maximum speed of 70–75 mph. Very few of these were sold, and for those that bought them results were hard. The only high spot was an 11th in the 1968 50 cc TT ridden by Rodney Gooch.

On the international front, Australian Malcolm Stanton put up some fine performances in the Grands Prix aboard a 350. He also rode at several of the major British meetings, including a star-studded Oulton Park, in which the results spoke for themselves – 1st Mike Hailwood, 2nd Kel Carruthers, 3rd Ginger Molloy, 4th Malcolm Stanton, 5th Rob Fitton and 6th Dave Simmonds. All but Stanton and Fitton were on works bikes.

At last Vic Camp's long years of sponsorship in long-distance events were to be rewarded, with several top placings for Ken Watson (now in his last season), Tom Dickie, Charles Mortimer and Reg Everett. Two highlights were a 3rd in the 500-miler, held at Brands Hatch – and even more importantly, another 3rd at Barcelona. Here the Everett/Smart pairing achieved an excellent result in spite of Smart sliding off.

For once the Manx Grand Prix was kind to Ducati and in return saw one of the largest groups of finishers. The leading Ducati rider that year was Gordon Thain, finishing in 13th position at 78·87 mph, just missing a replica. Ducatis also took 17th, 24th, 25th, 26th, 34th, 35th, 42nd, 44th and 46th positions.

1969 saw the arrival in Britain not only of the first of the new 250 and 350 wide-case models but also new Camp racers. These were still very much built to a price rather than to win races at any cost, and the 250 sold at £389 10s., with the 350 at £499 10s. Just why the larger model should have been almost 25 per cent more expensive, although it was identical in most respects, is a question that remains unanswered.

Specifications of these new Camp racers included Robinson racing front brakes, Dell'Orto carburettors (32 mm on the 250, 35 mm on the 350), twin plug cylinder heads, Girling hydraulic steering damper and rear suspension units,

Smiths rev counter, and Dunlop triangulated tyres. Fibreglass-ware was as usual by Duguid, and was now a replica of the style used on Spaggiari's works singles.

For 1969 Paul Smart was joined in the Vic Camp team by Charles Mortimer, and towards the end of the season a third rider was to emerge as a future Camp runner — Alan Dunscombe — who attracted his future sponsor's eye by winning the annual Stars of Tomorrow title at Brands Hatch. Meanwhile, the Vic Camp Racing School (now some three years old) assumed a new title, 'The Kirby/Camp Racing School', after the Ducati specialist was joined by Tom Kirby, a leading race sponsor and the man behind many a famous name of the period.

For my own part, the very quick 250 had been rebuilt as best it could following the Isle of Man fire and again provided several good placings at the beginning of the next season before being sold. After this I raced 350 and 500 BSA Gold

Paul Smart flat on the tank of his Vic Camp 350, Mallory Park 20 October 1968

Stars, owned and prepared by my brother Richard, followed by a spell on a Formula (Triumph) Tiger Cub. Although I hung up my leathers for a period at the end of 1968, I found it impossible to stay away from racing, and by 1970 had ridden a standard road-going 250 Mark 3 to Silverstone during April to use in some high-speed trials. Here the bug had bitten again, resulting in the same machine and rider finding themselves at the 1970 Thruxton 500. The bike, a Bill Hannah import, had been purchased in June of the previous year purely as day-to-day transport.

The Thruxton line-up was formidable, with one of the best entries of $\frac{1}{4}$-litre machines ever. In terms of numbers it was a fight between Suzuki and Ducati, with six of the Japanese twins pitted against five of the Italian singles. Also in the field were a factory-prepared Honda CB250, a Montesa and a BSA.

Cloudless skies greeted race day, as they had for many days before, including the practice session of the previous day. At 11.50 am the entrants, including myself, sprinted in a Le Mans-style start across the Thruxton tarmac. Down went the kickstarter, the little Mark 3 burst into life and the Ducati single and I were soon in the thick of the action. As the first laps unfolded I discovered that far from being left behind by the other machines, XML 962G was well able to hold its own — as confirmed by the class placings after the first hour. These read: 1st Dave Browning/ Charles Mortimer, 1970 Ducati Desmo; 2nd Ralph Guy/Graham Dixon, 1970 Honda CB250; 3rd Stuart Graham/Ralph Bryans, 1970 Suzuki; 4th Mick Walker/Tony Plumridge, 1969 (reg.) Ducati Mark 3. By the time it became necessary to hand over to my co-rider for the first time dark clouds had gathered, and shortly after Tony Plumridge had started out down came the first spots of rain. This quickly turned into far heavier stuff, and the ensuing storm was best summed up by the headline of the following week's *Motor Cycle News*: 'Deluge floods track as twenty-three retire at chilly 500 miler.'

With no fairing to hide behind and a single Barbour jacket to share between us, the Walker/Plumridge team was soon frozen. All I can remember now of the rest of the race was huddling in a blanket to keep warm between rides – even so my teeth still chattered. By the third hour, we had dropped to sixth spot, finally finishing as the seventh 250 and 27th overall, with a total of 170 laps completed at an average speed of 59·80 mph. Class winners Mortimer and Browning came home 11th at 67·00 mph, with Clive Thompsett and Jim Evans on another Ducati 4th in the class and 18th overall at an average of 63·50 mph.

Following its Thruxton success, Vic Camp's winning machine was ridden by Mortimer in the TT, three weeks later. Although a Honda ridden by Roy Boughey had been quickest in practice, race day was a different story, with Mortimer, John Williams on a Honda, Stan Woods on a Suzuki and Jim Curry on another Honda taking turns at leading through the early stages of the race. Williams had started his rise to fame three years earlier when he rode a Camp Ducati to his first win at Brands Hatch.

It was not until the last half lap that Mortimer was able to pull out a six-second gap, when he found that the Ducati had better acceleration on the climb out of Ramsey, and he was able to leave 2nd-place man Williams, winning the class at 84·47 mph. Of the fifteen 250 cc starters only eight finished, including two other Ducatis – Graham Hunter 4th at 83·05 mph, on an identical machine, and Clive Luton, whose earlier narrow-case model carried him to 8th at 72·50 mph. On the fast downhill section between Creg-ny-Baa and Brandish the official speed trap clocked Mortimer's fastest at 110·04 mph.

Although my Mark 3 had resumed its roadster duties following Thruxton, it had rekindled my will to return to racing. This was to find me heading once again to the Isle of Man to take part in the 1970 Lightweight Manx Grand Prix on a

A determined Chas Mortimer (partnered by Tom Dickie) in the 1968 500 miler; narrow case 250 Mark 3

rather ancient 200 Elite bought as a converted racer some weeks previously. What followed is typical of the problems and the comradeship which are a unique part of the annual amateur races held around the $37\frac{3}{4}$-mile Mountain circuit in early September.

Having only recently started my own business, after years of racing and owning the marque, my limited finances stretched no higher than spending the fortnight camped in the pits area next to the grandstand. Towards the end of practice week my two travelling companions decided to return to the mainland, taking with them everything except my bike, tools and belongings – which did not include the tent – so I was left with no sleeping quarters. Fellow competitors soon came to the rescue, however, including in particular Dennis Rapley's mechanic Tony Bright, who, with the help of his girlfriend, not only provided all my meals for the remainder of practice

1970
1ST. 250 CC. THRUXTON 500
VIC CAMP
1ST. 250 CC. T.T. PRODUCTION.

Vic Camp's logo/decal proudly proclaimed 250 production TT and Thruxton 500 class wins

and race week but also loaned me another bike to replace my rather tired 200 – a much more modern 1968 250 Mark 3 narrow case. And Junior (350 cc) competitor Brian (Snowy) Cammock placed his van at my disposal for sleeping accommodation. Even this had its funny side, for the first morning Brian promptly forgot this arrangement and drove off to Douglas with me still attempting to sleep in the back!

After the loan of the Tony Bright machine I had no more problems in qualifying. An unusual feature of his bike was its Gardiner carburettor, the first time I'd ever ridden with this instrument. To improve its braking, a Honda CB72 front brake had been grafted on to the standard early Ducati roadster front forks.

The race itself was disappointing for me after a long stop eight miles out on the first lap effectively killed all chances of a high place. However, the large Ducati entry secured many of the mid-field results as the record shows: 15th C. E. Crookes, 80·84 mph; 17th R. D. Wilson, 79·57 mph; 24th A. R. Vaughan-Jones, 78·16 mph; 25th W. M. Galbraith, 77·37 mph; 32nd M. J. G. Walker, 74·91 mph; plus seven more Ducati places. Forty-first finisher, Canadian Dale Nunn, had travelled all the way from British Columbia to compete, after racing Ducati singles for many years in North America.

At around this time the $\frac{1}{4}$-litre Ducati single was achieving great racing success on four

wheels, too. Although experiments with the British Formula IV car class had proved abortive, on the other side of the Atlantic Ducati engines were to power most of the field in American midget car racing. This was little publicized but was a popular form of cheap racing that prospered in the sixties. Midget racing took place on tracks that were similar to speedway ovals, with the competitors in full view of the spectators for the whole of the circuit. With the engine capacity limited to a mere 250 cc, the ohc four-stroke power of the Ducati proved ideal.

By the beginning of 1971 Vic Camp had reached a state of deadlock with the Ducati management in Italy. This was to result in very few Italian machines being exported to Britain during 1971/72, which led to his decision to bring in the Spanish Mototrans models (mainly the 24 Horas). Even in the USA Berliner was finding similar problems, which led to the introduction in America of the Spanish 'Road' models in place of Bologna singles.

The dispute with Ducati Meccanica rested on the prices of the single-cylinder range, although Camp's dispute went further because he turned them into racers. The supply of new machines thus began to dry up in Britain. Strangely, Camp's differences with the factory did not affect his sponsorship, which by now was concentrated on one man, Alan Dunscombe. In addition to the ex-works 350 dry clutch racer that Camp had purchased from the factory, Dunscombe had also achieved considerable success on a 450. This used an NCR-built engine in a standard chassis, and like the 350, which Camp had converted to front disc brake, used a Lockheed caliper with a Pagehiln hub and disc.

At club events throughout 1971 and 1972, Dunscombe strung together a series of top placings on both bikes. These successes were to lead Dunscombe both to a test ride on the 500 Grand Prix racing V-twin in 1971 and to becoming one of the back-up riders to support Spaggiari and Smart at Imola in 1972. Unfortunately, this ride was to end with a broken collarbone for Dunscombe when he came off a factory 750 at Imola.

The 1971 Manx Grand Prix was my last ride in the event. As in the year before my race mount was Tony Bright's 250 Mark 3, and we both hoped for an improvement. It was to be my most trouble-free Manx, although I again lost race time owing to a loose ignition coil. Even so, I managed to make it the third Ducati home. This time, the results of the Lightweight race included: 20th A. Vaughan-Jones, 82·24 mph; 21st R. H. Sheerhan, 81·05 mph; 30th M. J. G. Walker, 76·26 mph; plus seven more places.

In the Junior race, Snowy Cammock finished 20th, winning a replica, but without doubt the finest Ducati performance was newcomer Bob Sheerhan's ride to 21st in the Lightweight on a scruffy, well-used Mach 1, which was in full road-going trim. Bob, from Dublin, was a rider who could have gone much further with the right machinery.

During the Manx, my first taste of sponsoring itself had come about with the help of Andy Vaughan-Jones, Bob Sheerhan and Snowy Cammock. This was increased rapidly for the following year, when for the 1972 season I obtained rider Mick Taylor, the Yorkshireman who had put up such a stirling performance the previous year at Silverstone, overtaking a whole bunch of the world's leading riders, including Phil Read, in full view of the packed grandstand after they had sped past down Hangar Straight.

By the time of the 1972 Silverstone Grand Prix, Taylor had competed at a large number of meetings, including the TT, where he rode a 1972 24 Horas, which I had prepared for production racing after testing the machine myself at Snetterton. Although it went well in the TT, Mick was forced to retire because the clip came out of the carburettor needle during the race.

At Silverstone three bikes were ready for him to use. These were a 125 with a 160 Monza Junior-based engine, tuned and sleeved down to 124 cc in a 125 Ducati Grand Prix chassis; highly tuned 250 Mach 1, which had been the mainstay of his racing effort through the year; and the 24 Horas, which was entered for the production race. After coming off the 125 in practice his performances were below par, although he had a class leaderboard place in the production race. In the Manx Grand Prix, after lapping well over 80 mph in practice, he was an early retirement in the race.

Throughout 1972, while all this was happening, my shop manager, John Blunt, was racing the prototype of what was to become my most successful Ducati single racer. In essence this was a 350 Sebring engine tuned to the highest level we could obtain and fitted into a special chassis that retained only the standard Ducati rear hub. The spine frame was manufactured by

Kirby/Camp racing school, March 1970. Left to right Charles Mortimer Snr, Tom Kirby, Vic Camp and Brands Hatch officials; bikes are narrow case, 250 Mark 3s

Italian flavour – Augusto Brettoni, Castellina 1971. This talented rider later became an official Laverda race and test rider

Saxon (of go-kart fame) for a customer called Roger Cocks, who decided before the project was finished that he wanted to go racing with an Aermacchi instead. As a result, I was able to purchase the complete rolling chassis, into which the special Ducati engine was fitted. Initially the machine was completed with a Grimeca four-leading shoe front brake, Metal Profile front forks, an alloy tank, Yamaha TD2 fairing and a 35 mm Dell'Orto carburettor.

Although John Blunt would be first to admit that he raced only for fun, his entries did allow a lot of development work that otherwise would not have been possible with a rider working away from our base.

Because of our need to develop and sell replicas of the special frame, Mick Taylor and I parted company at the end of 1972, leaving a situation where it was possible for the machine to be entered for a full season during 1973 with a succession of riders, allowing different views to assist development. One of the first of these was Dave Arnold, who was to gain a victory in the Lightweight Manx Grand Prix later that year – on a Walker-entered Yamaha and not a Ducati.

From mid-1972 we had received a steady

demand for replicas of our spine-framed racer with 250, 350 and 450 cc engines. We also constructed a number of racers based on standard Ducati frames. During the close season an increase in demand meant Saxon were unable to meet our deadlines. This led to Spondon Engineering of Derby building frames instead. The two factories' products are easily distinguished – Saxon frames use square-section swinging-arms; Spondon, round-section.

On both versions of the spine frame construction was in T45 aircraft tubing throughout, and the steering head used Timken taper roller bearings. The engine was supported by the two rear engine mounting points and at the cylinder head. Braking was by the standard Ducati rear hub and a variety of proprietary units at the front. Although our own machine had finalized on a Fontana front brake, others used either Grimeca or Robinson; Oldani and Spondon were also fitted at various times. Likewise, forks varied from the Cerianis on our own bike to Metal Profile or Spondon units as specified by the customer. Front and rear wheels were laced to WM2 Borrani alloy rims and shod with 3·00 × 18 in. Dunlop triangulated tyres. Other fittings included a Bosch TJ6 oil-filled ignition coil (two were used if the twin-plug head was fitted), a Krober electronic rev counter, which read from 0–12,000 rpm, and Tomaselli clip-ons and levers.

Engine-wise, in 350 cc form we found the best compromise to be the following: green/white camshaft; a Monza/Sebring basic head casting with both the inlet and exhaust ports bored and flowed, but with Mach 1/Mark 3 internals including the valves, springs, collets and rockers. A 350 Desmo forged piston was fitted and, although a solid 'racing' points cam was available, we found it best to stick to the standard automatic advance/retard unit to permit easier starting. For short-circuit work we found the best carburettor to be the humble Amal Concentric Mark 1 at 32 mm, but for events such as the Isle of Man, or circuits with long straights, a Dell'Orto

in either 35 or 38 mm size was better. We tried a 42 mm, but found it too big on 350, although helpful on a 450. The larger engine that we used for these experiments was the NCR Dunscombe unit. Its new owner had decided to have it fitted into one of our frames, which we did in early 1973.

In all our bikes at the time we used Lodge spark plugs and Castrol R20 oil, although later converting to a mineral-based Shell/BP lubricant, since by then oil technology had caught up and made a vegetable lubricant unnecessary. To avoid clutch drag we used $3\frac{1}{2}$ pints in the narrow-case motors and 5 pints in the later wide-case engines.

The dry weight of our own finished 350 bike was right down to 220 lb. The only difference between this and the machines that we sold to the customers was that our bike contained a set of works close-ratio gears and was the subject of experiments with modified gear selectors, at last curing an Achilles heel of the Ducati singles in racing – missed gears. I cannot take the credit for this as it was solely the work of my brother Richard, who remained the mechanical man behind all my racing efforts, whether as rider or sponsor.

Towards the end of 1973 we suddenly began to achieve some very worthwhile results. At Silverstone, which had by then reached the importance it holds today as Britain's premier event, Dave Arnold won the 250 Production class on a Mach 1 entered by me. Stuart Morrell, in a one-off ride on our special 350, just missed a great result in the Junior Manx Grand Prix when, after lapping in the mid-90s, faster than any other Ducati single has before or since, he retired towards the end of the race when he looked set to finish in the first ten. This disappointment was caused by a misfire starting on the fourth lap which rapidly increased. Not wanting to risk serious engine damage, he pulled out. As these things often turn out to be, the cause was simple, nothing more than an inlet valve that was not seating properly. This was the result of one of our modifications when we shortened the inlet guide flush with the port. In short-circuit use this had never proved a problem, but the Island is different! Except for Morell's superb try, the 1973 Manx was a poor one for Ducati performances. By then the domination of Yamaha was almost complete, with even the Manx Grand Prix experiencing the trend.

Two other events brought the 1973 season to a close in fine style for us. Dave Arnold and Paddy Reid led the Thruxton 500 from the start almost to the finish, only to strike trouble just before the end. And Mick James made his début on the spine-framed 350 at the final race meeting of the season, held at Snetterton. This inaugural single-cylinder race, organized by Dave Bailey, the far-seeing secretary of the Newmarket club, was to be the forerunner of today's highly popular and much-loved classic racing.

By the early 1970s many owners and enthu-

1973 Silverstone Grand Prix production 250 race victor, Dave Arnold. 250 Mach 1; note non-standard exhaust layout

siasts with single-cylinder racers all had the same problem – Yamaha. So this Snetterton event had drawn a large entry from riders who wanted a chance to compete on equal footing. Many had to be turned down, but the result was to vindicate Dave Bailey's idea and at the same time provide a race that attracted the very best Manx Nortons, Matchless G50s, AJS 7Rs and Aermacchi racers – and of course, Ducatis – from all over Britain.

Mick James was a rider who was local to me and had put up some fine performances on a Weslake-engined machine before almost being forced to retire. His most ardent supporter, Rex Everitt, approached me to see if help could be found. I reasoned (correctly as it turned out) that if a spectator could be that keen, the rider must be something special. After a slow start Mick picked off one bike after another, snatching the lead from Dave Hughes on the Arter Matchless with two laps to go. Starting the last lap with victory in sight, Mick blasted past the pits still ahead of the field, only to throw away the bike, and the race, on someone else's oil patch in sight of the finish. Despite this blow Mick James was full of praise for the machine, in particular for the superb handling of the very light little Ducati.

The appointment in 1974 of Coburn and Hughes by the Ducati factory as their British importer led to vastly increased sales of the roadsters but did no service to those wishing to race the Italian bikes. For a start, it killed off Vic Camp's remaining enthusiasm, and it also meant that to cope with the high influx of additional work and sales of the roadsters I was forced to stop production of our own specials – just when demand was increasing and results were coming in. But most importantly, the factory had installed what were, for such an enthusiasts' marque, importers who had only one consideration – high-pressure, high-volume sales. Racing was something for which even their own employee, racer Doug Lunn, found no help or assistance forthcoming.

Although we could not continue building racers for sale, I decided that somehow time had to be found to allow us to prepare our own machine and continue to sponsor Mick James as our rider during 1974. This resolve was repaid by some excellent results, of which the highlight was probably the 6th place Mick gained at a Snetterton national meeting. This race, held on the full circuit, attracted an entry of 39 Yamahas. The Ducati was the only other machine in the race – a four-stroke-single at that! This event was to prove one of the very last occasions when a Ducati single would achieve a leaderboard placing in open class racing anywhere in the world. Thereafter, victories only came in protected forms of racing, such as single-cylinder or classic events.

But even though Mick James switched to riding our 750SS in production events midway through 1974, and our special 350 was sold, this was not to be the end of the Mick Walker involvement with single-cylinder racing Ducatis. This went on for many years in the form of help to Ian Gittens, first on his standard-framed, wide-case 250 and continuing when the engine was transferred to the very first prototype frame constructed by Hejira in 1976. The Hejira design was one of the very first of the now familiar single-shock frames anywhere in the world.

Elsewhere, with single-cylinder racing still in its infancy at the end of 1975, a Luton rider called John Wittman purchased a Mick Walker-built 350 narrow-case standard-frame racer from a rider named Barry Slipper, who had bought it new some two and a half years earlier. The main attraction of the machine at the time of purchase was the almost unused condition of the whole bike and its massive Grimeca front brake.

For 1976 John Wittman enlisted the help and sponsorship of Peter Coombes, who owned a transport company – part of the deal involved Wittman selling the bike to Coombes. At first the results were few and far between, but the two highlights of the season included 2nd position

John Wittman leading a works endurance Honda (France) during 1976 400 miler at Thruxton before engine blew on his race-kitted 350 Sebring

behind the Triumph of Paul Todd at Lydden Hill and a ride, still on the Ducati, in the Thruxton endurance race. This had by now been shortened to 400 miles, with the rules changed to allow a much wider variety of machinery to compete. Entries ranged from racers based on roadsters, like the Ducati, right through to bikes like the French works endurance racing Honda. After Wittman's stint at Thruxton he handed over to his co-rider for the event, Doug Cash. Cash suffered a major engine blow-up, which forced their retirement – but afterwards it was discovered that the rear subframe had cracked, so perhaps it was lucky that they had pulled out.

At the end of the season, Peter Coombes' support came to an end, with the result that the machine was repurchased. By that time Wittman had obtained Vic Camp's remaining spares and bikes, which included four machines from the racing school. Three of these were ex-pupils' mounts, while the other had been the instructor's. The first three of these were sold off, but the last machine, which had a Sebring-based engine, was kept to complement the ex-Slipper bike. These two were campaigned with 250 or 350 engines until the original bike was sold off during 1978. For 1979 Wittman had the use of at least two bikes and rates this as his best year for results, winning two club championships, the Newmarket and the BMCRC.

Since that superb season he has never quite recaptured the same consistent form, even though some very interesting machines have appeared with him in the saddle, including the ex-Dunscombe NCR 450 Desmo, housed in one of the Walker/Saxon frames. Before passing to him the bike had been sold to Vic Holliday, who at the time, during the mid-seventies, had been a mechanic in the Ducati importer's workshops.

This NCR 450 has recently become the subject of a conversion to 440 cc using an 87 mm Cosworth piston, but retaining the original 75 mm stroke, and is now mounted in a standard frame. But Wittman's most interesting machine is his home-brewed short stroke (called the USS), with a capacity of 344 cc, from a bore of 87 and a stroke of 57·8 mm. The engine of this special was based on a 450 Desmo with a 250 Desmo crankshaft, and an 11:1 Cosworth piston replacing the 440's 10·67:1. This made it impractical to use pump 4-star fuel and Avgas 50 was necessary to prevent piston detonation.

Reports on this machine suggested it to be very smooth between 6 and 10,000 rpm, but so far it has yet to prove itself in racing. Other detail modifications included a 350 wide-case bevel-drive top shaft, with the top of the cylinder barrel planed down by 10 mm. This permitted only 9 fins on the barrel instead of the usual 10. The gearbox was also basically 450, but with a larger mainshaft fixed gear, with a matching reduction on the first gear in the final drive shaft, resulting in an overall higher first gear. A Spanish Mototrans 24 Horas mainshaft second gear, with a matching cog on the final drive shaft, was also fitted. The inlet valve was changed to a 42 mm racing V-twin component, and the conrod was modified to take a 30 mm big end and rebushed from 22 to 20 mm at the small end.

Another modification of a standard 450 motor was carried out in Holland by Bert Bels to a full 500. This consisted of a standard 450 bottom end, together with the rear barrel, piston and cylinder head assembly from a 900SS. Another feature of this bike, which made its first public appearance in 1982, was the modified wide-case Ducati frame, with support tubes running from the rear engine mount to above and behind the cylinder head. The carburettor was a 40 mm Dell-'Orto pumper, again from a 900SS. Bel's bike was called simply the 'Imola 500'.

By 1982 several Ducati-mounted riders had begun to put up good performances at the various classic and vintage racing events staged in Europe and North America. The most popular of these events are those held by the British-based Classic Motorcycle Racing Club at several circuits throughout the summer months.

Typical Manx Grand Prix action. Richard Bool aboard his Mach 1 in the 1977 event

Peter Boast rounds Mere hairpin, Scarborough, 9 May 1982, with his John Smith sponsored 350 (a race-kitted Sebring with Oldani front brake and MP forks)

Typical of the machines from earlier days to be seen at these events was Mick Rodgers' production racing Mach 1, still to be seen in 1982 with its original green livery and underslung exhaust system running down the left of the machine – both features incorporated by the rider almost 20 years before.

1983 heralded, perhaps, a peak of interest and participation in classic events, with the leading Ducati-mounted riders proving to be Anthony Ainslie, Jim Porter and John Wittman. Porter was to be the most successful of these, campaigning his Saxon-Walker – the original Sebring-engined bike ridden by Mick James – to take the Classic Club and Brands Racing Committee championships in the 350 category. In addition he carried off the single-cylinder class in the annual Ducati-only race held at the Classic Race of the Year at Snetterton.

Also that year Wittman's short-stroke 350 USS had its most successful outing so far on 22 October at Brands, where in the important Kennings-sponsored classic race he finished 3rd, ahead of several top riders, and behind two Aermacchis in the 350 class. In the fiercely con-tested 250 category, Anthony Ainslie proved to be the Ducati rider to beat, even though some fine performances were put up by such riders as Peter Byrne and Kevin Bowman. In the 1983 Manx Grand Prix, Ainslie finished 3rd in the Lightweight Classic race, at an average speed of 82·02 mph. Such performances and similar battles continue to ensure without doubt the place of the tough little Bologna singles in racing for many years to come.

11 | Prototypes and frame-ups

Taglioni's range of overhead cam singles proudly flew the Ducati flag for two decades. Just how successful they were can be judged by how few alternative Ducati designs were taken even as far as the prototype stage during its production life span. In fact, the only periods during which the factory experimented with radically different road machines were the short times before and after the dominance of Taglioni's engine.

In the early days, experimental ideas were mainly restricted to those within the abortive co-operation agreement with the Caproni group, and resulted only in a few push-rod designs that did not get beyond the drawing board. The only machines that saw metal were a few forgotten prototypes using the Cucciolo engine.

It was not until way past the proper time for a suitable replacement for the design that had carried the factory's fortunes for so long that the Bologna plant actually set about building a successor. The first attempt appeared at the 1975 Milan Show, virtually hidden behind various of the ill-fated 350 and 500 parallel twins. This was not even a four-stroke, but a road-going adaptation of the recently announced six-speed Regolarita enduro bike. Although only a 125 was shown, the original plan offered a complete range of machines – enduro, motocross and roadsters – with engines spanning the full capacity classes from 125 to 400 cc.

The roadster was in what can best be described as the 'US Custom' style. At its heart was

Ducati showed this 125 Custom at the 1975 Milan Show, powered by an engine based on the Regolarita

a detuned version of the enduro engine, mounted in a twin cradle backbone frame. There were no frame tubes running down from the steering head to the front of the crankcase or indeed any tubes running under the engine at all – so the motor was supported entirely from its rear and top mountings. Paioli 31·5 mm front forks were fitted, and strangely, for a machine of just 125 cc, its cast alloy wheels carried triple disc brakes with Scarab calipers. The wheels and tyres themselves were an odd size, although in keeping with the American style, at 3·60 × 18 front and a massive 5·20 × 16 rear. All in all, the large-diameter

frame tubes and the triple discs confirmed that the machine was conceived with the idea of using a lot more power than was available from just 125 cc.

Handlebars from the 250/450 Scrambler were used, and the machine also carried a Veglia speedo and CEV lighting. The exhaust system swept back over the top of the cylinder head, between the twin frame tubes, back under the tank and seat, finally to exit on the left of the machine aft of the side panel. Although the exhaust system had the black finish of the Regolarita, the engine had polished alloy castings, with the massively finned radial head and cylinder barrel left unpainted as well. Other minor detail fittings included a side stand (no centre stand was provided), pillion footrests and a chrome-plated headlamp shell.

First attempt at a replacement 4-stroke single. This chain driven ohc engine, housed here in a modified 350 Sport Desmo chassis, appeared briefly in early 1977

Unlike the Regolarita (and later Six Days) the roadster two-stroke 'Custom' and a pure motocross version never went beyond the prototype stage. The next idea was a four-stroke single using parts from the the then-current parallel twin. This design featured a chain-driven sohc and could, like its twin cylinder brothers, be produced in either valve spring or Desmo form. A 30 mm Dell'Orto PHF carburettor from a 500 Sport Desmo was fitted and the gearbox is thought to have been a six-speeder. Although a kickstart was used on the sole prototype, an electric start would probably have been provided on a production version. This 350 cc engine, housed in a suitably modified 500 Sport Desmo chassis, never progressed further than factory 'hack', and was finally abandoned in the summer of 1977 in the light of the expected production of a new single design, loosely based on the Pantah V-twin, using a toothed belt in place of the cam chain.

Although most people assume that the Pantah engine concept is simply a V-twin design, its origins are somewhat different. These were evident at the Milan Show in November 1977, where, beside the 500 cc V-twin Pantah prototype, samples of a new 350 single also appeared for the first (and only) time. The two machines shown

were the Utah, a trail bike, and the Rollah, a conventional roadster. Both used identical engines based on the rear cylinder and numerous other parts of the 500SL Pantah. The then current idea was to develop a range of modular engines using as many interchangeable parts as possible, with the toothed belt drive to the overhead camshaft as a common theme. The 350 could also have been produced as a 250, so that together with the Pantah twin Ducati could offer a complete range of 250, 350, 500, 600, and 750 cc machines – and minimize their spares complications at the same time.

In the form in which the Rollah and Utah were shown in Milan the prototypes had identical engine units, but the cycle parts were quite different. The more conventional Rollah employed a frame not unlike that of the Ducati singles built towards the end of 1974. The Utah was completely different, with a full double cradle frame, cantilever suspension and a pair of 35 mm long-travel Marzocchi leading axle front forks. Both had cast alloy wheels; the Rollah used Grimeca-made wheels single front-wheel disc brake and rear drum; the Utah used Campagnolo wheels

At Milan in November 1977 Ducati exhibited a couple of 350 singles, the Utah trail (nearest camera) and Rollah roadster, these with a prototype Pantah are pictured behind. All used a 'modular' principle for the engine design

Billy Nelson's Doncaster Yamaha. A 125 Grand Prix
Ducati, housing a Yamaha TD1 engine

and followed the fashion of the 1975 Custom
prototype with triple Scarab discs. The appearance of the Rollah suggested the same mould
as the original Darmah and Sport Desmo parallel
twins – even to the extent of using a Darmah
seat and Sport Desmo fuel tank – but of the two
machines the Utah looked the most stylish and

purposeful, although the cast wheels and triple
discs were a strange choice for a serious off-road
iron.

Unlike the earlier singles, the gearchange followed the modern trend with the pedal on the
left, while the kickstart was fitted on the right.
The gearbox itself contained a five-speed cluster,
and primary drive was by gear. The electrics were
12-volt, and the Rollah alone had an electric
starter. Both engines used electronic ignition.
Camshaft-driven rev counters were fitted.

The Utah's engine was finished in black, while
the Rollah's was left unpainted. The Gilnisil-
coated cylinder barrels carried a forged 3-ring
piston of 9·5:1 in a bore and stroke of
83 × 64 mm, giving a capacity of 346 cc. The barrel and head were inclined foward 10 degrees
and the sohc desmodromic valve gear was
driven by a toothed belt identical to one of those
used on the Pantah. Taglioni had personal experience of the toothed belt because it had been
tried in the early 1970s works 500 V-twin racer
when in its four-valve head form. Following Pantah lines, the crankshaft was a one-piece cast-
iron component with a forged conrod using split

Rollah (with provision for electric starter motor)
crankcase; compare this with a Pantah V-twin to realize
the modular family likeness

Another interesting special was John Kirkby's 250 Alpha
Centuri two-stroke twin powered ex-Tom Phillips framed
Mach 1, with which the Lincolnshire rider consistently
beat the official Alpha team members during 1968

white-metal Vandervell bearing shells. Carburation was by 30 mm Dell'Orto pumper.

The power of this package was some 24 bhp at the rear wheel, but the performance of both bikes would have been unlikely to have matched that of the older, lighter, bevel-drive singles, for the apparent refinement had added considerable weight. However, it is also unlikely that this was a factor leading to the shelving of the designs immediately after the show. Indeed, I am sure that had the factory not been re-organized by its government-delegated administrators (within the state-owned VM group of companies), the Rollah and Utah singles would have appeared as planned – at around the same time as the first production 500SL Pantah, in 1979. That this did not occur was due to one simple reason, the severe financial drain that the mistakes of the mid-seventies had inflicted on Ducati Meccanica SpA.

Unfortunately, because of this the motorcycle division had been rapidly overtaken in both production capacity and earning power by the other branch of the company which made diesel industrial engines. By 1979, the motorcycle side constituted less than 30 per cent of the com-

Mick James at Cadwell Park, April 1974, in race winning form aboard the 350 Walker/Saxon prototype

pany's turnover, and far less in terms of the profits it generated. The hard truth was that at the time the less charismatic sections of Ducati were effectively keeping the famous name alive.

This meant that however good their plans, or however good their current production, the motorcycle division management had no chance when it came to justifying their case to the new board. The consequence was the end of the road for the modular belt-drive Rollah and Utah – and the end of the single-cylinder motorcycle at Ducati.

But even if the accountants and financial advisors in Rome could not appreciate the virtues of a Ducati with only one cylinder, there were those outside their range of influence who could – and still do – with the result that many Ducati singles have appeared in other makers' frames, and many other makers' engines have been transplanted into Ducati chassis. Such hybrids have occurred in both road and competition form although the Ducati engine has seldom worked in other chassis – mostly the work of the enthusiastic amateur, but some more official, even to the extent of the Swiss

Frame and engine installation details of the original 350 Walker/Saxon spine frame racer, built in 1972. It still survives today

police specifying 350 Ducati Mark 3 engine units for their Condor patrol motorcycles just before that unit went out of production.

But the most popular part of Ducati singles for most racing enthusiasts was the chassis. Even since the late 1950s riders have appreciated the race-bred qualities of Ducati handling, in much the same way as earlier enthusiasts claimed Norton as their favourite. Two of the most popular engines for insertion into Ducati tubes were the 490 cc unit construction Triumph twin, for road use, and the 246 cc Yamaha twin, for racing.

The roadster Ducati special almost certainly first appeared in 1965, when an Englishman from Reading had the idea of mounting a unit-construction Triumph T100A into his 200 Elite frame. This frame was lying dormant in his garden shed due to the lack of funds to repair its damaged engine. The owner of the resulting hybrid, one Michael Snaith, started a fashion, which, although it never nearly approached the vast popularity of the Triton (Triumph engine,

The same machine, now in road trim won the 'best special' at the British Ducati Owners' Club rally in September 1984

Norton frame), became well established with a name of its own – the Tricati.

In the racing world, the arrival of the twin-cylinder Yamaha TD1 – which had plenty of power, but suspect handling – caused many riders to consider another set of cycle parts. One of the first actually do do what so many had threatened was the Lincolnshire ace Derek Chatterton. At the time he found his Yamaha was not lacking speed, but that it possessed handling vices, which meant that using its power was quite another matter. Chatterton's first serious racing mount had been a 125 Ducati Grand Prix, on which he had learned how to win races before the little bike had become eclipsed by more modern two-strokes. Remembering how well it had handled, Chatterton wondered if a combination of the Yamaha's speed and the Ducati's handling would not make an ideal challenger in the 250 racing class. He was proven right; the Chat Yamaha, unbeatable at his local Cadwell Park circuit, proved competitive even at international level.

Chatterton soon proved just how successful the combination was. Another appeared, this

One of the world's first monoshock frames. Built by Hejira, it housed a wide case 250 Mark 3. Frame designer Derek Chittenden (left) and rider Ian Gittens at Snetterton, 1975

time ridden by Billie Nelson and called the Doncaster Yamaha, after Nelson's sponsor, Peter Doncaster. Both Chatterton's and Nelson's machines had 125 Grand Prix frames, but a third successful machine was one that used the ex-Ken Kavanagh 220 cc Duke as a basis. Barry Davis had purchased this for £120 during the winter of 1964/65, winning a number of races on it as a standard Ducati the following season. At the end of 1965, however, it was found that the Ducati was in need of several unobtainable engine parts, and taking note of the successes of Nelson and Chatterton with their Ducati Yamahas, Davis decided to commission frame manufacturer Rob North to carry out a similar conversion. This was undertaken by first cutting out the front downtube and the rear engine mounting plates. New plates were then welded in and two new tubes inserted to cradle the engine. These ran from in front of the swinging-arm, under the engine and up to the steering head. The resulting position of the Yamaha power unit was quite low and well forward, but the rest of the cycle parts were left largely unaltered.

All the work was carried out in the spring of 1967, and Davis had his first outing on the Ducati-Yamaha at Mallory Park, where he found that it felt good right from the start. His biggest problem was the unreliable TD1B engine and, after making a few enquiries, he decided to convert the existing power unit to the later TD1C specification. There proved to be a tremendous difference between the two, and soon, with both more power and better than average handling, he was competitive again.

After finishing a lowly 36th in the 1967 Manx Grand Prix, 1968 was completely different, with 6th spot at 84·39 mph. The following year, however, the little special flew round even quicker – although its average speed of 85·02 mph was only good enough for 10th place. During the 1968, 1969 and 1970 seasons' racing, Barry campaigned the Ducati-Yamaha in the British

Ian Gittens rushes through Union Mills during practice for the 1977 Lightweight Manx Grand Prix on the Hejira Ducati

internationals, experiencing racing in the company of such as Mike Hailwood, Ralph Bryans (on Honda sixes), Phil Read, Bill Ivy (on Yamaha fours), and Giacomo Agostini (on the MV). But in late 1969, during a Mallory Park meet, a high-speed crash halfway round Gerrards Bend resulted in a bent frame. While this did not affect the Ducati's handling for short-circuit events, it showed up badly in the Manx Grand Prix of 1970, held in very windy conditions. This effectively finished the career of the Ducati-Yamaha as a racer, although Barry Davis still has the machine and is currently rebuilding it back into its original form with the 220 cc double-knocker Ducati engine.

Another two-stroke twin-Ducati formula was a unique machine used by John Kirkby, a rider of no mean ability. Kirkby had notched up a series of excellent results during 1966/67, first on a standard Camp Mach 1, and later in 1967 on Tom Phillips's 1966 Camp racer. This bike featured an Oldani front stopper and heavily modified engine as described in the previous chapter.

At the beginning of 1968 Kirkby and his brother purchased the only private disc valve racing engine to be sold by Alpha Bearings of Dudley. Called the Centuri this engine showed great potential, but like many before it was never fully developed, with the final result that the entire stock of around 15 production engines were sold for scrap when American influence and money changed the direction of the parent company later in 1968.

Before this, Kirkby's Alpha/Ducati had proven more successful than the 'works' Alphas ridden by Browning and Wolfingdale. Like most Ducati-framed specials using British engines, the

NCR450 desmo power, Walker/Spondon chassis, John Wittman at Snetterton, May 1981

Mach 1's swinging-arm had to be reversed as the drive from the engine was on the opposite side. Two additional frame support tubes were welded from the front downtube to the rear loop to form a full cradle. In a successful attempt to retain the full road-holding qualities, the crankshaft on the Alpha engine was placed in an identical position to the Ducati's, so the centre of weight distribution remained the same; this was virtually achieved because the combined weight of the Centuri engine and five-speed Albion gearbox equalled that of the Ducati unit. The most serious problem was that of keeping the Albion box in line with the engine. This in turn created difficulty in maintaining the oil level in the primary crankcase, but as the works units suffered the same problem, it was a design fault rather than something which the different frame had shown up. John Kirkby's brother Roy worked long and hard on the project, completing it within a week, so that his brother could make his début on the new bike at a club meeting at nearby Cadwell Park. He was rewarded when the Alpha/Ducati screamed round to record two wins, beating Bob Heath riding a DMW in the first race, even though no rev counter was fitted, and the bike was hopelessly over-geared.

These first victories were followed by numerous wins and top places throughout the season against top riders of the day, including Derek Chatterton, Stan Woods and Steve Machin. Finally the season came to a dismal end with a series of piston problems, which caused several engine blow-ups when piston debris dropped into the crankcase, breaking the bottom end, including the disc valve. The result was that Alpha took back the engine after refusing to sell the Kirkby team more spares. A sad end to what in John Kirkby's words 'could have been a world beater'.

12 | Ducati off-road

Even though Ducati's name is now almost universally associated with road racing the Ducati single-cylinder engine has, in fact, been used in almost every other branch of the sport – motocross, trials, sprinting, grass track and even speedway! And even more surprisingly the initial sport participation was in an area far removed from their later road-racing triumphs, trials and record-breaking attempts.

Ducati were first attracted to both by the flamboyant, cigar-smoking veteran rider Ugo Tamarozzi. Besides breaking a large number of 50 cc world speed records on his near-standard Cucciolo-powered special during 1951 and 1952, Tamarozzi also represented both Ducati and his country in the 1951 International Six Days Trial. That year's ISDT was held in Italy, so Tamarozzi's bronze medal performance, and clean sheets for five out of the six days, was a particularly sweet victory.

In the days before Ing. Fabio Taglioni arrived and turned the factory's interests towards road racing, Ducati followed up the 1951 ISDT with a continued participation in similar off-road events. Pushrod-engined Ducatis of up to 100 cc were entered in both scrambles (motocross) events and long-distance trials. This even included a trip to the 1954 ISDT, which took place in Wales. In this event Ducati riders Alberto Farne and Giovanni Malaguti both took silver medals.

The pushrod engines of 48, 65 and 98 cc gave

sterling service in these off-road events, although the design was not suited to the rigours of road racing. A new engine was decreed necessary, and once the factory had developed their road-racing design and moved towards this sport, there was little further official interest in following up the early success in off-road competition. Except for the roadster-based Motocross and Scrambler models, and a brief flirtation with the ISDT in the early 1970s, it was usually left to various concessionaires, dealers and enthusiasts to produce their own versions of the Ducati dirt bike.

Ducati continued to catalogue 'off-road' models, but in truth these were in most cases merely styling exercises based on stock road-sters, not true competition machines. Neverthe-less, these machines continued to keep the spirit of competition alive, and in some cases became

potent tools in the hands of those who developed them.

The first off-road model that Ducati introdu-ced was in fact much closer to serious competi-tion than their later designs became. The 175 Motocross of 1958 was indeed what its name implied. It had a Taglioni-conceived engine, which had been his first roadster design, and was itself closely based on the 100 Gran Sport racer. All these engines shared a bevel-driven overhead cam in place of the earlier pushrod valve gear, but unlike the successful 175 Sport, the Motocross engine only survived for one year, before making way for the 200 cc version in the 1959 season.

Again, like the smaller bike, the engine was simply a suitably tuned production unit of 203·783 cc. However, both units were housed in similar special frames and had several non-stock parts, such as conical brake hubs, described in detail in Chapter 8. In Britain, at least one of the Ducati motocross machines was in competition use in 1959, ridden by Terry Cheshire. However, he found the bike too heavy to pose a serious

American picture of 350 desmo short track racer, year 1970

challenge to the then-dominant British two-strokes, which led the class.

Something of more significance to success and to sales was taking place on the other side of the Atlantic, where the Berliner brothers, Mike and Joe, had become Ducati's importer for the USA. Although the high-revving ohc single was not really suited to the often heavy-going of a British scrambles track, just the reverse was true for American Hare and Hounds scrambles, desert racing and flat-track events.

As soon as the new 250 line was introduced, in early 1961, the Berliners quickly contacted Ducati with an urgent request for a scrambles version. The outcome was the 250 Scrambler. The 250 engine was, like the 175 and 200, simply a reworked standard production unit, with a different camshaft, larger 27 mm SS1 carburettor, high-compression piston, and a flywheel

magneto-based QD competition lighting set. Other changes were a racing straight-through, one-piece exhaust pipe (not a megaphone), a large air filter, abbreviated chainguard and a sump guard. Unfortunately, unlike the earlier smaller motocross models, the brakes and frame were stock and these were to prove a serious weakness to the machine's competition potential. In particular, the brakes were far too large and cumbersome for use in off-road anger.

When delivered, the 250 Scrambler had a large number of 'extra' items supplied. Among these were a full set of control cables, valve adjustment caps, a pair of rigid frame units to

One day trials bike built from a 160 Monza Junior by Vic Camp's mechanic Bert Furness in 1967

replace the standard rear shocks for flat-track events, a tacho drive unit and cover, and three additional rear sprockets (45, 50 and 60 tooth), plus an extra 16 tooth gearbox sprocket. Gearing as shipped by the factory was 55 tooth rear and 14 tooth gearbox.

When tested by *Cycle World* magazine in August 1962, the 250's best one-way speed was 82 mph. But from this time, right through until it ceased production at the end of 1974 (going wide case from 1968 onwards), the 250 Scrambler became less and less of a dirt bike, as did the later 350 and 450 versions.

The only exceptions to this pattern were two developments of the 450, which showed the promise of becoming *real* dirt bikes. The first of these was only a prototype constructed for Berliner by Ducati in 1969. This had a frame with twin tubes running down from the cylinder head and then veering backwards on either side at the base of the cylinder barrel. The high-level open exhaust pipe ran down the left of the bike, and conical brake hubs cast in magnesium supported a 4·00 × 18 rear and 3·00 × 21 front tyre. Marzocchi 35 mm long-travel motocross forks and an oil radiator completed the specifications.

Although this model remained purely a prototype, another 450 motocross design did make it to the Ducati production line. This was the 450R/T, an extremely purposeful off-roader intended for full-blooded racing. As well as the Desmo engine it had a special frame with Marzocchi forks, plastic tank, mudguards and

A 1968 wide case 350 Scrambler converted into a pukka motocrosser

DESMO DUCATI
R/T 450

The motorcycle to be reckoned with.

Thrash it through the rough. Sweep it through the bends. The new Desmo Ducati R/T 450 is designed for action. With all the true sports features for any type of terrain, on or off the road.

A unique, desmodromic engine for special torque with a minimum rpm range to assure even power at any speed for smoother performance and longer engine life.

A smooth, unit construction, five-speed gearbox for sure shifting; special, highly-durable open cradle frame; heavy duty front fork allowing seven inches of travel; rugged swing arm rear with dampers adjustable for both load and degree of inclination.

Plus a heavy-duty rear chain and effective chain

guide with cam-type adjuster; spring-loaded, folding footpegs; durable skid plate; tuned exhaust; steering damper; reinforced motocross handlebars; 9.5 inch clearance; sports fenders; chrome headlight and brackets and taillight assembly for instant connection or detachment; and much, much more.

See the new Desmo R/T 450 at your nearest dealer today. One test ride will convince you. It's the motorcycle to be reckoned with.

DUCATI
The thoroughbred of motorcycles

BERLINER MOTOR CORP./Hasbrouck Heights, N.J. 07604/Sole U.S. Distributor

side panels, together with all the usual dirt bike trimmings, described in more detail in Chapter 6. From this model came the T/S, which was actually produced in two versions, one as a pukka Six Day enduro bike, the other as a street-legal machine complete with a stock, low-level Silentium silencer for the Italian home market.

For the 1971 International Six Day Trial, held in the Isle of Man, seven Italian riders rode Ducatis. Four aboard 450s, and three aboard 350s. All seven were actually 450T/S enduro machines with enduro equipment that consisted of a lighting set, centre stand, unbraced handle-

Left **Berliner advertisement of 1971 showing the 450R/T, Ducati's most serious four-stroke dirt bike**

Below **The 450 desmo which Eric Cheney built using one of his motocross frames in 1970**

bars and twin silencers branching from a single high-level exhaust pipe, although three had been fitted with 350 engines. Records of the event show that six of the Ducati riders were official members of the Italian Trophy team, while the seventh, the last of the 450 riders, was P. L. Laurenti, representing the manufacturer's team. The other 450 riders were A. Tarocchi, F. Dallara, and E. Dossena, while R. Consonni, F. Vegani and C. Rinaldi rode the 350 machines.

Although the T/S was reliable, it proved unequal to the challenge from machines of the calibre of the purpose-built Czechoslovakian Jawas, then the dominant Six Day bike. And the next time a Ducati was to be seen in the ISDT was some four years later, when ex BSA-rider Pat Slinn (then working for the British Ducati importers Coburn & Hughes) rode one of the new six-speed, two-stroke Regolarita models in the 1975 event, again held in the Isle of Man. This was not

1971 saw the ISDT held in the Isle of Man, seven Italian riders rode Ducatis, four on 450s, three aboad 350s; all looked like this

The 450R/T was for real, with one-off chassis and desmo power

to be a happy ride, however, because he was forced out of the competition with big end failure. That year he also rode in the Welsh Two Day Trial, where a finish was gained, albeit with only three gears left in the box. More successful was a finish in the Isca event held in mid-Wales, a 4th in class at the Beacons Enduro, and Best Guest Expert at the British Army championships in Pirbright, Surrey.

Apart from the factory's own machinery for use in competition, many enthusiasts picked Ducati power for their homebrewed efforts. As in the world of road racing, this enthusiastic participation ensured that Ducati's name stayed at the forefront, even in events that were not officially supported by the factory.

One such private effort secured Ducati's name in the statute books, when the British father and son team of Fred and Jim Wells was successful in capturing a number of world speed records in the 175 cc class. Fred Wells had previously held the world record with a Triumph

Italian Italo Forni campaigned this 125 Six Days in the 1977 Italian enduro championships, but although competitive, the gearbox was troublesome

The 1975 125 Regolarita engine, forerunner of the Six Days

Tiger Cub engine mounted in a modified Capriolo chassis. For 1968/69 he picked Ducati power for the bikes with which he was to contest the 250/350 classes, and Jim Wells was to take on the 175. Although the Well's Ducatis still retained the Capriolo front forks and wheel hubs, the frames were home made. And while the engines were all basically standard roadster units, the compression ratio was upped to run them on a 25/30 ratio of nitro. The Well's Ducatis only ever used narrow-case engines fitted with higher-lift camshafts and coil valve springs, Wal Phillips fuel injectors and BTH magneto ignition.

Recalling Ducati's early record-breaking victories of the 1950s, the father and son team captured all the existing records in the 175 cc class during 1968/69, although success in the larger-capacity groups eluded them. And, sadly, this was to be the final attempt to take a world speed record with the Ducati single engine.

Another was the limited use of both narrow- and wide-case ohc singles in American flat-track events throughout the 1960s, culminating with machines such as Sydney Tunstall's 350 Desmo in 1970.

In default of really suitable stock machines from Ducati, trials and motocross enthusiasts built up their own. Among countless of these privateer efforts three British Ducati single conversions are particularly outstanding. The first of these was the well-known trials rider Peter Gaunt's effort with a 340 Sebring-based motor housed in a frame of his own design. For a couple of seasons he used the Ducati engine, which was

left standard with the exception of substituting the 60-watt alternator with the heavier brass flywheel magneto from a 156 cc Monza Junior, so that no battery was required. The Scottish Six Days was Peter Gaunt's main event, but he also used the Ducati in many one-day trials.

A second successful conversion was of a 160 Monza Junior, which was built into a really purposeful one-day trials mount by Bert Furness, then mechanic to Vic Camp. The machine was based on the standard 156 cc engine and carb, housed in an original frame and retaining the standard forks, rear suspension units and brake hubs. However, the forks had their shrouds and lamp brackets removed, with rubber gaiters installed instead. The 16 in. wheel rims were replaced by more suitable 19 in. front and 18 in. rear, both shod with Dunlop Universal Trials tyres.

All-up weight was reduced by fitting a fibreglass tank and trials saddle, plus lightweight

A purposeful looking bike, a 125 Six Days enduro outside the factory in early 1977

alloy guards. The standard air filter box was retained, but this was cut in half to leave just the actual filter section. The rear frame tube was bent to allow the larger and wider rear wheel and tyre to clear, and a 250 swinging-arm was fitted. The rider's footrests went where the original pillion ones were mounted, with the kick-start lever curving outwards to clear the folding nearside footrest. Completing the transformation were a pair of trials handlebars and a high-level exhaust system with Triumph Trials Cub silencer.

The third machine was a full-blooded Cheney motocross chassis with a 450 Desmo power unit. This was built in 1970, in a tie-up between Eric Cheney and Vic Camp. Cheney had by that time become a highly respected figure in motocross with his Cheney-framed BSA machines ridden by Jerry Scott, amongst others. Originally the Cheney machines used Gold Star engines, and later went on to the unit-construction BSA, and it would be no exaggeration to say that these (apart from the BSA factory efforts) were the most successful frames ever to house the BSA engines until CCM arrived.

Cheney's Ducati showed similar promise, but the project never passed beyond the development stage. Vic Camp lost interest and went

back to concentrating his efforts on his original love, road racing, and a new venture in grass-tracking. This was a shame, because the Cheney Ducati, with its dry weight of only 222 lb and plans to market replicas in Britain and the USA, had the promise to help brighten an increasingly two-stroke dominated motocross scene.

The Cheney Ducati frame had no under-loop as such, but used massive $1\frac{3}{4}$ in. diameter top and front downtubes. Duplex 1 in. seat tubes extended downwards and rearwards from the back of the top tube to meet the rear subframe and form the swinging-arm mounting. A traditional Cheney hallmark was the nickel-plated finish given to the whole frame. A Cheney telescopic front fork, Electron wheel hubs and a light alloy $1\frac{1}{2}$-gallon fuel tank, mudguards and side panels were also included in the specification.

Although this machine went no further, Camp's grass-track efforts were just as interesting. At the time he turned his attention to the sport it was dominated by the ancient JAP motors in the 350 and 500 classes, and the BSA C15 in the 250. On paper the Ducati engines seemed admirably capable of taking on both. Two of the first riders to try the Italian singles were Denny Barber and the British champion Brian Maxted. Both quickly achieved success, although the Ducati engine could not make full use of dope fuel, which had allowed the JAP and BSA engines to run on a compression ratio as high as 15:1! All the way through the Ducati engine's grass-track career the problems of misfiring at high rpm were never successfully cured, despite a relatively low compression ratio of around 10:1 (for use with alcohol). Reverting back to petrol meant that the motors just did not give sufficient power.

Both Barber and Maxted produced their own frames, called the Barber and the Maxmade, respectively. Another frame kit soon appeared when Alf Hagon obtained a 250 Ducati engine to enable him to market his own Hagon-Ducati as a complete bike, less engine and carburettor.

Ducati developed a motocrosser from the 125 Six Days; here's the first prototype

1972 was to be the most successful season for Ducatis on the grass, with a full-blown assault on the British ACU Grass Track Championships. By June of that year Camp's original two riders had been joined by Chris Rodwell, Richard Moore, Julian Wigg and Graham Hurry. Hurry was the last of Camp's signings, making his début on a 350 narrow-case Sebring-based machine. The Ducati powered him to victory at the fourth British Championship qualifying round, held on 4 June in Folkestone.

Although it was not a success, the 450 was tried in the same year by Richard Moore. The same engine was also put into a Hagon speedway frame and entered at the Hackney Wick Speedway Stadium in East London. This attempt was another failure, although as a publicity stunt Camp managed to enlist the services of road racer Derek Minter to do a demonstration lap during the interval at a British League match staged at the track.

Vic Camp's was not the only concern to be experimenting with the Ducati singles' grass track potential. Mick Walker Motorcycles built several Hagon-framed grass-track machines (all 250s) and sponsored the leading Northern rider, Brian Havelock, on his machine using a 250 Ducati Mach 1-based engine.

After all this time the factory proved they had not lost all interest in sport outside road racing, for 1977 saw a surprising new launch, which was to be their last serious off-road attempt. This was the 125 Six Days, an improved version of the 125 Regolarita that Pat Slinn had campaigned in 1975. For this attack on enduro honours, Ducati signed an Italian rider, Italo Forni. With the engine power upped to 25 bhp at 10,250 rpm (at the crankshaft, 19·5 bhp at the rear wheel), enough was available to take on the very best any other factory could put up against it in Italian events. Unfortunately, if the engine was up to the job the gearbox was not, and this fickle unit now began to complain at the additional load put on it. As a result there were more retirements

Factory test rider poses with the final layout for the 125 motocross project, but a change of policy in 1978 killed it off

than finishes, even though Forni was always up near the front when the gearbox let him down. Finally, continuing poor sales of the production version forced Ducati to terminate their support for the rider and no fresh agreement was signed for 1978.

In parallel, at least two complete motocross prototypes were built, clearly based on the same piston port, six-speed power unit. These, too, did not meet any better fate than their enduro brothers, even though the power produced was impressive.

Prompted no doubt by Mike Hailwood's TT victory and the ensuing publicity, compared to the poor return from their participation in the off-road sector, this period marked a new revival of Ducati's interest in road racing. It also caused the final curtain to be drawn over their interest and enthusiasm in anything off-road. And with the end of the Bologna-produced singles, there were to be no more enthusiastic amateur specials.

Appendix

1 Specifications

Bologna singles

Model	60 Sport	65TS	98N	98T
Year from	**1950**	**1952**	**1952**	**1952**
Year to	**1951**	**1958**	**1958**	**1958**
Bore (mm)	42	44	49	49
Stroke (mm)	43	43	52	52
Capacity (cc)	59·57	65·38	98·058	98·058
Compression ratio (to 1)	8	8	8	8
Valve type	ohv	ohv	ohv	ohv
bhp	2·25	2·5	5·8	5·8
@ rpm	5000	5500	7500	7500
Oil system	wet sump	wet sump	wet sump	wet sump
Inlet opens BTDC			30	30
Inlet closes ABDC			69	69
Exhaust opens BBDC			69	69
Exhaust closes ATDC			30	30
Tappets, inlet (mm)	0·03	0·03	0·03	0·03
Tappets, exhaust (mm)	0·03	0·03	0·03	0·03
Ignition timing fully advanced			42	42
Primary drive gearing			3·454	3·454
Final drive gearing			2·706	2·706
Box gearing: 4th			1	1
Box gearing: 3rd			1·365	1·365
Box gearing: 2nd			1·85	1·85
Box gearing: 1st			2·69	2·69
No. gears	3	3	4	4
Front tyre	2·00 × 18		2·75 × 17	2·75 × 17
Rear tyre	2·00 × 18		2·75 × 17	2·75 × 17
Front suspension	teles	teles	teles	teles
Rear suspension	cantilever **1**	s/a	s/a	s/a
Ignition system	flywheel mag	flywheel mag	flywheel mag	flywheel mag
Wheelbase (mm)			1245	1245
Seat height (mm)			762	762
Length (mm)			1890	1890
Dry weight (kg)	46	54	88	88

1 Later version had a different frame with swinging arm suspension

Model	Cruiser	65T	65TL	98TL
Year from	**1952**	**1953**	**1953**	**1953**
Year to	**1953**	**1958**	**1958**	**1958**
Bore (mm)		44	44	49
Stroke (mm)		43	43	52
Capacity (cc)	175	65·38	65.38	98·058

Compression ratio (to 1)	8	8	8	8
Valve type	ohv	ohv	ohv	ohv
bhp	7·5	2·5	2·5	5·8
@ rpm		5500	5500	7500
Oil system	wet sump	wet sump	wet sump	wet sump
Inlet opens BTDC				30
Inlet closes ABDC				69
Exhaust opens BBDC				69
Exhaust closes ATDC				30
Tappets, inlet (mm)		0·03	0·03	0·03
Tappets, exhaust (mm)		0·03	0·03	0·03
Ignition timing fully advanced				42
Primary drive gearing				3·454
Final drive gearing				2·706
Box gearing: 4th				1
Box gearing: 3rd				1·365
Box gearing: 2nd				1·85
Box gearing: 1st				2·69
No. gears	automatic with torque converter	3	3	4
Front tyre				2·50 × 17
Rear tyre				2·75 × 17
Front suspension	teles	teles	teles	teles
Rear suspension	s/a with one sus. unit	s/a	s/a	s/a
Ignition system	electric start	flywheel mag	flywheel mag	flywheel mag
Dry weight (kg)		59	59	89
Battery	12v			

Model	**98S**	**98 Super Sport**	**55E**	**55R**
Year from	**1953**	**1954**	**1955**	**1955**
Year to	**1958**	**1955**	**1957**	**1957**
Bore (mm)	49	49	39	39
Stroke (mm)	52	52	40	40
Capacity (cc)	98·058	98·058	47.78	47.78
Compression ratio (to 1)	9	10	6·7	6·7
Valve type	ohv	ohv	ohv	ohv
bhp	6·5	7·5	1·35	1·35
@ rpm	7800	8000	5500	5500
Oil system	wet sump	wet sump	wet sump	wet sump
Tappets, inlet (mm)	0·04	0·06	0·15	0·15
Tappets, exhaust (mm)	0·06	0·08	0·25	0·25
Ignition timing fully advanced	42	44		
No. gears	4	4	2	2
Front tyre	2·50 × 17	2·50 × 17	2·00 × 18	2·00 × 18
Rear tyre	2·75 × 17	2·75 × 17	2·00 × 18	2·00 × 18
Front suspension	teles	teles	leading link	leading link

Rear suspension	s/a	s/a	s/a	s/a
Wheelbase (mm)			1092	1092
Seat height (mm)			648	648
Length (mm)			1890	1890
Dry weight (kg)	81	79	44	44
Generator/output			6v/12w	6v/12w
Battery			none	none

Model	**55M**	**125T**	**125TV**	**85N 1**
Year from	**1955**	**1956**	**1956**	**1958**
Year to	**1957**	**1960**	**1958**	**1960**
Bore (mm)	39	55·2	55·2	45·5
Stroke (mm)	40	52	52	52
Capacity (cc)	47.78	124·443	124·443	84.55
Compression ratio (to 1)	6·7	8	8	8
Valve type	ohv	ohv	ohv	ohv
bhp	1·35	7	7	5·5
@ rpm	5500	6500	6500	7200
Oil system	wet sump	wet sump	wet sump	wet sump
Tappets, inlet (mm)	0·15	0·04	0·04	0·03
Tappets, exhaust (mm)	0·25	0·06	0·06	0·03
No. gears	2	4	4	4
Front tyre	2·00 × 18	2·50 × 17	2·50 × 17	2·50 × 17
Rear tyre	2·00 × 18	2·75 × 17	2·75 × 17	2·75 × 17
Front suspension	leading link	teles	teles	teles
Rear suspension	s/a	s/a	s/a	s/a
Length (mm)	1890			
Dry weight (kg)	44	93	94	79
Generator/output	6v/12w			
Battery	none			

1 85 also produced in Sport version during same period, but with 9:1 comp. ratio and 1 more bhp

Model	**85 Bronco 1**	**98TS**	**175S**	**175T**
Year	**1960**	**1958**	**1957**	**1957**
Year to	**1963**	**1960**		
Bore (mm)	45·5	49	62	62
Stroke (mm)	52	52	57·8	57·8
Capacity (cc)	84.55	98.058	174·5	174·5
Compression ratio (to 1)	9	8	8	7
Valve type	ohv	ohv	ohv	ohv
bhp	6·5	5·8	14	11
@ rpm	7500	7500	8000	7500
Oil system	wet sump	wet sump	wet sump	wet sump
Inlet opens BTDC			44	35
Inlet closes ABDC			73	65
Exhaust opens BBDC			73	65
Exhaust closes			38	35

Tappets, inlet (mm)	0·04	0·03	0·06	0·05
Tappets, exhaust (mm)	0·06	0·03	0·08	0·07
Primary drive gearing			2·522	2·522
Final drive gearing			2·875	3·066
Box gearing: 4th			0·97	0·97
Box gearing: 3rd			1·18	1·18
Box gearing: 2nd			1·65	1·65
Box gearing: 1st			2·75	2·75
No. gears	4	4	4	4
Front tyre			2·50 × 18	2·50 × 18
Rear tyre			2·75 × 18	2·75 × 18
Front brake (mm)			drum 180	drum 180
Rear brake (mm)			drum 160	drum 160
Front suspension			teles	teles
Rear suspension			s/a	s/a
Ignition system			coil	coil
Wheelbase (mm)			1320	1320
Ground clear. (mm)			130	130
Seat height (mm)			790	790
Width (mm)			580	580
Length (mm)			1950	1980
Dry weight (kg)	79	89	103	104
Generator/output			6v/40w	6v/40w
Battery			6v 13·5ah	6v 13·5ah

1 Bronco was also produced in 98 and 125 versions with the same specification as the 98T and 125T/TV models

Model	125S	100 Sport	125 Sport	125TS
Year from	1957	1958	1958	1958
Year to		1960	1965	1965
Bore (mm)	55·2	49	55·2	55·2
Stroke (mm)	52	52	52	52
Capacity (cc)	124·443	98·058	124·443	124·443
Compression ratio (to 1)	8	9	8	7
Valve type	ohc	ohc	ohc	ohc
bhp	10	8	10	6·2
@ rpm	8500	8500	8500	6500
Oil system	wet sump	wet sump	wet sump	wet sump
Inlet opens BTDC	48	44	48	24
Inlet closes ABDC	65	68	65	56
Exhaust opens BBDC	67	72	67	40
Exhaust closes ATDC	45	41	45	22
Tappets, inlet (mm)	0·05	0·05	0·05	0·05
Tappets, exhaust (mm)	0·07	0·07	0·07	0·07
Primary drive gearing	2·533	3·000	3·000	3·000
Final drive gearing	2·875	3·066	2·750	2·875
Box gearing: 4th	0·96	0·97	0·97	0·97
Box gearing: 3rd	1·18	1·18	1·18	1·18

Ducati Singles

Box gearing: 2nd	1·54	1·65	1·65	1·65
Box gearing: 1st	2·38	2·75	2·75	2·75
No. gears	4	4	4	4
Front tyre	2·50 × 17	2·50 × 17	2·50 × 17	2·50 × 17
Rear tyre	2·75 × 17	2·75 × 17	2·75 × 17	2·75 × 17
Front brake (mm)	drum 180	drum 180	drum 180 **1**	drum 158
Rear brake (mm)	drum 160	drum 160	drum 160 **2**	drum 136
Front suspension	teles	teles	teles	teles
Rear suspension	s/a	s/a	s/a	s/a
Ignition system	coil	coil	coil	coil
Wheelbase (mm)	1320	1320	1320	1310
Ground clear. (mm)	140	140	140	120
Seat height (mm)	750	750	750	760
Width (mm)	580	580	580	680
Length (mm)	1910	1910	1910	1890
Dry weight (kg)	100·5	100	100·5	98·5
Generator/output	6v/40w	6v/40w	6v/40w	6v/40w
Battery	6v 13·5ah	6v 13·5ah	6v 13·5ah	6v 13·5ah

1 after 1960—158   **2** after 1960—136

Model	**175 Americano**	**175 Sport**	**175 Tourist**	**175TS**
Year from	**1958**	**1958**	**1958**	**1958**
Year to		**1961**	**1961**	**1960**
Bore (mm)	62	62	62	62
Stroke (mm)	57·8	57·8	57·8	57·8
Capacity (cc)	174·502	174·502	174·502	174·502
Compression ratio (to 1)	7	8	7	7
Valve type	ohc	ohc	ohc	ohc
bhp	11	14	11	11
@ rpm	7500	8000	7500	7500
Oil system	wet sump	wet sump	wet sump	wet sump
Inlet opens BTDC	35	44	35	35
Inlet closes ABDC	65	73	65	65
Exhaust opens BBDC	65	73	65	65
Exhaust closes ATDC	35	38	35	35
Tappets, inlet (mm)	0·05	0·06	0·05	0·05
Tappets, exhaust (mm)	0·07	0·08	0·07	0·07
Primary drive gearing	2·522	2·522	2·522	2·522
Final drive gearing	3·066	2·875	3·066	3·066
Box gearing: 4th	0·97	0·97	0·97	0·97
Box gearing: 3rd	1·18	1·18	1·18	1·18
Box gearing: 2nd	1·65	1·65	1·65	1·65
Box gearing: 1st	2·75	2·75	2·75	2·75
No. gears	4	4	4	4
Front tyre	2·50 × 18	2·50 × 18	2·50 × 18	2·50 × 18
Rear tyre	2·75 × 18	2·75 × 18	2·75 × 18	2·75 × 18
Front brake (mm)	drum 180	drum 180	drum 180	drum 180

Rear brake (mm)	drum 160	drum 160	drum 160	drum 160
Front suspension	teles	teles	teles	teles
Rear suspension	s/a	s/a	s/a	s/a
Ignition system	coil	coil	coil	coil
Wheelbase (mm)	1320	1320	1320	1310
Ground clear. (mm)	110	110	130	130
Seat height (mm)	800	790	790	750
Width (mm)	640	580	580	640
Length (mm)	1980	1990	1980	1950
Dry weight (kg)	118	103	104	108
Generator/output	6v/40w	6v/40w	6v/40w	6v/40w
Battery	6v 13·5ah	6v 13·5ah	6v 13·5ah	6v 13·5ah

Model	**175 Motocross**	**200 Elite**	**200 Supersport 1**	**200 Americano**
Year from	**1958**	**1959**	**1959**	**1959**
Year to		**1965**	**1960**	
Bore (mm)	62	67	67	67
Stroke (mm)	57·8	57·8	57·8	57·8
Capacity (cc)	174·500	203·783	203·783	203·783
Compression ratio (to 1)	8	8·5	8·5	7·5
Valve type	ohc	ohc	ohc	ohc
bhp	14	17	18	16
@ rpm	8000	7500	7800	7500
Oil system	wet sump	wet sump	wet sump	wet sump
Inlet opens BTDC		34	44	34
Inlet closes ABDC		56	68	56
Exhaust opens BBDC		70	72	70
Exhaust closes ATDC		24	41	24
Tappets, inlet (mm)	0·07	0·06	0·07	0·05
Tappets, exhaust (mm)	0·10	0·08	0·10	0·07
Primary drive gearing		2·520	2·500	
Final drive gearing		2·812	2·647	
Box gearing: 4th	0·97	0·97	0·97	0·97
Box gearing: 3rd	1·18	1·18	1·18	1·18
Box gearing: 2nd	1·65	1·65	1·65	1·65
Box gearing: 1st	2·75	2·75	2·75	2·75
No. gears	4	4	4	4
Front tyre	2·75 × 21	2·75 × 18	2·75 × 18	2·75 × 18
Rear tyre	3·00 × 19	3·00 × 18	3·00 × 18	3·00 × 18
Front brake (mm)	drum 180	drum 180	drum 180	drum 180
Rear brake (mm)	drum 180	drum 160	drum 160	drum 160
Front suspension	teles	teles	teles	teles
Rear suspension	s/a	s/a	s/a	s/a
Ignition system	coil	coil	coil	coil
Wheelbase (mm)	1380	1320	1320	1320
Ground clear. (mm)		110	130	110
Seat height (mm)	830	800	800	800
Width (mm)	800	580	580	800

Length (mm)	2060	1990	1990	2000
Dry weight (kg)	122	111	109	118
Generator/output	6v/40w	6v/40w	6v/40w	6v/40w
Battery	6v 13·5ah	6v 13·5ah	6v 13·5ah	6v 13·5ah

1 With high lift camshaft, and 27 mm SS1 carburettor

Model	**200 Motocross**	**200TS**	**200GT**	**250 Monza (n/case)**
Year from	**1959**	**1960**	**1962**	**1961**
Year to	**1960**	**1961**		**1967**
Bore (mm)	67	67	67	74
Stroke (mm)	57·8	57·8	57·8	57·8
Capacity (cc)	203·783	203·783	203·783	248·589
Compression ratio (to1)	8·5	7	7	8
Valve type	ohc	ohc	ohc	ohc
bhp	1959|1960 19 | 18	17	14	16·4
@ rpm	7800	7500	7000	7200
Oil system	wet sump	wet sump	wet sump	wet sump
Inlet opens BTDC		34	34	20
Inlet closes ABDC		56	56	70
Exhaust opens BBDC		70	70	50
Exhaust closes ATDC		24	24	30
Tappets, inlet (mm)	0·07	0·05	0·05	0·05
Tappets, exhaust (mm)	0·10	0·07	0·07	0·07
Box gearing: 5th				**1**
Box gearing: 4th	0·97	0·97	0·97	0·97 **2**
Box gearing: 3rd	1·18	1·18	1·18	1·18 **3**
Box gearing: 2nd	1·65	1·65	1·65	1·65 **4**
Box gearing: 1st	2·75	2·75	2·75	2·75 **5**
No. gears	4	4	4	4 **6**
Front tyre	2·75 × 21	3·00 × 18	2·75 × 18	2·75 × 18
Rear tyre	3·00 × 19	3·00 × 18	3·00 × 18	3·00 × 18
Front brake (mm)	drum 180	drum 180	drum 180	drum 180
Rear brake (mm)	drum 180	drum 160	drum 160	drum 160
Front suspension	teles	teles	teles	teles
Rear suspension	s/a	s/a	s/a	s/a
Ignition system	coil	coil	coil	coil
Wheelbase (mm)	1380	1320	1320	1320
Ground clear. (mm)		130	130	130
Seat height (mm)	830	800	750	800
Width (mm)	800	800	580	800
Length (mm)	2060	2000	2000	2000
Dry weight (kg)	124	118	116	125
Generator/output	6v/40w	6v/40w	6v/40w	61/64 | 64/67 6v/40w | 6v/60w
Battery	6v 13·5ah	6v 13·5ah	6v 13·5ah	6v 13·5ah

1 For 5 gear version—0·97   **2** For 5 gear version—1·10   **3** For 5 gear version—1·35   **4** For 5 gear version—1·73   **5** For 5 gear version—2·53   **6** 1961–mid-1964, from mid-1964–1967—5 gears

Model	Diana (Europe)	Diana (USA)	250 Mark 3 (n/case)	250 Scrambler (n/case)
Year from	**1961**	**1961**	**1967**	**1962**
Year to	**1964**	**1966**		**1967**
Bore (mm)	74	74	74	74
Stroke (mm)	57·8	57·8	57·8	57·8
Capacity (cc)	248·589	248·589	248·589	248·589
Compression ratio (to 1)	8	9	10	9·2
Valve type	ohc	ohc	ohc	ohc
bhp	17·6			
@ rpm	7400	8000	8500	8000
Oil system	wet sump	wet sump	wet sump	wet sump
Inlet opens BTDC	20 degrees	62	62	32
Inlet closes ABDC	70 degrees	68	76	71
Exhaust opens BBDC	50 degrees	75	70	50
Exhaust closes ATDC	30 degrees	55	48	44
Tappets, inlet (mm)	0·05	0·15	0·15	0·15
Tappets, exhaust (mm)	0·07	0·20	0·25	0·20
Primary drive gearing	2·500	2·500	2·500	2·500
Final drive gearing	2·647	2·647	2·222	3·929
Box gearing: 5th		**1**	0·97	**1**
Box gearing: 4th	0·97	0·97 **2**	1·10	0·97 **2**
Box gearing: 3rd	1·18	1·18 **3**	1·35	1·18 **3**
Box gearing: 2nd	1·65	1·65 **4**	1·73	1·65 **4**
Box gearing: 1st	2·75	2·75 **5**	2·53	2·75 **5**
No. gears	4	4 **6**	5	4, 62–mid 64 **7** 5, mid 64–67
Front tyre	2·75 × 18	2·75 × 18	2·50 × 18	3·00 × 19
Rear tyre	3·00 × 18	3·00 × 18	2·75 × 18	3·50 × 19
Front brake (mm)	drum 180	drum 180	drum 180	drum 180
Rear brake drum	160	160	160	160
Front suspension	teles	teles	teles	teles
Rear suspension	s/a	s/a	s/a	s/a
Ignition system	coil	flywheel magneto	coil	flywheel magneto
Wheelbase (mm)	1320	1320	1350	1350
Ground clear. (mm)	130	130	130	130
Seat height (mm)	750	750 **8**	800	750
Width (mm)	580	800	590	820
Length (mm)	2000	2000	2000	2020
Dry weight (kg)	120	110	116	109 **9**
Generator/output	6v/40w	6v/40w	6v/40w	6v/40w
Battery	6v 13·5ah	None	6v 13·5ah	None

1 For 5 gear version—0·97　**2** For 5 gear version—1·10　**3** For 5 gear version—1·35　**4** For 5 gear version—1·73　**5** For 5 gear version—2·53　**6** 1961–mid-1964, mid-1964–1965—5 gears　**7** 1962–mid-1964, mid-1964–1967—5 gears　**8** 1961–1964, 1965–1966—800 mm　**9** 1962–1965, 1966–1967—120

Model	Mach 1	250GT	250 Monza (w/case)	250 Mark 3 (w/case)
Year from	**1964**	**1964**	**1968**	**1968**
Year to	**1966**	**1966**		**1974**
Bore (mm)	74	74	74	74
Stroke (mm)	57·8	57·8	57·8	57·8
Capacity (cc)	248·589	248·589	248·589	248·589
Compression ratio (to 1)	10	8	8	9·7
Valve type	ohc	ohc	ohc	ohc
@ rpm	8500	7200	7000	7800
Oil system	wet sump	wet sump	wet sump	wet sump
Inlet opens BTDC	62	52	20	62
Inlet closes ABDC	76	52	70	76
Exhaust opens BBDC	70	75	50	70
Exhaust closes ATDC	48	27	30	48
Tappets, inlet (mm)	0·15	0·05	0·05	0·15
Tappets, exhaust (mm)	0·25	0·07	0·07	0·20
Primary drive gearing	2·500	2·500	2·500	2·500
Final drive gearing	2·222	2·647	3·008	2·812
Box gearing: 5th	0·97	0·97	0·97	0·97
Box gearing: 4th	1·10	1·10	1·10	1·10
Box gearing: 3rd	1·35	1·35	1·35	1·35
Box gearing: 2nd	1·73	1·73	1·73	1·73
Box gearing: 1st	2·53	2·53	2·46	2·46
No. gears	5	5	5	5
Front tyre	2·50 × 18	2·75 × 18	2·75 × 18	2·75 × 18 **1**
Rear tyre	2·75 × 18	3·00 × 18	3·00 × 18	3·00 × 18 **2**
Front brake (mm)	drum 180	drum 180	drum 180	drum 180 **3**
Rear brake (mm)	drum 160	drum 160	drum 160	drum 160
Front suspension	teles	teles	teles	teles
Rear suspension	s/a	s/a	s/a	s/a
Ignition system	coil	coil	coil	coil **4**
Wheelbase (mm)	1350	1320	1365	1360
Ground clear (mm)	130	130	130	130
Seat height (mm)	'64/'65 | '66 760 | 800	800	800	735
Width (mm)	590	800	850	780
Length (mm)	2000	2000	2000	2000
Dry weight (kg)	116	125	127	128
Generator/output	6v/60w	6v/60w	6v/70w	6v/70w
Battery	6v 13·5ah	6v 13·5ah	6v 13·5ah	6v 13·5ah

1 1968–1972, 1973–1974—3·00 × 19   **2** 1973–1974—3·50 × 18   **3** 1973–1974—dual drum 180   **4** 1968–1972, 1973–1974—electronic

Model	250 Mark 3D	250 Scrambler (w/case)	250 Desmo	239 Desmo
Year from	1968	1968	1971	1974
Year to	1971	1974	1974	
Bore (mm)	74	74	74	72·5
Stroke (mm)	57·8	57·8	57·8	57·8
Capacity (cc)	248·589	248·589	248·589	238·613
Compression ratio (to 1)	9·7	9·2	9·7	10
Valve type	ohc	ohc	ohc	ohc
@ rpm	9000	7000	9000	9000
Oil system	wet sump	wet sump	wet sump	wet sump
Inlet opens BTDC	70	27	70	70
Inlet closes ABDC	82	75	82	82
Exhaust opens BBDC	80	60	80	80
Exhaust closes ATDC	65	32	65	65
Tappets, inlet (mm)	upper rocker 0·15 lower rocker 0	0·10	upper rocker 0·15 lower rocker 0	upper rocker 0·15 lower rocker 0
Tappets, exhaust (mm)	upper rocker 0·15 lower rocker 0	0·15	upper rocker 0·15 lower rocker 0	upper rocker 0·15 lower rocker 0
Primary drive gearing	2·500	2·500	2·500	2·500
Final drive gearing	2·647	3·000	2·647	2·647
Box gearing : 5th	0·97	0·97	0·97	0·97
Box gearing : 4th	1·10	1·10	1·10	1·10
Box gearing : 3rd	1·35	1·35	1·35	1·35
Box gearing : 2nd	1·73	1·73	1·73	1·73
Box gearing : 1st	2·46	2·46	2·46	2·46
No. gears	5	5	5	5
Front tyre	2·75 × 18	3·50 × 19	2·75 × 18	2·75 × 18
Rear tyre	3·00 × 18	4·00 × 18	3·00 × 18 [1]	3·25 × 18
Front brake (mm)	drum 180	drum 180	dual drum 180 [2]	disc 280
Rear brake (mm)	drum 160	drum 160	drum 160	drum 160
Front suspension	teles	teles	teles	teles
Rear suspension	s/a	s/a	s/a	s/a
Ignition system	coil	coil	electronic	electronic
Wheelbase (mm)	1360	1380	1360	1360
Ground clear. (mm)	130	130	130	130
Seat height (mm)	735	770	735	735
Width (mm)	600	940	600	600
Length (mm)	2000	2120	2000	2000
Dry weight (kg)	128	132	128	128
Generator/output	6v/70w	6v/70w	6v/70w	6v/70w
Battery	6v 13·5ah	6v 13·5ah	6v 13·5ah	6v 13·5ah

1 1971–1972, 1973–1974 — 3·25 × 18   2 1971–1972, 1973–1974 — disc 280 mm

Model	239 Mark 3	Monza Junior	Piuma Standard	Piuma Sport
Year from	**1974**	**1964**	**1961**	**1962**
Year to		**1967**	**1968**	**1966**
Bore (mm)	72·5	61	38	38
Stroke (mm)	57·8	52	42	42
Capacity (cc)	238·613	151·968	47·663	47·663
Compression ratio (to 1)	10	8·2	6·3	9·5
Valve type	ohc	ohc	t.s.	t.s.
bhp		13	1·5	4·2
@ rpm	8000	8000	5200	8600
Oil system	wet sump	wet sump	petrol/oil mix	petrol/oil mix
Inlet opens BTDC	62	24		
Inlet closes ABDC	76	40		
Exhaust opens BBDC	70	51		
Exhaust closes ATDC	48	30		
Tappets, inlet (mm)	0·05	0·05		
Tappets, exhaust (mm)	0·10	0·07		
Primary drive gearing	2·500	3·000	3·666	3·666
Final drive gearing	2·812	2·875	3·250	3·000
Box gearing: 5th	0·97			
Box gearing: 4th	1·10	0·97		
Box gearing: 3rd	1·35	1·18	1·14	1·14
Box gearing: 2nd	1·73	1·65	1·61	1·61
Box gearing: 1st	2·46	2·75	2·61	2·61
No. gears	5	4	3	3
Front tyre	3·00 × 19	2·75 × 16	2·25 × 18	2·25 × 18
Rear tyre	3·50 × 18	3·25 × 16	2·25 × 18	2·25 × 18
Front brake (mm)	dual drum 180	158	drum 90	drum 105
Rear brake (mm)	160	136	drum 90	drum 105
Front suspension	teles	teles	teles	teles
Rear suspension	s/a	s/a	s/a	s/a
Ignition system	electronic	flywheel mag	flywheel mag	flywheel mag
Wheelbase (mm)	1360	1330	1170	1170
Ground clear. (mm)	130			
Seat height (mm)	735	760	760	760
Width (mm)	780	735	720	570
Length (mm)	2000	1980	1910	1910
Dry weight (kg)	128	108	50	52
Generator/output	6v/70w	6v/40w	6v/18w	6v/18w
Battery	6v 12ah	6v 7ah	none	none

Model	Piuma De-Luxe	Brisk	Sport 48	80 Standard
Year from	**1962**	**1961**	**1962**	**1962**
Year to	**1967**	**1967**	**1965**	**1963**
Bore (mm)	38	38	38	
Stroke (mm)	42	42	42	
Capacity (cc)	47·632	47·632	47·632	79

Compression ratio (to 1)	6·3	6·3	9·5	
Valve type	ts	ts	ts	ts
bhp	2·2	1·5	4·2	
@ rpm	5800	5200	8600	
Oil system	petrol/oil mix	petrol/oil mix	petrol/oil mix	petrol/oil mix
Primary drive gearing	3·666		3·666	
Final drive gearing	3·250		3·000	
Box gearing: 3rd	1·14		1·14	
Box gearing: 2nd	1·61		1·61	
Box gearing: 1st	2·61		2·61	
No. gears	3	1	3	3
Front tyre	2·25 × 19	2·00 × 18	2·25 × 19	
Rear tyre	2·25 × 19	2·00 × 18	2·25 × 19	
Front brake (mm)	drum	drum 90	drum 105	drum 118
Rear brake (mm)	drum	drum 90	drum 105	drum 118
Front suspension	teles	teles	teles	teles
Rear suspension	s/a	s/a	s/a	s/a
Ignition system	flywheel mag	flywheel mag	flywheel mag	flywheel mag
Wheelbase (mm)	1170	1160	1180	
Seat height (mm)	770	760	780	
Width (mm)	720	720	570	
Length (mm)	1910	1900	1800	
Dry weight (kg)	52	45	54	
Generator/output	6v/18w	6v/18w	6v/18w	6v/30w
Battery	none	none	none	none

Model	**Sport 80**	**48SL**	**100 Cadet (51 mm bore)**	**100 Cadet (52 mm bore)**
Year from	**1962**	**1964**	**1964**	**1967**
Year to	**1963**	**1965**	**1966**	
Bore (mm)		38	51	52
Stroke (mm)		42	46	46
Capacity (cc)	79	47·633	93·969	97·691
Compression ratio (to 1)		9·5	8·5	9
Valve type	ts	ts	ts	ts
Oil system	petrol/oil mix	petrol/oil mix	petrol/oil mix	petrol/oil mix
Primary drive gearing		3·666	3·000	3·000
Final drive gearing		3·250	3·000 **1**	
Box gearing: top				
Box gearing: 5th			3 speed **2**	
Box gearing: 3rd		1·04	1·14	
Box gearing: 2nd		1·61	1·76	
Box gearing: 1st		2·83	3·18	
No. gears	3	3	3 **3**	4
Front tyre		2·25 × 18	2·25 × 18	2·25 × 18
Rear tyre		2·50 × 17	2·50 × 18	2·50 × 18
Front brake (mm)	drum 118	drum 118	drum 118	drum 118

Ducati Singles

Rear brake (mm)	drum 118	drum 118	drum 118	drum 118
Front suspension	teles	teles	teles	teles
Rear suspension	s/a	s/a	s/a	s/a
Ignition system	flywheel mag	flywheel mag	flywheel mag	flywheel mag
Wheelbase (mm)		1150	1160	1160
Seat height (mm)		730	750	750
Width (mm)		550	660	660
Length (mm)		1770	1810	1810
Dry weight (kg)		59	66	66
Generator/output	6v/30w	6v/18w	6v/30w	6v/30w
Battery	none	none	none	none

1 1964–1965—3 speed   **2** 1964–1965, 1966—4 speed   **3** 1964–1965, 1966—4 gears

---

Model	100 Mountaineer (51 mm bore)	100 Mountaineer (52 mm bore)	Brio 48 scooter	Brio 50 scooter
Year from	**1964**	**1967**	**1963**	**1967**
Year to	**1966**		**1966**	**1968**
Bore (mm)	51	52	38	38
Stroke (mm)	46	46	42	42
Capacity (cc)	93·969	97·691	47·633	47·633
Compression ratio (to 1)	8·5	9	7	7
valve type	ts	ts	ts	ts
bhp			1·5	1·5
@ rpm			5200	5200
Oil system	petrol/oil mix	petrol/oil mix	petrol/oil mix	petrol/oil mix
Primary drive gearing	3·000	3·000	3·666	3·666
Box gearing: 5th	3 speed **1**			
Box gearing: 3rd	1·14		1·04	1·04
Box gearing: 2nd	1·76		1·61	1·61
Box gearing: 1st	3·18		2·83	2·83
No. gears	3 **2**	4	3	3
Front tyre	2·50 × 16	2·50 × 16	1·75 × 9	1·75 × 9
Rear tyre	3·50 × 16	3·50 × 16	1·75 × 9	1·75 × 9
Front brake (mm)	drum 118	drum 118	drum 105	drum 105
Rear brake (mm)	drum 118	drum 118	drum 105	drum 105
Front suspension	teles	teles	leading link	leading link
Rear suspension	s/a	s/a	s/a	s/a
Ignition system	flywheel mag	flywheel mag	flywheel mag	flywheel mag
Wheelbase (mm)	1170	1170		
Seat height (mm)	760	760		
Width (mm)	700	700		
Length (mm)	1830	1830		
Dry weight (kg)	68	68	63·5	63·5
Generator/output	6v/30w	6v/30w	6v/18w	6v/18w

1 1964–1965, 1966—4 speed   **2** 1966—4 gears

Model	Brio 100 scooter	Brio 100/25 scooter	48 Cacciatore	50SL
Year from	1964	1968	1964	1966
Year to	1967		1967	
Bore (mm)	51	51	38	38·8
Stroke (mm)	46	46	42	42
Capacity (cc)	93·969	93·969	47·633	49·659
Compression ratio (to 1)	8·5	8·5	9·5	11
Valve type				
bhp	6	6	4·2	
@ rpm	5200	5200	8600	
Oil system	petrol/oil mix	petrol/oil mix	petrol/oil mix	petrol/oil mix
Primary drive gearing	3·000	3·000	3·666	3·666
Final drive gearing			3·500 **1**	4·083
Box gearing: 4th				1·04
Box gearing: 3rd	1·14	1·14	1·04	1·35
Box gearing: 2nd	1·76	1·76	1·61	1·94
Box gearing: 1st	3·18	3·18	2·83	3·27
No. gears	3	3	3	4
Front tyre	3·50 × 8	3·50 × 8	2·50 × 18	2·25 × 19
Rear tyre	3·50 × 8	3·50 × 8	3·25 × 16	2·25 × 19
Front brake (mm)	drum 105	drum 105	drum 118	drum 118
Rear brake (mm)	drum 105	drum 105	drum 118	drum 118
Front suspension	leading link	leading link	teles	teles
Rear suspension	s/a	s/a	s/a	s/a
Ignition system	flywheel mag	flywheel mag	flywheel mag	flywheel mag
Wheelbase (mm)			1170	1150
Seat height (mm)			760	730
Width (mm)			700	550
Length (mm)			1830	1770
Dry weight (kg)	80	80	63	59
Generator/output	6v/30w	6v/30w	6v/18w	6v/18w
Battery	none	none	none	none

1 With 42T rear wheel sprocket; 5·000 dirt, 60T

Model	50SL1	50SL2	Rolly 50	50 Scrambler
Year from	1967	1968	1968	1969
Year to	1968	1969		1970
Bore (mm)	38·8	38·8	38	38·78
Stroke (mm)	42	42	42	42
Capacity (cc)	49·660	49·660	47·663	49·660
Compression ratio (to 1)	11	11	6·3	10·5
Valve type	ts	ts	ts	ts
bhp			1·5	3·27
@ rpm			5200	6500
Oil system	petrol/oil mix	petrol/oil mix	petrol/oil mix	petrol/oil mix
Primary drive gearing	3·666	3·666		3·000

Final drive gearing	4·083	4·083		3·818
Box gearing: 4th	1·04	1·04		1·04
Box gearing: 3rd	1·35	1·35		1·35
Box gearing: 2nd	1·94	1·94		1·94
Box gearing: 1st	3·27	3·27		3·27
No. gears	4	4	1	4
Front tyre	2·25 × 19	2·25 × 19		2·50 × 18
Rear tyre	2·25 × 19	2·25 × 19		2·50 × 17
Front brake (mm)	drum 118	drum 118	drum 90	drum 118
Rear brake (mm)	drum 118	drum 118	drum 90	drum 118
Front suspension	teles	teles	teles	teles
Rear suspension	s/a	s/a	solid	s/a
Ignition system	flywheel mag	flywheel mag	flywheel mag	flywheel mag
Wheelbase (mm)	1150	1150		1180
Seat height (mm)	730	730		730
Width (mm)	550	650		800
Length (mm)	1770	1770		1840
Dry weight (kg)	59	60	43	64
Generator/output	6v/18w	6v/18w	6v/18w	6v/18w
Battery	none	none	none	none

Model	**100 Scrambler**	**125 Cadet/4**	**Sebring**	**350 Scrambler**	
Year from	**1969**	**1967**	**1965**	**1968**	
Year to	**1970**		**1967**	**1974**	
Bore (mm)	52	53	76	76	
Stroke (mm)	46	55	75	75	
Capacity (cc)	97·690	121·340	340·235	340·235	
Compression ratio (to 1)	11·2	8·4	8·5	9·5	
Valve type	ts	ohv	ohc	ohc	
bhp	6·27				
@ rpm	6000		6250		
Oil system	petrol/oil mix	wet sump	wet sump	wet sump	
Inlet opens BTDC		30	20	1968	1969–74
				65	70
Inlet closes ABDC		70	70	76	84
Exhaust opens BBDC		70	50	80	80
Exhaust closes ATDC		30	30	50	64
Tappets, inlet (mm)		0·05	0·07	0·10	
Tappets, exhaust (mm)		0·05	0·10	0·15	
Primary drive gearing	3·000	3·000	2·111	2·111	
Final drive gearing	3·000	3·000	2·647	3·214	
Box gearing: 5th			0·97	0·97	
Box gearing: 4th	1·04	1·043	1·10	1·10	
Box gearing: 3rd	1·35	1·35	1·35	1·35	
Box gearing: 2nd	1·94	1·937	1·73	1·73	
Box gearing: 1st	3·27	3·181	2·53	2·46	
No. gears	4	4	5	5	

Front tyre	2·50 × 18	2·50 × 18	2·75 × 18	3·50 × 19
Rear tyre	2·50 × 17	2·75 × 18	3·00 × 18	4·00 × 18
Front brake (mm)	drum 118	drum 118	drum 180	drum 180
Rear brake (mm)	drum 118	drum 118	drum 160	drum 160
Front suspension	teles	teles	teles	teles
Rear suspension	s/a	s/a	s/a	s/a
Ignition system	flywheel mag	coil	coil	coil
Wheelbase (mm)	1180	1160	1330	1330
Ground clear. (mm)	150		130	130
Seat height (mm)	730	770	800	770
Width (mm)	800	670	850	940
Length (mm)	1840	1810	2000	2120
Dry weight (kg)	67	72	123	133
Generator/output	6v/30w	6v/28w	6v/60w	6v/70w
Battery	none	6v 13·5ah	6v 13·5ah	6v 13·5ah

Model	**350 Mark 3**	**350 Mark 3D**	**350 Desmo**	**450 Scrambler**
Year from	**1968**	**1968**	**1971**	**1969 5**
Year to	**1974**	**1971**	**1974**	**1974**
Bore (mm)	76	76	76	86
Stroke (mm)	75	75	75	75
Capacity (cc)	340·235	340·235	340·235	435·661
Compression ratio (to 1)	9·5	9·5	9·5	9·3
Valve type	ohc	ohc	ohc	ohc
Oil system	wet sump	wet sump	wet sump	wet sump
Inlet opens BTDC	70	70	70	27
Inlet closes ABDC	84	82	82	75
Exhaust opens BBDC	80	80	80	60
Exhaust closes ATDC	64	65	65	32
Tappets, inlet (mm)	0·10	upper rocker 0·15 lower rocker 0	upper rocker 0·15 lower rocker 0	0·10
Tappets, exhaust (mm)	0·15	upper rocker 0·15 lower rocker 0	upper rocker 0·15 lower rocker 0	0·15
Primary drive gearing	2·111	2·111	2·111	2·111
Final drive gearing	3·214	2·500	2·500	2·692
Box gearing : 5th	0·97	0·97	0·97	0·97
Box gearing : 4th	1·10	1·10	1·10	1·10
Box gearing : 3rd	1·35	1·35	1·35	1·35
Box gearing : 2nd	1·73	1·73	1·73	1·73
Box gearing : 1st	2·46	2·46	2·46	2·46
No. gears	5	5	5	5
Front tyre	2·75 × 18 **1**	2·75 × 18	2·75 × 18	3·50 × 19
Rear tyre	3·00 × 18 **2**	3·00 × 18	3·25 × 18	4·00 × 18
Front brake (mm)	180 **3**	180	dual drum 180 **4**	drum 180 **6**
Rear brake (mm)	160	160	160	160
Front suspension	teles	teles	teles	teles
Rear suspension	s/a	s/a	s/a	s/a

Ignition system	coil **7**	coil	coil **8**	coil
Wheelbase (mm)	1360	1360	1360	1380
Ground clear. (mm)	130	130	130	130
Seat height (mm)	735	735	735	770
Width (mm)	780	600	600	940
Length (mm)	2000	2000	2000	2120
Dry weight (kg)	128	128	128	140
Generator/output	6v/70w	6v/70w	6v/70w	6v/70w
Battery	6v 13·5ah	6v 13·5ah	6v 13·5ah	6v 13·5ah

1 1968–1972, 1973–1974—3·0 × 19 **2** 1968–1971, 1971–1974—3·50 × 18 **3** 1973–1974—dual drum 180 mm **4** 1971–1972, 1973–1974 280 disc. Also available with a dual drum 180 mm **5** 450SCR, marketed as the Jupiter in the USA during 1970 season **6** 1969–1973, 1973–1974 dual drum 180 **7** 1968–1972, 1973–1974—electronic **8** 1971–1972, 1973–1974—electronic

Model	**450 Mark 3**	**450 Mark 3D**	**450 Desmo**	**450R/T**
Year from	**1969**	**1969**	**1971**	**1971**
Year to	**1974**	**1971**	**1974**	**1972**
Bore (mm)	86	86	86	86
Stroke (mm)	75	75	75	75
Capacity (cc)	435·661	435·661	435·661	435·661
Compression ratio (to 1)	9·3 **1**	9·3	9·3	9·3
@ rpm	7500	8000	8000	8500
Inlet opens BTDC	27	70	70	70
Inlet closes ABDC	75	82	82	82
Exhaust opens BBDC	60	80	80	80
Exhaust closes ATDC	32	65	65	65
Tappets, inlet (mm)	0·10	upper rocker 0·15 lower rocker 0	upper rocker 0·15 lower rocker 0	upper rocker 0·15 lower rocker 0
Tappets, exhaust (mm)	0·15	upper rocker 0·15 lower rocker 0	upper rocker 0·15 lower rocker 0	upper rocker 0·15 lower rocker 0
Primary drive gearing	2·111	2·111	2·111	2·111
Final drive gearing	2·666	2·666	2·666	2·692
Box gearing: 5th	0·97	0·97	0·97	0·97
Box gearing: 4th	1·10	1·10	1·10	1·10
Box gearing: 3rd	1·35	1·35	1·35	1·35
Box gearing: 2nd	1·73	1·73	1·73	1·73
Box gearing: 1st	2·46	2·46	2·46	2·46
No. gears	5	5	5	5
Front tyre				3·00 × 21
Rear tyre				4·00 × 18
Front brake (mm)	180 **2**	drum 180	dual drum 180 **3**	drum 158
Rear brake (mm)	drum 160	drum 160	drum 160	drum 160
Front suspension	teles	teles	teles	teles
Rear suspension	s/a	s/a	s/a	s/a
Ignition system	coil **4**	coil	coil **5**	flywheel mag
Wheelbase (mm)	1360	1360	1360	
Ground clear. (mm)	130	130	130	

Seat height (mm)	735	735	735	790
Width (mm)	780	600	600	930
Length (mm)	2000	2000	2000	2180
Dry weight (kg)	130	130	130	124
Generator/output	6v/70w	6v/70w	6v/70w	6v/40w
Battery	6v 13·5ah	6v 13·5ah	6v 13·5ah	none

1 Some 450 Mark 3s in touring trim had a concave 8 to 1 piston in 1972   **2** 1969–1971, 1971–1974 dual drum 180 mm   **3** 1971–1972, 1973–1974—disc 280 mm   **4** 1969–1972, 1973–1974—electronic   **5** 1971–1972, 1973–1974—electronic

Model	450T/S	450 Mark 3 Tourer	Regolarita	Six Days
Year from	**1971**	**1970**	**1975**	**1977**
Year to	**1972**	**1972**	**1976**	
Bore (mm)	86	86	54	54
Stroke (mm)	75	75	54	54
Capacity (cc)	435·661	435·661	123·672	123·672
Compression ratio (to 1)	9·3	8	12·4	14·6
Valve type	ohc	ohc	ts	ts
bhp			21·8	25
@ rpm	8500	6800	9000	10250
Inlet opens BTDC	70	27		
Inlet closes ABDC	82	75		
Exhaust opens BBDC	80	60		
Exhaust closes ATDC	65	32		
Tappets, inlet (mm)	upper rocker 0·15 lower rocker 0	0·10		
Tappets, exhaust (mm)	upper rocker 0·15 lower rocker 0	0·15		
Primary drive gearing	2·111	2·111		
Final drive gearing	2·692	2·666		
Box gearing: top			2·65	2·65
Box gearing: 5th	0·97	0·97	3·05	3·05
Box gearing: 4th	1·10	1·10	3·77	3·77
Box gearing: 3rd	1·35	1·35	4·87	4·87
Box gearing: 2nd	1·73	1·73	6·61	6·61
Box gearing: 1st	2·46	2·46	9·5	9·5
No. gears	5	5	6	6
Front tyre	3·00 × 21	3·00 × 18	3·00 × 21	3·00 × 21
Rear tyre	4·00 × 18	3·25 × 18	3·75 × 18	4·00 × 18
Front brake (mm)	drum 158	drum 180	drum 125	drum 125
Rear brake (mm)	drum 160	drum 160	drum 125	drum 125
Front suspension	teles	teles	teles	teles
Rear suspension	s/a	s/a	s/a	s/a
Ignition system	flywheel mag	coil	Motoplat electronic	Motoplat electronic
Wheelbase (mm)		1360		
Ground clear. (mm)		130		
Seat height	790	735	851	856

Width (mm)	930	800		
Length (mm)	2180	2000		
Dry weight (kg)	128	133	108	101
Generator output	6v/40w	6v/70w	6v/60w	6v/60w
Battery	none	6v 13·5ah	6v 7ah	6v 7ah

Model	**125 Scrambler**	Box gearing: 4th	1·10
Year from	**1971**	Box gearing: 3rd	1·35
Bore (mm)	55·2	Box gearing: 2nd	1·65
Stroke (mm)	52	Box gearing: 1st	2·39
Capacity (cc)	124·443	No. gears	5
Compression ratio (to 1)	8·5	Front tyre	2·50 × 19
Valve type	ohc	Rear tyre	3·50 × 18
bhp	10	Front brake (mm)	drum 158
@ rpm	8500	Rear brake (mm)	drum 136
Oil system	wet sump	Front suspension	teles
Inlet opens BTDC	24	Rear suspension	s/a
Inlet closes ABDC	40	Ignition system	coil
Exhaust opens BBDC	56	Wheelbase (mm)	1340
Exhaust closes ATDC	22	Ground clear. (mm)	180
Tappets, inlet (mm)	0·20	Seat height (mm)	850
Tappets, exhaust (mm)	0·20	Width (mm)	860
Primary drive gearing	3·000	Length (mm)	2040
Final drive gearing	3·714	Dry weight (kg)	105
Box gearing: 5th	0·97	Battery	6v 11ah

Model	**Sebring (w/case)**	Box gearing: 3rd	1·35
Year	**1968**	Box gearing: 2nd	1·73
Bore (mm)	76	Box gearing: 1st	2·46
Stroke (mm)	75	No. gears	5
Capacity (cc)	340·235	Front tyre	2·75 × 18
Compression ratio (to 1)	9·5	Rear tyre	3·00 × 18
Valve type	ohc	Front brake (mm)	drum 180
@ rpm	8000	Rear brake (mm)	drum 160
Oil system	wet sump	Front suspension	teles
Inlet opens BTDC	20	Rear suspension	s/a
Inlet closes ABDC	70	Ignition system	coil
Exhaust opens BBDC	50	Wheelbase (mm)	1365
Exhaust closes ATDC	30	Ground clear. (mm)	130
Tappets, inlet (mm)	0·05	Seat height (mm)	800
Tappets, exhaust (mm)	0·10	Width (mm)	850
Primary drive gearing	2·111	Length (mm)	2000
Final drive gearing	3·214	Dry weight (kg)	127
Box gearing: 5th	0·97	Generator/output	6v/70w
Box gearing: 4th	1·10	Battery	6v 13·5ah

Mototrans singles

Model	175 Turismo	175 Sport	200 Elite	160 Turismo
Bore (mm)	62	62	67	62
Stroke (mm)	57·8	57·8	57·8	52
Capacity (cc)	174·502	174·502	203·783	156·992
Compression ratio (to 1)	8·2	8·5	8·5	8·2
Valve type	ohc	ohc	ohc	ohc
bhp	12	14	18	8
@ rpm	7800	8000	7500	7500
Oil system	wet sump	wet sump	wet sump	wet sump
Inlet opens BTDC	45	45	45	40
Inlet closes ABDC	85	85	85	50
Exhaust opens BBDC	65	65	65	60
Exhaust closes ATDC	45	45	45	55
Tappets, inlet (mm)	0·05	0·06	0·06	0·05
Tappets, exhaust (mm)	0·07	0·08	0·08	0·07
Ignition timing degree static	13	13	10	12
Ignition timing fully advanced	41	41	37	39
Primary drive gearing	2·520	2·520	2·520	3·000
Final drive gearing	3·066	3·066	2·625	2·411
Box gearing : 4th	0·96	0·96	0·96	0·96
Box gearing : 3rd	1·18	1·18	1·18	1·18
Box gearing : 2nd	1·65	1·65	1·65	1·65
Box gearing : 1st	2·38	2·38	2·38	2·38
No. gears	4	4	4	4
Front tyre	2·75 × 18	2·50 × 18	2·75 × 18	2·50 × 17
Rear tyre	2·75 × 18	2·75 × 18	2·75 × 18	2·75 × 17
Front brake (mm)	drum 180	drum 180	drum 180	drum 180
Rear brake (mm)	drum 160	drum 160	drum 160	drum 160
Front suspension	teles	teles	teles	teles
Rear suspension	s/a	s/a	s/a	s/a
Ignition system	coil	coil	coil	coil
Wheelbase (mm)	1320	1320	1320	1320
Ground clear. (mm)	130	130	130	140
Seat height (mm)	790	790	790	750
Width (mm)	640	540	540	580
Length (mm)	1980	1980	1980	1910
Dry weight (kg)	112	114	114	106
Generator/output	6v/80w	6v/80w	6v/80w	6v/80w
Battery	6v 16ah	6v 16ah	6v 16ah	6v 16ah

Model	160 Sport	250 De-Luxe	250 24 Horas	250 Road 3
Bore (mm)	62	69	69	74
Stroke (mm)	52	66	66	57·8
Capacity (cc)	156·992	246·793	246·793	248·589
Compression ratio (to 1)	8·5	8	10	8

Valve type	ohc	ohc	ohc	ohc
bhp	10	20	23	20
@ rpm	8500	7000	8000	7000
Oil system	wet sump	wet sump	wet sump	wet sump
Inlet opens BTDC	65	45		20
Inlet closes ABDC	80	85		70
Exhaust opens BBDC	86	65		50
Exhaust closes ATDC	62	45		30
Tappets, inlet (mm)	0·05	0·05	0·15	0·05
Tappets, exhaust (mm)	0·07	0·07	0·20	0·07
Ignition timing degree static	12	10		
Ignition timing fully advanced	39	37		
Primary drive gearing	3·000	2·520	2·520	
Final drive gearing	2·625	2·411		
Box gearing: 5th				0·97
Box gearing: 4th	0·96	0·96		0·10
Box gearing: 3rd	1·18	1·18		1·35
Box gearing: 2nd	1·65	1·65		1·73
Box gearing: 1st	2·38	2·38		2·46
No. gears	4	4	5	5
Front tyre	2·50 × 17	2·75 × 18	2·75 × 18	3·00 × 19
Rear tyre	2·75 × 17	3·00 × 18	3·00 × 18	3·50 × 18
Front brake (mm)	drum 180	180 **1**	drum 2LS 200	drum 180
Rear brake (mm)	drum 160	180 **1**	drum 200	drum 160
Front suspension	teles	teles	teles	teles
Rear suspension	s/a	s/a	s/a	s/a
Wheelbase (mm)	1320	1320	1320	1360
Ground clear. (mm)	140	130	130	130
Seat height (mm)	750	770	780	780
Width (mm)	540	580 **2**	540	700
Length (mm)	1910	1980	1990	2000
Dry weight (kg)	107	118	118	128
Generator/output	6v/80w	6v/80w	6v/80w	6v/80w
Battery	6v 16ah	6v 16ah	6v 16ah	6v 16ah

1 First version, 2nd version—200 mm 1972/73 **2** Normal bars, clip ons—540 **3** Also produced in 350 form, sold in USA

Model	**200 Turismo**	**125 Sport**	**48 Cadet**	**Mini 1**
Bore (mm)	67	55·2	38	38
Stroke (mm)	57·8	52	42	42
Capacity (cc)	203·783	124·443	47·632	47·632
Compression ratio (to 1)	7·5	8	6·3	6·3
Valve type	ohc	ohc	ts	ts
bhp	14	10	2·5	2·2
@ rpm	7200	8500	6000	5800
Oil system	wet sump	wet sump	petrol/oil mix	petrol/oil mix
Inlet opens BTDC	45	45		

Inlet closes ABDC	85	85		
Exhaust opens BBDC	65	65		
Exhaust closes ATDC	45	45		
Tappets, inlet (mm)	0·05	0·20		
Tappets, exhaust (mm)	0·07	0·20		
Ignition timing degree static	13	12		
Ignition timing fully advanced	41	39		
Primary drive gearing	2·520	3·000	3·666	3·666
Final drive gearing	2·933	2·750	3·000	
Box gearing: 5th		0·97		
Box gearing: 4th	0·96	1·10		
Box gearing: 3rd	1·18	1·35	1·14	1·14
Box gearing: 2nd	1·65	1·65	1·61	1·61
Box gearing: 1st	2·38	2·39	2·61	2·61
No. gears	4	5	3	3
Front tyre	2·75 × 18	2·50 × 17	2·25 × 17	3·00 × 12
Rear tyre	3·00 × 18	2·75 × 17	2·50 × 17	3·00 × 12
Front brake (mm)	drum 180	drum 180	drum 105	drum 100
Rear brake (mm)	drum 160	drum 160	drum 105	drum 100
Front suspension	teles	teles	teles	teles
Rear suspension	s/a	s/a	s/a	s/a
Ignition system	coil	coil	flywheel mag	flywheel mag
Wheelbase (mm)	1320	1320		985
Ground clear. (mm)	130	140		
Seat height (mm)	790	750		430
Width (mm)	580	540		680
Length (mm)	1980	1910		1570
Dry weight (kg)	112	110	48	56
Generator/output	6v/80w	6v/80w	6v/18w	6v/18w
Battery	6v 16w	6v 16w	none	none

Model	**Mini 2**	**Mini 3**	**50 Pronto**	**100 Pronto**
Bore (mm)	38	38	38	52
Stroke (mm)	42	42	42	46
Capacity (cc)	47·632	47·632	47·632	97·641
Compression ratio (to 1)	6·3	6·3		11
Valve type	ts	ts	ts	ts
bhp	2·2	2·2		10
@ rpm	5800	5800		6500
Oil system	petrol/oil mix	petrol/oil mix	petrol/oil mix	petrol/oil mix
Box gearing: 3rd	1·14	1·14	1·14	1·14
Box gearing: 2nd	1·61	1·61	1·61	1·61
Box gearing: 1st	2·61	2·61	2·61	2·61
No. gears	3	3	4	4
Front tyre	3·00 × 12	3·00 × 12	2·25 × 17	2·50 × 17
Rear tyre	3·00 × 12	3·00 × 12	2·50 × 17	2·75 × 17
Front brake (mm)	drum 100	drum 100	drum 110	drum 110

Ducati Singles

Rear brake (mm)	drum 100	drum 100	drum 110	drum 110
Front suspension	teles	teles	teles	teles
Rear suspension	s/a	s/a	s/a	s/a
Ignition system	flywheel mag	flywheel mag	flywheel mag	flywheel mag
Wheelbase (mm)	985	985	1182	1182
Seat height (mm)	430	430	740	740
Width (mm)	680	680	650	650
Length (mm)	1570	1570	1240	1240
Generator/output				6v 50w

Model	300 Electronic	50 Senda TT	75 Senda TT	250 Strada	350 Forza
Bore (mm)	66	38	45	74	76
Stroke (mm)	75	42	46	57·8	75
Capacity (cc)	256·590	47·633	73·160	248·589	340·235
Compression ratio (to 1)	9			8·5	9
Valve type	ohc	ts	ts	ohc	ohc
bhp	20	4·2	7·5	21	22
@ rpm	6500	6500	6000	8000	6650
torque (Kg-m)				2·15	8·2
@ rpm				5000	4250
Starting system		ks	ks	ks	electric
Oil system	wet sump	petrol/oil mix	petrol/oil mix	wet sump	wet sump
Inlet opens BTDC					68
Inlet closes ABDC					95
Exhaust opens BBDC					84
Exhaust closes ATDC					78
Box gearing : 5th				0·97	0·97
Box gearing : 4th		1·04	1·04	0·10	0·10
Box gearing : 3rd		1·35	1·35	1·35	1·35
Box gearing : 2nd		1·94	1·94	1·73	1·73
Box gearing : 1st		3·27	3·27	2·46	2·46
No. gears	5	4	4	5	5
Front tyre	3·25 × 18	2¼ × 19	2¼ × 19	3·25 × 18	3·25 × 18
Rear tyre	4·00 × 18	3·00 × 18	3·00 × 18	3·50 × 18	3·50 × 18
Front brake (mm)	disc 275	drum 95	drum 95	drum 180 **1**	disc 260
Rear brake (mm)	drum 160	drum 110	drum 110	drum 160 **1**	drum 200 **2**
Front suspension	teles	teles	teles	teles	teles
Rear suspension	s/a	s/a	s/a	s/a	s/a
Ignition system	electronic	flywheel mag	flywheel mag	coil	coil
Wheelbase (mm)	1355	1250	1250	1410	1410
Seat height (mm)	785	750	750	740	740
Width (mm)	740	775	775		
Length (mm)	2050	1885	1885		
Dry weight (kg)	130			136	146
Generator/output	12v			12v	12v
Battery	12v 12ah	none	none	12v 12ah	12v 12ah

1 Also produced in 1980–1981 with front disc (260 mm) and drum rear brake, 1982 with discs front and rear
2 Up to 1981, 1982 onwards—disc 260 mm

Model	350 Vento 1	MTV Cross	MTV Sport	MTV Yak 410
Bore (mm)	76	39	39	86
Stroke (mm)	75	41·9	41·9	70
Capacity (cc)	340·235	450·053	50·053	406·41
Compression ratio (to 1)	10			9
Valve type	ohc	ts	ts	ohc
bhp	28·8	2·9	2·9	39
@ rpm	8050	5600	5600	8500
torque (Kg-m)	8·4			
@ rpm	5900			
Starting system	ks	ks	ks	electric
Oil system	wet sump	petrol/oil mix	petrol/oil mix	wet sump
Inlet opens BTDC	72			60
Inlet closes ABDC	100			99
Exhaust opens BBDC	98			97
Exhaust closes ATDC	80			70
Tappets, inlet (mm)	0·7			
Tappets, exhaust (mm)	0·10			
Primary drive gearing	2·190			
Final drive gearing	3·000			
Box gearing: 5th	0·97			
Box gearing: 4th	1·10			
Box gearing: 3rd	1·35			
Box gearing: 2nd	1·73			
Box gearing: 1st	2·46			
No. gears	5	4	4	6
Front tyre	3·25 × 18	2·25 × 19	2·50 × 18	2·75 × 21
Rear tyre	3·50 × 18	3·00 × 18	2·50 × 18	4·00 × 18
Front brake (mm)	twin disc 260	drum 95	drum 120	drum 160
Rear brake (mm)	disc 260	drum 110	drum 120	drum 140
Front suspension	teles	teles	teles	teles
Rear suspension	s/a	s/a	s/a	s/a
Ignition system	coil	flywheel mag	flywheel mag	electronic
Wheelbase (mm)	1410	1250	1250	1444
Seat height (mm)	735	800	570	
Width (mm)		800	760	
Length (mm)		1900	1865	
Dry weight (kg)	141 1			128
Battery	12v 12ah	none	none	12v 14ah

1 Early Vento had following differences; 9:1 comp. ratio, 32 bhp @ 6500, weight 120 kg

Specifications

2 Colours

Only the well-known models have been listed here—no pushrod, Mototrans or early two-stroke machines—because of the vastness of the range.

125 Sport 1958/65

Metallic blue for all painted parts except mudguards, suspension units, headlamp shell and front section of fuel tank, which were finished in metallic gold. The exceptions were the horn, battery strap and seat brackets, in black.

Transfers: tank sides 'Ducati Meccanica' and 'Made in Italy' at rear of filler cap. 'Ducati' on front mudguard. Many earlier singles used this colour scheme including 100 Sport, 125TV and several early two-strokes, plus the 125 Formula III racer.

175 Sport 1958/61

Metallic cherry red for mudguards, headlamp shell, suspension units, chainguard, toolboxes, rear light/number plate support and rear section of fuel tank. Metallic gold for frame, swinging-arm, bottom yoke, spring covers and fork bottoms, engine mounting plates and centre stand.

The 1957 175S was identical except for gold-painted tank fluting, not chrome, which was used in this area from 1958 onwards. The 200 Elite and SS models used an identical paint finish to the 175S.

Transfers: toolbox sides and front mudguards with steel tank badge.

175T 1957 and Tourist 1958/61

Overall dark crimson with the following in black—suspension units, rear light number plate/support, headlamp shell horn and battery strap. White for tank flutes, outlined in yellow striping as were toolboxes. Other colour options were tank finishes in black overall with contrasting white or red.

Transfers: toolboxes and front mudguard, with 'Ducati 175' metal badges for tank in the same style as the Sport model.

250 Monza 1961/65

Overall metallic kingfisher blue with chrome areas on tank and side panels, with striping in red. Metallic gold was used on sections of the toolboxes, the headlamp shell, suspension unit top spring covers and mudguards.

Transfers: 'Moto Ducati' eagle on tank sides, 'Made in Italy' rear of filler cap and '250 Monza' on toolboxes. 'Ducati' on front mudguard. Later Monzas up to the end of 1965

were usually finished in black with silver relief for mudguards, and part of the tank and toolboxes. Some had metallic cherry red tanks, not black.

250 Diana, Diana Mark 3 1961/64

As 1961 250 Monza (kingfisher blue) except for silver not gold for parts of the toolboxes, both mudguards, headlamp shell and tank panels. Lining in red.

Transfers: Monza except '250 Diana' on toolboxes ('250 Daytona' for UK).

250 Scrambler 1962/67

All narrow crankcase 250 Scramblers were black, with silver mudguards, headlamp shell, tail-light and air cleaner box. Tank and side panels were in silver with yellow striping.

Transfers: 'Moto Ducati' eagle for tank sides, with 'Made in Italy' behind filler cap and 'Ducati' on front mudguard.

250 Mach 1 1964/66 and Mark 3 1965/67

Italian racing red except silver mudguards, headlamp shell, toolboxes and tank flutes, which were lined in yellow. Toolbox lids were lined in yellow (Mark 3) or red (Mach 1).

Transfers: both had 'Moto Ducati' eagle on tank, with 'Made in Italy' and 'Ducati' in traditional places. Toolbox had either 'Mach 1' or 'Mark 3'.

200GT 1962

Deep claret except black headlamp shell, rear light/number plate support, horn and rear suspension unit top spring covers. Silver for tank side flutes as Diana and Mach 1, lining in yellow.

Transfers: 'Ducati Meccanica' for tank, with '200GT' on toolboxes. 'Made in Italy' and 'Ducati' in traditional places.

250GT 1964/65

Black except silver mudguards, headlamp shell and fluting on tank and side panels, pinstriping in yellow.

Transfers: tank 'Moto Ducati', toolboxes '250GT' ('Daytona 250' for UK), 'Made in Italy' and 'Ducati' in usual areas.

Sport 48 1962/65

Metallic gold frame, swinging-arm, forks, stand and tank/toolboxes flutes, with white pinstriping. Metallic cherry red main area of tank/toolboxes, mudguards, headlamp shell, chainguard and rear light.

Transfers: 'Moto Ducati' tank, 'Sport 48' toolboxes, 'Made in Italy' and 'Ducati' in usual areas. Also in metallic kingfisher blue and silver.

Piuma Sport 1962/66, De Luxe 1962/67

Metallic kingfisher blue, with silver forks and headlamp shell, suspension units and tank flutes. Red pinstriping. On De Luxe full chain enclosure in silver.

Transfers: 'Moto Ducati' tank, and either 'Piuma Sport 48' or 'Piuma 48' on toolboxes ('Puma' for UK).

48SL, Cacciatore, 50SL and 100 Mountaineer

Italian racing red or metallic cherry with silver mudguards, toolboxes (red flutes) and headlamp shell. Tanks had silver flutes. Yellow pinstriping for tank and toolboxes. Air cleaner box in matt black.

100 Cadet (fan cooled) 1964/66)

Either – black overall with Italian red tank and silver flutes; silver for mudguards, headlamp shell and toolbox; pinstriping in yellow for tank, black for toolbox. Or – red overall (metallic cherry) replacing areas which were black in the first finish. Both versions had black rear light/number plate assembly, with matt black air cleaner box.

Transfers: 'Moto Ducati' eagle tank sides, 'Cadet 100' on toolbox, 'Made in Italy' and 'Ducati' in usual positions.

100 Cadet (not fan-cooled) 1967

Overall black, with silver for tank flutes, side panel and mudguards.

Brio scooters 1963/68

48 and 50 cream overall; 100 light green overall.

No transfers, but chromed badges 'Ducati' and 'Brio' in 48, 50 or 100 version. The last batch of 100s had '100/25'. All were on the nearside front leg shield, near the top. Another 'Ducati' chromed badge was mounted above the rear light.

Monza Junior (160) 1964/67

This was produced in three versions. Version 1 used the same colour scheme as the 1964 Monza; version 2 and 3 had black cycle parts, with silver mudguards, tank and side panels, with about 50 per cent of the bikes having a metallic cherry red tank. On the black/silver bikes all pinstriping was in black, while the red tank models had their tank pinstriped in gold, with silver panels.

250 Monza and 350 Sebring (square styling) 1966/68

These were finished as the second and third version of the 160 Monza Junior, but both the Monza and Sebring were also in a metallic green for both the tank and side panels, with silver tank flutes and gold pinstriping.

250/350 Mark 3 1968/69

Italian racing red, but with silver for mudguards, headlamp shell and tank flutes.

Transfers: three-star effect, for toolboxes with inscription '250' or '350' 'Mark 3' in silver. Pinstriping in gold on the tank. 'Made in Italy', rear of filler cap, 'Ducati' on front mudguard. Metal tank badges.

250/350 Mark 3D (Desmo) 1968/69

Overall black, but with metallic cherry red for tank and toolboxes. Chrome replaced the silver paint of the Mark 3s for mudguards, headlamp shell and fluting on the tank sides. Pinstriping was in gold, silver for three-star effect on toolboxes, with inscription '250' or '350'-'Mark 3' with 'D' in yellow with black edging. 'Mark' in black, '3' in yellow and '250' or '350' in black.

As the mudguards were in chrome no 'Ducati' transfer was applied to front.

250/350/450 Mark 3 and Mark 3D 1970/71

With the arrival of the new 450 both Mark 3 and 3D were finished as the 1968/69 Mark 3Ds; in black with the exception of the chrome headlamp shell and tank flutes, but whereas only metallic cherry had been available, colours were white, yellow or blue (all non-metallic) but as the red only for the tank and toolboxes. Stainless steel replaced chrome for the mudguards.

250/350 Scrambler 1968/74 and 450 Scrambler 1969/74

Initially colours were red, white or black for the tank (with chrome flute). Black was the main colour, and silver mudguards. In late 1969 yellow plus orange/red were added. The metal tank badge of the 1968/71 Mark 3 and Desmos was carried on the Scramblers until the end of production in late 1974. The 250 Scrambler remained unchanged for minor details; its last year of production saw it produced only in yellow for the tank (still with chrome flute) and mudguards, which with the tank had black stripes running lengthways. From the beginning of 1973 the 350/450s had large plastic side panels and double-sided front brakes. These were an overall black finish with gold pinstriping, or the metallic gold used on the 1973/74 750GT for the tank and mudguards, lined in a similar way to the late 250 Scrambler. The 1973/74 350/450 Scramblers had their side panels moulded in black and were therefore 'unpainted', but usually had '350' or '450' decals.

450 Jupiter 1970

USA market name for 450 Scrambler, only sold in yellow and black, see 450 Scrambler 1969/74 above.

125 Scrambler 1971/72

Black with white side number plates/panel covers. Tank and mudguards in orange/red with black lining from front to back. Tank same as other SCR models of the period, but without the chrome fluting or metal badges.

Transfers: 'Ducati' in same style as Desmo and 750S and SS models.

450R/T and T/S 1971/73

Silver frame and swinging-arm assembly and stands/chainguard. All plastic parts such as side panels, tank, mudguard, headlamp cowling (T/S) moulded in yellow, except the R/T front number plate, which was white. Both models had competition number backgrounds on side panels in white. Rear number plate/light-support mounting (T/S) in moulded black rubber.

250/350/450 Desmo 1971/72

Referred to in some countries as the 'Silver Shotgun'; the reason – metalflake silver fibreglass for the tank, side panels, seat and mudguards. The rest was finished in black.

The bikes used exclusively transfers with a large 'Ducati' in the same style as the 750S and SS and the later yellow Desmos. 'Made in Italy', plus special 'Desmo' transfers for the side panels, in a contrasting shade of silver were used. Chrome headlamp shell.

450 Mark 3 (touring version) 1972

Colour scheme as 1968/69 Mark 3Ds (even though the fuel tank was based on the earlier Mach 1).

Mark 3 1973/74

Black with exception of tank, mudguard and side panels. Gold fluting on tank and side panels.

Transfers (not paint): early models had 'Ducati' transfer for tank and fibreglass lids for toolbox/air cleaner with black metal backs – later models, a chromed plastic tank badge and one-piece metal toolbox/air cleaner (one each side) all in blue, except gold flute transfer and either '250', '350' or

'450' transfer in white. Other transfers were the 'Made in Italy' behind the filler cap and matching gold stripes for the mudguards to go with those on the tank and panels.

Note: the Mark 3 was available with both clip-on and conventional handlebars and had black-painted top and bottom yokes and fork bottoms. None left the factory with polished components.

Desmo models 1973/74

Black but for yellow tank, side panels, seat base and front mudguard. Same colour scheme for disc and drum variants. Rear mudguard in matt black.

Transfers: black for striping on top of and on the side of tank. 'Ducati' transfer used earlier on 1971/72 'Silver Shotgun', but side panel transfer design was new for 1973 with thick stripes and word 'Desmo'. Capacity ('239', '250', '350' or '450') was on seat base.

Regolarita 1975/76

Silver frame, swinging-arm, front forks and cycle parts, except plastic or fibreglass items. Tank in non metallic blue or red, with 'Ducati' decal and 860GT/Darmah style lining (transfers) in white/black. Mudguards in moulded black plastic, matt black rubber number plate/light holder. Rear lamp body in black, as was headlamp shell and control lever supports. Complete exhaust system in matt black, including sump/exhaust shield. Leg guard heat grille chrome. Side panels in black moulded plastic, with yellow competition number as was the front background number plate. Headlamp grille chrome plated. A small black, simulated-leather map/tool kit bag was located on top of the rear mudguard.

Six Days 1977

Red polished alloy tank with 'Six Days Ducati' decals, white moulded plastic mudguards and side panels, with yellow competition number backgrounds. Silver chain guard, with same colour used for front fork bottoms.

Transfers

As a general rule all Ducati single-cylinder models between 1957 and 1974 had 'Made in Italy' positioned at the rear of the filler cap, facing towards the rider. The gold 'Ducati' for the front mudguard (positioned facing so it could be read from the front) was only retained on machines up to the middle of 1971. None of the wide-case Scramblers used this, however. Other transfers and badges were used, usually, for only a short period of time, except for the 'Moto Ducati' decal.

3 Carburettor settings

Bologna singles

Model	Year	Dell'Orto type	Size	Needle	Main	Pilot	Slide	Needle pos.	Needle jet
60 Sport	1950–51	MA 16 B	16	D15	70	45	50	2	260B
98N	1952–58	MA 16 B	16	D12	75	35	40	2	260B
98T	1952–58	MA 16 B	16	D12	75	35	40	2	260B
98TL	1953–58	MA 16 B	16	D12	75	35	40	2	260B
98S	1953–58	MA 18 B	18	D16	82	35	60	2	260B
98 Super Sport	1954–55	MB 20 B	20	E10	72	35	50		
55E	1955–57	14 MFC			60	45			
55R	1955–57	14 MFC	Weber type		60	45			
55M	1955–57	14 MFC			60	45			
125T	1956–60	MA 18 B	18	D12	80	40	50	2	260A
125TV	1956–58	MB 20 B	20	E10	82	35	50	2	260B
85N	1958–60	ME 15 BS	15	G4	70	35	50	2	258A
85 Sport	1958–60	ME 15 BS	16	G4	70	35	50	2	258A
98TS	1958–60	ME 16 BS	16	G1	74	35	50	3	258A
175S	1957	MB 22·5 B	22·5	E14	98	80	40	2	260B
175T	1957	MB 22 B	22	E12	92	45	80	2	260B
125S	1957	MB 20 B	20	E9	78	38	70	3	262A
100 Sport	1958–60	MA 18 B	18	D17	78	35	50	2	260A
125 Sport	1958–65	UB 20 BS	20	E10	85	35	50	2	260B
125 Sport (optional)	1958–61	SS1 22 C	22	R4	92	50	80	3	260
125TS up to 1500th engine	1958	UA 20 BS	20	E10	85	35	50	2	260B
125TS	1959–65	ME 18 BS	18	G4	76	38	50	3	258B
175 Americano	1958	MB 22 B	22	E12	92	45	80	2	260B
175 Sport	1958–61	UB 22·5 BS2	22·5	E14	98	40	80	2	260B
175 Sport (optional)	1959–61	SS1 25 A	25	M14	120	50	100	2	265
175 Tourist	1958–61	MB 22 B	22	E12	92	45	80	2	260B
175TS	1958–60	MB 22 B	22	E12	92	45	80	2	260B
175 Motocross	1958	SS1 25 A	25	M14	118	50	100	2	265
200 Elite	1959–65	UBF 24 BS	24	E10	98	40	70	2	260B
200 Super Sport	1959–62	UBF 24 BS	24	E10	98	40	70	2	260B
200 Super Sport (optional)	1959–60	SS1 27 A	27	M13	108	50	80	3	265
200 Americano	1959	UBF 24 BS	24	E10	92	40	70	2	260B
200 Motocross	1959–60	SS1 27 A	27	M13	105	50	80	3	265
200TS	1960–61	UBF 24 BS	24	E10	92	40	70	2	260B
200GT	1962	UBF 24 BS	24	E11	95	40	70	2	260A
250 Monza (n/case)	1961–67	UBF 24 BS	24	E11	108	40	70	2	260B
Diana Europe	1961–64	UBF 24 BS	24	E11	103	35	70	2	260A
Diana USA	1961	UBF 24 BS	24	E11	108	40	70	2	260B
Diana Mk3 USA	1962–65	SS1 27 D	27	M14	120	50	100	2	265
Diana Mk3 USA	1966–67	SS1 29 D	29	M14	125	50	60	2	265
250 Mark 3 (n/case)	1967	SS1 29 D	29	M14	125	50	60	2	265
250 Scrambler (n/case)	1962–67	SS1 27 D	27	M14	112	50	100	3	265

Model	Year	Dell'Orto type	Size	Needle	Main	Pilot	Slide	Needle pos.	Needle jet
Mach 1	1964–66	SS1 29 D	29	M14	122	50	60	2	265
250GT	1964–66	UBF 24 BS	24	E19	108	40	60	2	260B
250 Monza (w/case)	1968	UBF 24 BS	24	E11	108	45	80	2	260H
250 Mark 3 (w/case)	1968–69	SS1 29 D	29	M14	112	45	60	2	260
250 Mark 3 (w/case)	1970–74	VHB 29 AD	29	V13	110	40	40	2	265M
250 Mark 3D	1968–69	SS1 29 D	29	M14	115	45	60	2	
250 Mark 3D	1970–71	VHB 20 AD	20	V13	110	40	40	2	265M
250 Scrambler (w/case)	1968–69	SS1 27 D	27	M14	112	50	80	3	265
250 Scrambler (w/case)	1970–73	VHB 26 BD	26	E17	95	45	40	2	260R
250 Desmo	1971–74	VHB 29 AD	29	V13	110	40	40	2	265M
239 Desmo	1974	PHF 30 AD	30	K3	125	65	503	2	265AB
239 Mark 3	1974	PHF 30 AD	30	K3	125	65	503	2	265AB
Monza Junior	1964–67	UB 22 BS	22	E16	98	42	60	2	260A
Piuma Standard	1961–68	T4 12 D1	12	A4	58			2	1–210
Piuma Sport	1962–66	UAO 15 S	15	C1	68	45	65	3	260
Piuma De-Luxe	1962–67	T4 12 D1	12	A4	58			2	1–210
Brisk	1961–67	T4 12 D1	12	A4	58			2	1–210
Sport 48	1962–65	UA 1SS	15	C1	68		45	3	260
180 Standard	1962–63	ME 1S BS	15	G1	63	40		3	258A
Sport 80	1962–63	UA 18 S	18	C1	92	35	55	3	260
48SL	1964–65	UA 15 S	15	C1	68	45	65	3	260
100 Cadet (51 mm bore)	1964–66	UA 18 S	18	C2	82	38	50	2	260
100 Cadet (52 mm bore)	1967	UBF 24 BS	24	E2	102	40	70	2	260A
100 Mountaineer (51 mm bore)	1964–66	UA 18 S	18	C2	82	38	50	2	260
100 Mountaineer (52 mm bore)	1967	UBF 24 BS	24	E2	102	40	70	2	260A
Brio 48	1963–66	SHA 14 12	12		52	40	6493/01		
Brio 50	1967–68	SHA 14 12	12		56	40	6108/01		
Brio 100	1964–68	SHB 18 16	16		82	40	6493/01		
Brio 100/25	1968	SHB 18 16	16		88	50	6493/02		
48 Cacciatore	1964–67	UA 15 S	15	C1	68	45	65	3	260
50SL	1966	UA 18 S	18	D10	85	40	55	1	260F
50SL1	1967–68	UAO 18 S	18	D10	85	40	55	1	260F
50SL2	1968–69	UAO 18 S	18	D10	85	40	55	1	260F
Rolly 50	1968	SHA 14 12	12		52	40	6493/01	1	
50 Scrambler	1969–70	UA 18 S	18	C8	85	40	50	3	260F
100 Scrambler	1969–70	UBF 24 Bs	24	E2	102	40	70	2	260A
125 Cadet/4	1967	ME 18 BS	18	G3	85	38	50	2	258A
125 Cadet/4 Motocross	1967	ME 18 BS	18	G3	85	38	50	2	258A
Sebring (n/case)	1965–67	UBF 24 BS	24	E16	108	40	70	2	260A
Sebring (w/case)	1968	UBF 24 BS	24	E16	108	40	70	2	260A
350 Scrambler	1968–69	SS1 29 D	29	M14	125	50	100	2	265
350 Scrambler	1970–74	VHB 29 AD	29	V13	110	40	40	2	265M
350 Mark 3	1968–69	SS1 29 D	29	M14	112	45	60	2	260
350 Mark 3	1970–74	VHB 29 AD	29	V13	115	40	40	2	265M
350 Mark 3D	1968–69	SS1 29 D	29	M14	115	45	60	2	260
350 Mark 3D	1970–71	VHB 29 AD	29	V13	120	40	40	2	265M

Model	Year	Dell'Orto type	Size	Needle	Main	Pilot	Slide	Needle pos.	Needle jet
350 Desmo	1971–74	VHB 29 AD	29	V13	118	40	40	2	265M
450 Scrambler	1969–74	VHB 29 AD	29	V7	130	50	60	2	265T
450 Mark 3	1969–74	VHB 29 AD	29	V7	135	50	60	2	260T
450 Mark 3D	1969–71	VHB 29 AD	29	V8	135	50	60	2	260T
450 Desmo	1971–74	VHB 20 AD	29	V8	135	50	60	2	260T
450R/T (open pipe)	1971–72	VHB 29 AD	20	V7	140	50	60	2	265T
450T/S	1971–73	VHB 29 AD	20	V7	135	50	60	2	265T
450 Mark 3 Tourer	1970–72	VHB 29 AD	29	V7	130	50	60	2	265T
Regolarita	1975–76	PHB 30 BS	30	K3	125	65	50/3	2	265AB
Six Days	1977	PHBE 32 GS	32	K1	140	55	40	2	265AR
125 Scrambler	1971	375/20*	20	A1	95	12	373/3	1	105/DA

* Amal carburettor

Bologna production road racers

Model	Year	Dell'Orto type	Size	Needle	Main	Pilot	Slide	Needle pos.	Needle jet
98 Competizione	1955	SS1 20 C	20	R4	88	50	70	3	260
125 Gran Sport	1956	SS1 20 C	20	R4	80	45	70	3	260
175 Gran Sport	1957	SS1 22·5 c	22·5	R4	98	50	70	3	260
175 Formula III	1959	SS1 27 A	27	M14	108	50	80	3	260
220 Grand Prix	1960	SS1 29 A	29	M14	115	50	80	3	260
250 Formula III (Manxman)	1961	SS1 29 A	29	M14	118	50	100	3	260
250 Mach 1/s	1965	SS1 30 A	30	M14	132	50	60	2	260

Mototrans singles

Model	Year	Amal type	Size	Needle	Main	Pilot	Slide	Needle pos.	Needle jet
175 Turismo		375/22 or	22		85	15			
		UB 22 1352*	22	E11	90	42	80	2	260B
175 Sport		UB							
200 Elite		UB 24 B*	24	E11	110	40	70	2	260
160 Turismo		375/20	20		85	15			
160 Sport		375/20	20		100	12			
250 De Luxe		376/25 or	25		240	20			
		UBF 24 BS*	24	E11	112	42	70	2	260A
250 24 Horas		376/27D	27		240	25			
250 Road									
200 Turismo		375/22	22		100	15			
50 Pronto		625	25						
250 Strada		627							
350 Forza		PHF30*	30						
350 Vento		PHF32*	32	K3	160	55	50	1	AB 265
MTV Yak 410		PHB34*	34						

* Dell'Orto carburettor

4 Prices

1958 (March) importer: S D Sullam Ltd, Africa House, Kingsway, London WC2

65T	£105. 4s. 7d.
65TS	£117.13s.10d.
98S	£163. 8s. 6d.
98T	£162.17s. 8d.
100S	£222.16s. 1d.
125S	£237. 2s. 3d.
125T	£181.13s.10d.
125TV	£187. 2s. 6d.
175S	£259. 9s. 7d.
175T	£222.16s. 1d.

1959 (March) importer: Ducati Concessionaires, 80, Burleigh Rd, Stratford, Manchester

100 Sport	£221. 9s. 4d.
•125 Sport	£225.19s. 9d.
125 Super Sport	£254. 4s. 8d.
175 Tourist	£236. 2s.11d.
175 Sport	£259. 2s. 6d.
175 Americano	£259. 2s. 6d.
200 Elite	£279. 1s.10d.
200 Americano	£279. 1s.10d.
200 Motocross	£299. 8s. 0d.
125 Formula III	£493.15s. 0d.
175 Formula III	£538.19s. 6d.

1960 (October) importer: Ducati Concessionaires

125 Monza	£218.10s. 3d.
175 Silverstone	£250.11s. 2d.
175 Silverstone Super	£278.12s. 2d.
200 Super Sports	£274. 4s. 7d.
125 Formula III	£477. 8s. 5d.
175 Formula III	£521. 3s.11d.

1961 (May) importer: Ducati Concessionaires

200 Super Sports	£234. 4s. 4d.
250 Daytona	£254. 6s. 1d.
250 Manxman Formula III	£481. 5s. 7d.

1962 (October) importer: Ducati Concessionaires

48 Piuma De-Luxe	£68. 16s. 2d.
48 Piuma De-Luxe (with speedo)	£72. 11s. 2d.
48 Sport	£89. 19s. 6d.

80 Sport	£107.19s.11d.
125 Sport Monza	£208.19s.11d.
200GT	£229.10s. 0d.
200 Super Sports	£239.19s. 4d.
250 Daytona	£249. 0s. 6d.

1963 Unchanged. Importer: Ducati Concessionaires

1964 (October) importer: Ducati Concessionaires

48 Piuma De-Luxe	£79.10s. 0d.
48 Sport	£89.19s. 6d.
200 Super Sport (Elite)	£199.0s. 0d.
250 Daytona	£249.0s. 6d.
250 Mach 1	£269.0s. 0d.

1965 (October) importer: Ducati Concessionaires

48 Sport	£95. 0s. 0d.
200 Super Sport (Elite)	£210. 0s. 0d.
250GT	£262.10s. 0d.
250 Mach 1	£275.10s. 0d.

1966 Unchanged. Importer: Ducati Concessionaires

1967 (August) importer: Vic Camp Motor Cycles, 131 Queens Rd, Walthamstow, London E17

50SL1	£119.10s. 0d.
160 Monza Junior	£228. 0s. 0d.
250 Mark 3	£287. 0s. 0d.
350 Sebring	£299. 0s. 0d.

1968 (October) importer: Vic Camp Motor Cycles (two importers, with Hannah)

50SL1	£109.10s. 0d. (Camp)
250 Mark 3	£287. 0s. 0d. (Camp)

Other importer:
Bill Hannah (Imports) Ltd 41–61 Gt George St, Liverpool

100 Cadet	£122.19s. 1d.
Brio 100/25	£127.17s. 0d. (Hannah)
160 Monza Junior	£211.15s. 0d. (Hannah)
250 Monza	£275.17s. 0d. (Hannah)
250 Mark 3	£281. 7s. 9d. (Hannah)
350 Sebring	£299. 9s.11d. (Hannah)

Hannah Ducati's were machines originally ordered by Berliner, the USA importer, some remained unsold into 1972, although only one shipment, it consisted of 3400 bikes.

1970 (May) importer: Vic Camp Motor Cycles

250 Mark 3D	£341.10s. 1d.
350 Mark 3D	£373.14s.11d.
450 Mark 3D	£405.19s. 1d.

1971 (August) importer: Vic Camp Motor Cycles

250 24 Horas	£346.45p.

1972 (August) importer: Vic Camp Motor Cycles

50 Mini 2	£146.02p.
48 Cadet	£143.63p.
250 De-Luxe	£341.11p.
250 24 Horas	£352.52p.
450 Mark 3	£469

1972 (November) importer: Vic Camp Motor Cycles

450 Mark 3 Special	£502.69p.

1973 (November) importer: Coburn & Hughes, 21 Crawley Rd, Luton, Bedfordshire

250 Mark 3	£499
350 Mark 3	£529
450 Mark 3	£549

1974 (November) importer: Coburn & Hughes

250 Scrambler	£479
239/250 Mark 3	£519
239/250 Desmo	£599
350 Mark 3	£549
450 Mark 3	£579
450 Desmo	£699
450 Scrambler	£579

Note: Britax Ltd imported Ducati Cucciolo engines from 1950 to 1956 for assembly into machines of their own construction, usually with parts supplied by the Enfield Cycle Co.

5 Model recognition

Bologna singles

1950
60 Sport introduced, telescopic forks and cantilever rear suspension, ohv engine, development of factory's Cucciolo power unit, but with different bore and stroke.

1951
60 Sport continues.

1952
60 Sport discontinued, replaced by 65TS using a new frame and again updated styling. 98 introduced in commuter, touring and sport guises. All used same pressed-steel open frame, with telescopic forks and swing-arm rear suspension. Cruiser scooter introduced with 175 ohv engine and electric start.

1953
Range increased to include 65T, 65TL, 98TL and improved version of 98 Sport, featuring a deeply finned front area of the crankcase.

1954
Cruiser scooter dropped. 98 Super Sport introduced. The 98SS was a tuned version of the ohv 98 Sport using a 20 mm carburettor in place of the Sport's 18 mm instrument.

1955
Three mopeds 55E, 55R, 55M introduced using improved version of the 48 cc Cucciolo two-speed engine with enclosed valve gear and improved primary transmission.

1956
98 Super Sport dropped from production in favour of 100 Gran Sport racer. First 125 cc from Ducati featuring ohv (bore and stroke 55·2 × 52 mm) and four speeds. There were two versions, 125T with single saddle and open headlamp, the 125TV had dual saddle and a headlamp nacelle.

1957

First ohc models introduced. 174 cc in two versions S – Sport, T – Touring, and 124 cc in Sport form only. 175S had 22·5 mm carburettor, round Bakelite fuel cap, twin silencers, whilst 175T had 22 mm carburettor, chrome quick-action handle filler cap, single silencer and valanced mudguards. All existing models continued.

1958

The previous year's ohc S and T were thereafter known as Sport and Touring. The only changes to the 175 were the exhaust pipe shape and end cone to the Silentium silencers. Gear lever was modified. The 125 had its carburettor changed from an MB20B to a UB20BS, in addition an optional SS1 22C was offered. Other changes included the petrol tank paint style and front engine plates (four hole, instead of three hole for 1957). New introductions for the year were 85N and 85 Sport, both with 85 cc ohv engines. The 98TS ohv and several new ohc models. 100 Sport, 125TS, 175 Americano, 175TS and 175 Motocross. The 100 Sport was a 125 Sport with the bore reduced to 49 mm, in place of the metal tank badge was a 'Ducati Meccanica' transfer, and the headlamp rim did not have a peak like the 125. The 125TS had a tank of different shape with a black Bakelite filler cap. Conventional handlebars with the top fork yoke having clamps. The headlamp brackets and top spring covers were a combined black-painted steel pressing and the brake drum diameter was reduced to 158 and 136 mm front and rear. Carburettor size was 18 mm, against 20 mm for the 125 Sport. The 175 Americano was a model with US styling including high-rise bars, larger dual saddle with a large number of metal studs, two horns, a crashbar and a smaller capacity tank taken from the 100/125 Sport. 175S, different tank (like the 125TS), deeply valanced mudguards and conventional, flat handlebars. The 175 Motocross had a black open megaphone, 21 in. front wheel, braced bars and scrambler tyres. The following models were discontinued: 55E, 55R and 55M.

1959

200 (203 cc) introduced in four versions: Elite, Super Sport, Americano and Motocross. The Elite and Super Sport were identical to 175 Sport except carburettor size increased to 24 mm, the Elite and Americano featured valanced mudguards and twin silencers, the SS a single silencer. The Motocross was larger bore version of 175 Motocross. Several machines were discontinued: 65TS, 98N, 98T, 65T, 65TL, 98S, 125TV, 175 Motocross and Americano.

1960

200 engine modified as forerunner to test items for new 250 unit. These changes were crankshaft (one long shoulder, in place of previous equal crankpin type), clutch housing and cylinder head. The 175 type had fins running across front to back in between four head bolts 250-type, 200 did not. Elite introduced with identical lightweight mudguards as 200SS. 200 Motocross now had lower front mudguard and chrome silencer fitted, restricting noise and power output. 200 Americano dropped. New model introduced to replace it called the 200TS; different saddle and tank design, to be used the following year on the 250 Monza. Also equipped with crash bar, valanced mudguards and high bars.

1961

248 cc engine introduced initially in two versions: Monza (touring), Diana (sport). The latter was marketed in Britain as the Daytona. Monza had prop stand, high bars, small tank with chrome fluting and valanced rear mudguard. Diana clip-ons, larger tank, mudguard similar to 175 Sport/200SS and later Elite but longer at front. Both had larger toolbox/air cleaner, cover on front offside brake hub. These models also introduced alloy oblong rear light used on many later models. Both featured 24 mm UBF24BS carburettor with air filter hose and 4-ring pistons. Some Dianas were sold in the USA with 27 mm SS1 carburettor, higher compression 3-ring piston and large Veglia tachometer. Others were kitted out in a like manner elsewhere after being sold. Brisk and Piuma two-stroke introduced. The following were discontinued: 125T, 85N, 85 Sport, 98TS, 100 Sport, 175TS, 200SS and 200 Motocross.

1962

250 Scrambler introduced, this like the USA models. Diana used a flywheel magneto without a battery. No toolboxes, horn or charging system. 27 mm SS1 carburettor, abbreviated mudguarding, 19 in. wheels and special tank and saddle. Also available for American flat-track events with solid struts replacing conventional rear units. Also introduced was 200GT. This was essentially a 250 with 200 engine unit, main changes from Diana styling were the valanced mudguards and deep claret paint finish. More two-strokes were added, a De Luxe version of the three-speed Piuma with dual saddle and fully enclosed chaincase, Sport version with downdraught 15 mm carburettor, motorcycle style tank, saddle and exhaust system. All Piumas, however, employed the same pressed-steel open frame.

Sport 48 introduced using Piuma Sport engine, but in a

full double cradle frame with racing styling, including clip-ons and bump stop saddle. 175/200 Bakelite screw filler cap used. 80 cc version of Sport 48 was introduced in two forms, both with same single downtube frame and larger tank. Sport model had clip-ons, standard version conventional handlebars.

1963

48 Brio scooter introduced, using fan cooled version of Piuma engine, producing 1·5 bhp. Three-speed hand gear change, 9 in. tyres and single seat. 200GT discontinued.

1964

All 250 models received five-speed gear boxes, in addition two new models were introduced — 250 Mach 1, 250GT. The Mach 1 was the star performer with its highly tuned engine featuring high-lift camshaft, 10 to 1 piston, larger valves and 29 mm Dell'Orto SS1 carburettor. Tank had cutaway underneath to enable larger carburettor to be fitted. Specification also included clip-ons, rear sets and ball end control levers. 250GT was a soft tourer with even less performance than the Monza and used tank, panels and mudguards from 200GT. A distinctive feature was the fitment of swan neck clip-on handlebars which provided a touring riding position.

160 Monza Junior introduced, engine developed from ohc 125. Capacity 156 cc 22 mm carburettor, four-speeds. Original version used tank from early 250 Monza, with round 130 mm headlight and round section mudguards. Touring guise complemented by parcel carrier, crashbars and prop stand. 16 in. wheels as standard, many parts from 125TS model. New two-strokes were: 48SL, 100 Cadet, 100 Mountaineer, Brio 100 scooter and 48 Cacciatore. 48SL was restyled version of Sport 48, but with fan-cooling and new tank, saddle, toolbox and mudguards. Unlike the Sport 48, the SL had an air cleaner fitted. Cadet and Mountaineer were brand new designs, both used identical engine unit with three speeds and fan-cooling. The Brio 100 also used this 94 cc engine, but in a full-size scooter, with 8 in. wheels and a dual saddle. For their American launch the 100s were marketed as '90 cc' by the US importers. With the introduction of the five-speed ohc 250s, all the four-speed models in this size were discontinued, in addition both 80 cc two-strokes ceased production.

1965

Mark 3 updated to Mach 1 specification, but retained high bars and flywheel magneto ignition. All 250s now fitted ball-end levers. GT fitted with Monza handlebars and Mark 3 saddle. Monza Junior produced with different square styling, but retaining original round headlamp 340 cc version of five-speed 250 introduced. Two versions produced in 1965, USA edition had Monza styling, whereas Sebring sold in other markets was identical to the 1965 250GT. 125TS, 125 Sport, 200 Elite and Sport 48 all discontinued.

1966

Touring 250s and 350s extensively restyled. 250 Scrambler now fitted battery, and tyre sizes altered to 3·50 × 19 in. front/4·00 × 18 in. rear. Mach 1 fitted Mark 3 saddle. Mark 3 fitted Monza footrests and pedals. GT and Monza fitted tank, saddle, sidepanels and mudguards introduced on Series 2, 160 Monza Junior previous year, also Sebring produced in same guise. All three and the Monza given hexagonal Aprilia cast alloy headlamp shell and matching chrome-plated rim to complete new styling package. All four-stroke models now with matching air scoop on speedo drive mounting plate and wheel hubs with less number of ribs across hub than previously, three front and four rear (against seven front and rear on all previous ohc models). Four-speed version of the two-strokes introduced in both capacity classes, also changed from hand- to foot-change. The only new model was the two-stroke 50SL. This was clearly based on the earlier 48SL, but the engine had its bore increased to 38·8 giving a capacity of 49·660 cc, in addition to a high-level exhaust system with head shield run all the way along the offside, other changes were a plastic moped-type headlight, square-section mudguards and the saddle from a 100 Cadet. The other major change was the use of 19 in. wheels. Piuma Sport discontinued.

1967

50SL discontinued in favour of the new SL1, this retained the SL four-speed engine, but introduced chromed bore alloy cylinder barrel, which was also carried through into the Cadet and Mountaineer, at the same time their bore size increased by 1 mm to 52 mm, raising the capacity to 98 cc. The SL1 had a completely new tank, with twin filler cap and clip-ons and small single saddle. Mach 1 discontinued, replaced by a revised Mark 3 which now had the battery/coil electrics from the Mach 1. For America this model was still offered with the high bars and 'race kit' comprising large Veglia tachometer, black megaphone, racing flyscreen and number plates and an assortment of jets. In other countries it simply replaced the Mach 1 and therefore had clip-ons and rearset footrests, but like the 1966 Mach 1 had the larger Mark 3 saddle. The 125 Cadet/4 pushrod was introduced, but by the end of the year had been taken out of production, essentially using the cycle parts of the 100 Cadet two-stroke, with a different tank, headlight and exhaust system. It also differed in having a battery. Brio scooter title change front '48' to '50'. 48 Cacciatore discontinued.

1968

All the existing four-stroke models were replaced by new machines featuring larger capacity sumps and much wider rear engine mounting points. First model was the 350 Scrambler introduced in May, followed by 250 and 350 Desmo (Mark 3D) and Mark 3, plus a 250 Scrambler. Scramblers had 19 in. front wheels, enclosed rear suspension units and heavy-duty front forks. Mark 3s had painted mudguards, Mark 3Ds had chrome trim for tank, with chromed mudguards and Desmo emblem on nearside cam and cover. 1968 models of Mark 3 and Desmo had twin filler caps and SS1 carburettors. Besides the discontinued four-strokes, the following two-strokes were taken out of production: Piuma Standard, De Luxe, Brisk, Cadet, Mountaineer, Brio scooters and SL1. Rolly 50, a single-speed automatic moped with no rear suspension was introduced together with a Piuma with hexagonal headlamp and whitewall tyres. 50 SL2 introduced. 250 Monza, 350 Sebring, Rolly 50 and Piuma discontinued at end of year.

1969

436 cc ohc single introduced in Scrambler, Mark 3 and Desmo versions known as 450. 250, 350 and 450 singles standardized with single filler cap and square slide VHB29 carburettors. 50 and 100 Scramblers introduced with four-speed two-stroke engines.

1970

Four-stroke models unchanged. All two-strokes discontinued. 450 Scramber called Jupiter for US market.

1971

Scramblers discontinued, mid-season new version of Mark 3 and Mark 3D (now called Desmo). These had 35 mm Marzocchi forks, dual-sided front brakes, alloy rims and metal-flake silver finish. Fork legs and yoke polished alloy finish 450R/1 and T/S models introduced. Both had in common brand new heavy-duty frames, braced swinging-arms, plastic tanks, side panels and mudguards. R/T was an off-road scrambler T/S enduro/six days bike with lights and

silencer, initially high-level, later fitted with low-level Mark 3 system. 125 Scrambler introduced using Spanish-built five-speed engine and Amal carburettor.

1972

Touring versions of the 450 introduced, simply called Mark 3, one had old-style forks, tank and touring bars with concave low-compression piston, the other was a custom-built tourer with valanced mudguards, panniers, prop stand and crashbars. R/T and 125 Scrambler discontinued.

1973

New versions of Mark 3 and Desmo introduced. Mark 3 with 19 in. front wheel and choice of clip-ons or touring bars, the 35 mm Marzocchi forks now had black-painted yokes and fork bottoms. Mudguards were similar to those fitted to the 750GT with chrome front stays. Desmos in two version, disc or drum front brakes. Disc version had Ceriani forks and the front mudguard bolted on to the forks. Drum, Marzocchi forks, with the mudguard retained by jubilee clips. Both Mark 3 and Desmo featured fibreglass side panel covers, both instruments mounted in a black hard rubber moulded surround and fully enclosed rev counter drive unit. The 350 and 450 Scramblers utilized parts from the 1973 Mark 3, but retained their own tank and saddle. They also used the side panels from the 1971/72 Mark 3/Desmos. The 250 Scrambler remained unchanged. At the end of the year the touring 450s and the T/S were discontinued.

1974

Mark 3, Desmo and Scramblers continued. 250 Scramblers now with Spanish-made engine and Amal carburettor. 239 version of Mark 3 and Desmo introduced for French market, some imported later into Britain. Identified by DM239 on crankcase, used coil valve springs (Mark 3), slipper piston, 30 mm PHF carburettor and Lafranconi silencer. Some 350 Mark 3s used Spanish-built engines towards the end of the year and last Mark 3s produced utilized steel wheel rims, earlier (1968/71) steel toolboxes and chromed plastic 'Ducati' tank badges. All production of the bevel-driven ohc singles stopped at the end of the year.

1975

New 125 six-speed two-stroke introduced. The Regolarita had left-hand gearchange, chrome bore alloy barrel, plastic tank, mudguards and panels. 105 mm headlamp glass with chromed grille and conical brake hubs.

1976
Regolarita continued.

1977
Regolarita discontinued. New model introduced. Six Days, with polish alloy tank, redesigned chassis and more highly tuned engine. Only a few produced before production ceased later in the year.

Mototrans singles

175 Turismo, 175 Sport, 200 Elite, 200 Turismo
All licence-built versions of Italian originals.

160 Turismo
17 in. wheels, larger brakes and round styling distinguish this from Italian 160.

160 Sport
Almost the same bike as the Italian 125 Sport, but with larger capacity and Amal carburettor.

250 Deluxe
Spanish styling copy of Italian Diana, but with different bore and stroke, external speedo drive (as on Italian 175), and in common with several other earlier Mototrans models 125/160 outer engine casings.

250 24 Horas
Early version had dual saddle and smaller brakes, later ones had racing saddle and 200 mm brakes front and rear. Fibreglass tank and mudguards, clip-ons and rearset footrests.

250 Road
Mototrans version of Italian Scrambler, old-style brakes, longer forks and smaller capacity tank.

125 Sport
Almost identical to 160 Sport except five-speed gearbox.

48 Cadet
Based on Italian two-strokes, this first model had 17 in. wheels.

Mini, 1, 2 and 3
Small-wheeled city bike, 12 in. tyres, telescopic forks and swinging-arm, usually has front and rear carriers.

50 and 100 Pronto
Full-size motorcycle with duplex frame, but still only three-speed.

50 and 75 Senda
Style like a pure trials bike, both have four-speed gearbox, and plastic panels, tank and mudguards.

250 Strada
First of the later wide-crank Italian-size (bore and stroke) Mototrans models. Original bikes had 180/160 front/rear drum brakes, 1981 featured disc front, 1982 discs front and rear with cast-alloy wheels.

350 Forza
Electric start, originally at front of crankcase, later 1981 onwards mounted at rear of cylinder. Touring guise like other late Mototrans singles have square finning on barrel and eccentric chain adjustment in swinging-arm. Also like Strada had only one engine mounting bolt at front, unlike Vento and Italian models which had four. 1982 model had gold-painted cast-alloy wheels.

350 Vento
Mototrans answer to Italy's last Desmo singles, but had twin front discs, single rear disc, cast-alloy wheels and plastic fuel tank.

MTV Cross
Zundapp-powered 50 enduro-styled moped, four gears, tank, mudguards and panels in plastic. Monoshock frame and wire wheels.

MTV Sport
Uses same Zundapp engine as Cross but cast alloy wheels with racer-style bikini fairing and cast-alloy wheels.

MTV Yak 410
Six-speed, belt-driven trail bike in a similar style to the Suzuki SP370. 21 in. front wheel and Telesco forks.

**Tail end – Cucciolo – found inside a Britax handbook of
the early 1950s**